"Lord, Please Don't Take Me in August"

To Pastor & Jeanne
From
Dorothy and Gayle
We Thought you would
like to have This
with
love

BLACKS IN THE NEW WORLD
Edited by August Meier and John H. Bracey

A list of books in the series appears at the end of this book.

"Lord, Please Don't

Take Me in August"

African Americans in Newport and

Saratoga Springs, 1870–1930

Myra B. Young Armstead

University of Illinois Press • Urbana & Chicago

Library of Congress Cataloging-in-Publication Data
Armstead, Myra Beth Young, 1954–
Lord, please don't take me in August : African Americans in Newport and
Saratoga Springs, 1870–1930 / Myra B. Young Armstead.
p. cm.—(Blacks in the New World)
Includes bibliographical references (p.   ) and index.
ISBN 0-252-02485-0 (alk. paper)
ISBN 0-252-06801-7 (pbk. : alk. paper)
1. Afro-Americans—Rhode Island—Newport—Social conditions.
2. Afro-Americans—New York (State)—Saratoga Springs—Social conditions.
3. Rural-urban migration—Rhode Island—Newport—History.
4. Rural-urban migration—New York (State)—Saratoga Springs—History.
5. Resorts—Rhode Island—Newport—History.
6. Resorts—New York (State)—Saratoga Springs—History.
7. Newport (R.I.)—Social conditions—19th century.
8. Newport (R.I.)—Social conditions—20th century.
9. Saratoga Springs (N.Y.)—Social conditions—19th century.
10. Saratoga Springs (N.Y.)—Social conditions—20th century.
I. Title. II. Series.
F89.N5A76   1999
974.5′700496073—dc21   98-58092
CIP

For my mother, Bethsheba Young;
my father, Frank Young;
and the memories of my maternal grandparents,
Gratnie and Maggie Smith
—with a grateful heart to God

CONTENTS

ILLUSTRATIONS FOLLOW PAGE 86

ACKNOWLEDGMENTS

THIS BOOK, A MUCH-REVISED VERSION OF MY 1987 DOCTORAL THESIS, was unusually long in the making; not surprisingly, therefore, it owes its appearance to a rather long list of helpers. Faculty at the University of Chicago when I was there as a graduate student contributed to this book's genesis as a dissertation. These included Kathleen Conzen, James Grossman, William J. Wilson, Ed Cook, and Neil Harris. Later comments that I received from David Katzman at the University of Kansas at Lawrence, the members of the 1996 National Endowment for the Humanities summer seminar in U.S. labor history directed by Melvyn Dubofsky at Binghamton University, Thomas Dublin at Binghamton University, and participants in the 1997 NEH summer seminar on the Atlantic plantation complex directed by Phillip Curtin also helped me to sculpt the manuscript. My colleagues in the history department at Bard College offered professional encouragement all along: John Fout, Gennady Shkliarevsky, and Alice Stroup served as cheerleaders; Mark Lytle and Joel Perlmann reviewed drafts and offered helpful critiques. I wish to thank the series editors, August Meier and John H. Bracey, for their invaluable contributions to this book. August Meier especially deserves mention for both his erudition in African-American history and his patience with me.

My research at the community level was greatly assisted by numerous public historians and supervisors of local archives. Regarding Saratoga Springs, I thank Field Horne, former director of the Saratoga County Historical Society; Jean Stamm, former librarian at the Saratoga Springs Public Library; Bea Sweeney, former Saratoga Springs city historian; Heidi Fuge, former director of the Saratoga Springs Historical Society; Jane Rehl, former director of the Saratoga Springs Historical Society; and Susan Brome, Holly Hallanan, and Michael Noonan at the Bolster Collection (photographs) of the Saratoga Springs Historical Society. Of all my Saratogian assistants, I am particularly indebted to Field for his friendship and tireless research aid.

My Newport archival research would not have been possible without the help of Rowena Stewart and Linda A'Vant Deshinni, former directors of the Rhode Island Black Heritage Society; Bert Lippincott of the Newport Historical Society's library; and Joan Youngken, photograph curator at the Newport Historical Society.

Several individuals shared their memories with me as I attempted to construct my narrative of resort towns. In Saratoga Springs, these include Edna Bailey Miller, Joseph Jackson, Edward Pilkington, Ernest Jackson, Carol Daggs, Margaret Daggs, George Ellis, Susan Jackson, Harvey Reid, Harvey Reid Jr., Robert and Mamie Simms, and Shirley Webb. Regarding Newport, these include Leonard J. Panaggio, Ed Dunbaugh, and Richard Berry. Transcripts of and/or notes taken during these interviews, from which I quote throughout this book, are in my possession.

At the institutional level, at various points I received research support from the New York State African American Research Institute, Bard College, and, through their summer seminars, the National Endowment for the Humanities.

The clerical staff at Bard College, particularly Evelyn Krueger, kindly accommodated years of typing revisions. Juliet Meyers in the Bard Publications Office is responsible for the lovely maps contained in this volume.

I am grateful to the various Christian communities to which I have belonged for the spiritual support they provided as I prepared this book: Chatham Fields Lutheran Church of Chicago; St. Timothy Lutheran Church of Hyde Park, New York; Everlasting Covenant Christian Ekklesia, formerly of Fishkill, New York; and Full Gospel Family Center of Lagrangeville, New

York. I am thankful to James Server for his quiet, steady, and prayerful undergirding.

My family—extended and immediate—has been my most tangible rudder throughout this project. My mother, Bethsheba Young, and late mother-in-law, Virginia Coad Armstead Boddy, provided moral support and practical help in the area of child care at critical moments. Siblings Vanessa, Roxanne, Letise, Larin, and Cosby buoyed me with their persistent expectations that this project would be completed. My husband, LeRoi, has understood the necessity of this book for me. He and my children, Matthew and Nathan, bolstered me with their pride in my work even as they endured my absences, anxieties, irritability, and general preoccupation with this research. I especially hope that Matthew and Nathan will take from these pages a better understanding and deeper appreciation of themselves.

Portions of this manuscript appeared earlier in the following publications:

"Black Families in Saratoga Springs, N.Y., 1870–1930." *Grist Mill.* 19 (July 1985): n.p.

"The Black Family in an Unfamiliar Setting." *Colorlines* 3 (Fall 1986): 8–10.

"Blacks in Saratoga: Putting Everything in Focus." *Annandale* 129.1 (Dec. 1989): 49–52.

"Dimensions of African-American Community Life in Saratoga Springs, New York, 1930–1989." *Documents in the History of Saratoga Springs* 1 (Feb. 1992): 3–28.

"An Historical Profile of Black Saratoga." In *A Heritage Uncovered: The Black Experience in Upstate New York, 1800–1925.* Ed. Cara A. Sutherland. 27–35. (Elmira, N.Y.: Chemung County Historical Society, 1988).

PREFACE

MY AUTOBIOGRAPHICAL LINK TO THE SUBJECT OF THIS BOOK IS INESCAP-
able. I grew up in South Fallsburg, New York—a resort town nestled in the
famed Borscht Belt region of New York's Catskills. The town and area have
stagnated in the economic doldrums for well over one quarter of a century
now, but the opposite was true during my childhood in the 1950s and 1960s.
As a youngster, I experienced firsthand the special rotation in local life
brought about by the yearly tourist population. "The season" brought a surge
of business and social activity on the Fourth of July weekend that continued
unabated through Labor Day weekend. In my little hamlet, which claimed a
commercial strip not even one-half mile long, I often rode my bicycle to
either one of the two four-way intersections on Main Street to watch the
police direct the ceaseless flow of automobile traffic. If I chose to walk
through town, I would have to compete with the jostling crowds, which
appeared as seamless as the sea to a girl of elementary school age, for a literal
foothold on the sidewalk. On Sunday nights, my extended family often
gathered in lawn chairs on the front yard of my grandparents' home—
enjoying ice cream, coffee, summer fruit, and each other's company—to
observe the spectacle of the bumper-to-bumper chain of weekenders' cars

snaking its way from the hotels and bungalow colonies down the road onto Main Street and the highway southeast to New York City. The relative privilege of the vacation world of bungalow colonists, campers, and hotel guests was external to ours. The distance and apparent material advantages of this world, however, made ogling an exciting pastime.

Through the summer black service workers it attracted, that vacation world connected to mine. My maternal grandparents ran a rooming house for African-American seasonal workers from New York, New Jersey, and mainly the South who came to our area each summer to earn money as waiters, commercial laundry workers, drivers, domestics, and assorted help for the invigorated local businesses. During the Depression, my grandmother had been the first in our family to migrate seasonally to the area from her native Virginia. It was partly the salary and tips from a hotel chambermaid's jobs that had lured her, but these had combined with the physical beauty of the mountains to convince her that she, her husband, and children could make a better life for themselves in Sullivan County, New York. Even then, the relocation was not sudden. It proceeded in stages: grandmother, leaving the family in Virginia, had first come up every summer to work. Next, the entire family moved to Harlem and used it as their base while spending summers in the Catskills. Finally, in the late 1940s, they bought a house in South Fallsburg, expanded it, and established their rooming house business. Their summer income was augmented by my grandfather's barbering business and my grandmother's home-based laundry operation. Since my grandfather was also a licensed, ordained minister, he held services in his home for African-American seasonal workers. In many ways, this Smith homestead functioned as a local black community center in the 1950s and the early 1960s, and this world—one that was very close to me—was as thrilling as the one I watched at a distance.

There was nothing gradual about the finish of each season. Relentless in its return, "the end" appeared suddenly and cruelly every September. I was always stunned by its arrival. On Labor Day Monday, the restaurants, roads, and stores stood dismally quiet, starkly abandoned. The desolation left me reeling with an overwhelming sadness, an acute withdrawal from the adrenalin rush of warm-weather frenzy. While many locals bemoaned the coming of summer and rejoiced at the exodus of those wretched "summer people," I missed them and intuitively understood our social and economic dependence on them. Within the week, we year-rounders regained our off-season cadence and returned to the slower pace of small-town life; but in late spring, we all prepared ourselves for the inevitable return of the city people.

The "inevitable" element in this cycle, in fact, serves as a kind of imperceptible canopy overshadowing the framing of this book. That is, the large, scholarly questions lurking behind the case studies contained in the following pages were born out of certain early observations and intuitive musings of mine concerning the deep contrast between "the season" and "the winter" in my hometown: summer differed sharply from the rest of the year for us permanent residents. The city folk who visited our county in July and August were faster, ruder, and wealthier than we. Yet, for a brief period each year, the two ostensibly opposite worlds united. I wondered, What drove the city people to us? Why were we so dependent on them? In time, I realized that these questions were another way of formulating a more basic question about the relationship between urban and rural life, between cities and towns.

Early sociological writings on the distinctive features of modern city life have combined with a perennial antiurban strain in American thought to fix in many minds the erroneously simplistic notion of an alien and antithetical relationship between cityscape and countryside. On the other hand, scholars of American urban development—from Richard Wade to William Cronon—have correctly emphasized the inescapable interconnections between the city mouse and its country cousin by pointing out that city growth is an essential feature of frontier expansionism, that rural needs propel metropolitanism, and that cities have a reciprocal influence on the hinterland. What binds the country to the city is urbanization, a societal process comprehensive in its penetration and not confined to specific locations. In other words, urbanization—the progressive movement of increasingly dense concentrations of people toward greater degrees of economically specialized activity—is not restricted to cities per se. It is possible, therefore, to imagine urbanization as a continuum along which may be identified more and less urbanized areas and places urbanized in differing ways.

Resort towns like Saratoga Springs, New York, and Newport, Rhode Island—geographically "pastoral" yet serving the "citified"—are fine manifestations of this tight urban-rural nexus. And the extent to which such resort towns differed in their level of dependence on tourist trade, farming, manufacturing activity, and/or otherwise diversified economic pursuits illustrates the possible range of positions on the horizontal line of urbanization.

Urbanization is also integral to the more specific analysis of the African-American populations of the two resort towns that follows. Inasmuch as this research explores the extent and essence of black community, it also locates the mechanism for the transmission of an African-American identity in those racialized dimensions of the urbanization processes in the United States during the late nineteenth and the early twentieth centuries: special migration streams away from more rural, less industrialized areas; residential segregation; exclusion from industrial jobs; and institutional separatism.

INTRODUCTION

THIS IS A STUDY OF THE BLACK COMMUNITIES OF NEWPORT, RHODE IS-
land, and Saratoga Springs, New York, during a six-decade period spanning
the last years of the nineteenth and the early years of the twentieth centuries.
The blindness of the historical eye to this subject on the part of African-
American specialists and urbanists suggests the two questions that drive this
investigation: How much, if at all, did the relatively small group of African
Americans living in Newport and Saratoga Springs resemble their contemporary counterparts, especially those in other larger cities? In what ways does
it make sense to see the individual African Americans in these resorts as a
whole, as a coherent community set apart in experience from the general
population of their towns? The answers to these questions can deepen and
expand our understanding of the historical meaning of racial identity for
African Americans and how this identity was formed, experienced, and
transmitted in areas of relatively sparse black concentration.

The cultural, social, economic, and political networks linking Cordelia
Howard, Edith Pilkington, and Carrie Pilkington in the years preceding
World War I, for example, provoke these queries. In 1911, Cordelia, a twenty-
nine-year-old black woman, worked aboard a steamship that traveled be-

tween New York City and her home in Newport. On a spring day that year while her boat was docked in New York, Cordelia was introduced by a mutual acquaintance to two other young black women—sisters Edith and Carrie Pilkington. The meeting took place on Thirty-seventh Street between Eighth and Ninth Avenues in one of Manhattan's several "small and densely populated [black] ghettoes . . . surrounded by white people."[1] With Cordelia stopping by to visit Carrie and Edith whenever her boat made layovers, the women's friendship lasted seven years until Mrs. Viola Pilkington, mother and widow, removed her family to Saratoga Springs—her own mother's birthplace.[2]

The concurrence of events represented by the New York City–based friendship of Cordelia, Carrie, and Edith, in which black resort-town residents came together in a burgeoning national center of African-American concentration surrounded by a white majority, neatly encapsulates the concentric circles of historical analysis traced in this study. It is specifically a historical investigation of the experiences of African Americans living in two resort towns between 1870 and 1930. The significance of its findings, however, will be located in the relationship between black Newporters and black Saratogians, on the one hand, and the larger national African-American and American experience, on the other.

A double-faceted basis for community feeling and identity is assumed here. First, the restrictive options uniquely imposed on African Americans of the period forced a commonality on them. Thus, blacks finding themselves sharing the same migration imperatives, jobs, houses, streets, and neighborhoods constituted a community by default. However, a secondary cohesive dynamic was in operation when African Americans transformed this circumscribed space into an autonomous world. In other words, community building became a deliberate act when African Americans created their own institutional life.

The five chapters that unfold in the following pages reflect this understanding of the multiple sources of black community. The first chapter is a necessary preliminary, a chronologically broad consideration of the general development of resort towns as urban places in the United States and of the situation of blacks as workers, tourists, and residents in these locales. Special attention is given in this chapter to Newport, Saratoga Springs, and their African-American populations in the years prior to 1870. Chapter 2 is a demographic profile of the two black communities covering population size and growth, the dynamics of migration, household structuring, and residential patterns as phenomena shaped by economic conditions and/or cultural imperatives. The economic dimensions of African-American life through home-based and workplace labors in Saratoga Springs and Newport are explored in chapter 3 as lacunae in which gender, race, and class intersect in multiple ways, such that race generally emerges as the most salient variable. Chapter 4 examines black institutional, social, and political life—formal and informal—making a case for the replication of a racial identity for African Americans in the resorts that had universal applicability during this period in U.S. history. At the same time, throughout the ensuing narrative, the details emerging from the comparison of Newport and Saratoga Springs serve to highlight the variation in experience subsumed under the category "black racial identity," even for African Americans in resort towns. Therefore, besides summarizing the racialized experience of blacks in Newport and Saratoga Springs, the concluding chapter places the findings within a framework that highlights the importance of structural and internal factors in shaping the details of African-American history.

It is argued here that, in at least two ways, the experience of black residents and workers in northern resort towns like Saratoga Springs and Newport stretches and questions the utility of older African-American historiographic models that initially offered two basic loci for studying the black community: the nineteenth-century, largely antebellum, rural South, focusing mainly on the plantation; and the twentieth-century, chiefly post–World War I, urban North, targeting primarily national major metropolises.[3] First, this research singles out a special type of setting—*small* northern towns. Second, in viewing resort towns as urban places, this study does not interpret movement from the rural South to the urban North as a disruptive, jarring passage necessarily resulting in that web of social pathology labeled "the ghetto."[4] Like the post-1970 slave historiography that emphasized the internal life of the slave, treating such issues as work, family, religion, resistance, and gender, this investigation demonstrates the adaptive aspects of African-American experience within a world of constricted options.[5] Like the newer black urban historiography, it emphasizes black agency, the continuity between rural and urban lifestyles, and the logic of alternative values in a world in which these are deemed unacceptable "race" traits.[6]

Several continuous threads linking both the South with the North and the rural with the urban in the historical experience of African Americans surface in the study of resort towns. In typical mode, separate race-specific national institutions like churches and fraternal societies connected the northerner and the southerner, the citified and the countrified, among blacks in the vacation spots. Also, the race-advancement and/or self-advancement strategies utilized by the African Americans studied here have a fairly permanent resonance in the black experience. One involved rationalized, formally organized alliances between bourgeois black elites and the black masses in the cause of race uplift—an urban approach employed in the South and the North.[7] Another device, especially used by slaves and African Americans in less-populous northern towns, entailed personalized, oblique, and non-institutionalized modes of self-advocacy—sometimes subterfuges, sometimes kinship and acquaintance networks.[8] Moreover, the seasonal economic rhythms of such places in which periods of intense tourist activity were followed by relatively dormant phases resembled the work patterns of agricultural societies in which planting, cultivating, and harvesting times are succeeded by cycles of passive waiting. Southern workers migrating to the North from rural regions therefore discovered the familiar ebb and flow of prosperity and leanness, activity and unemployment, in resort towns. Furthermore, black wage earners in resort towns repeated the servant roles with which they were well acquainted as domestic slaves in the rural and urban South during the antebellum period and as domestic servants in urban households, North and South, following the Civil War. As unique sorts of urban places, resort towns were therefore special milieux in which black Americans simultaneously experienced aspects of southern life, country life, northern life, and modern city life. In them, a span joining two conventional foci of black American history may be discerned.

African Americans in U.S. history represent a counterplot in the American success story. Their labors and presence help define it, yet their experiences often oppose it. Nowhere was this more true than in American resort towns in which the presence of black servants solidified the middle- and upper-class status of a white element anxious to affirm its social attainments.[9] The years 1870 to 1930, when both Saratoga Springs and Newport were in their heydays as celebrated retreats for America's wealthy, and when racial conventions severely limited the social, economic, and political prospects of African Americans, provide an especially fruitful laboratory for observing this historical process.

At the same time, for Afro-Newporters and Afro-Saratogians, the decision to live in these tiny resort communities was conscious and deliberate. Like their sisters and brothers elsewhere in the nation, they could not escape a web of racial proscriptions. But rather than make their way in older or larger black enclaves, they preferred to adapt coping and race-advancement strategies to their locations and small numbers. They recognized that, as resort-town dwellers, they could claim unique annual gifts from their special hometowns: cosmopolitan experiences in pastoral settings; expanded employment opportunities; recharged and enhanced social life and political activity; and a general renewed sense of efficacy and optimism that yoked them, perhaps chimerically, to the promise of the American Dream. In short, each year they had their "season," and it always came back.

⟡ I ⟡

Flattering Anticipations Had Seduced Them

THE AFRICAN-AMERICAN PEOPLE WHO LIVED IN NEWPORT AND SARATOGA Springs during the period studied here were inhabitants of a relatively new type of urban place in the United States—the resort town. These first appeared in the antebellum period and then proliferated as the nineteenth century wore on, with Saratoga Springs and later Newport emerging as premier summer tourist meccas. From the beginning of their histories, resort towns claimed African Americans as residents, workers, and guests, so it is not surprising that Newport and Saratoga Springs contained black communities even before 1870. This chapter, the chronological focus of which is broad but chiefly antebellum, will provide a summary of the rise of resort towns, the initial development of Newport and Saratoga Springs, the place of blacks in national resorts, and the early historical location of African Americans in Newport and Saratoga Springs. The major point is that notable differences in political advocacy between Afro-Newporters and Afro-Saratogians had surfaced by 1870—a difference that must be taken into account in considering the later narratives of these two groups of people.

The Rise of Resort Towns

Fashionable resort towns resulted from several simultaneous trends in America: the secularization of culture, especially in the North; the emergence of a middle class and a leisured, prosperous element; transportation improvements; and urbanization. During the seventeenth and the early eighteenth centuries, when most American settlers lived in a rural and often inhospitable wilderness that demanded their full energies for survival, colonial authorities harshly condemned inactivity, forbade amusements, and adopted severe legal measures "in detestation of idleness." Puritan Calvinism reinforced this emphasis on work and productivity. In this atmosphere, the drinking of alcoholic beverages stood as one of the few purely recreational activities permitted. Other forms of amusement often were "legitimate" survival activities, civic rituals, and religious events turned into occasions for group sport and socializing: barn raisings, hunting parties, corn huskings, militia-training days, wedding receptions, and the like. The rise of a colonial aristocracy and the decline of Puritanism's restraining influence during the latter half of the eighteenth century fostered a climate in which more spirited play took place. In Boston, there were now dancing and card-playing parties. Horse racing, sleigh riding, theater, balls, and epicurean banquets highlighted the list of social activities in the middle colonies. The gayest merrymaking, however, occurred in the South. There, heavy gambling accompanied horse races and cockfights. Dancing schools prepared partners for balls. Even christenings provided occasions for grand parties, and many southern gentleman rode and hunted for sport. Still, the poor condition of roads in an era of overland transportation made pleasure travel difficult. Outside of private homes, socializing among the wealthy was limited to sporting and social clubs.[1]

The national demographic and economic evolution shaped nineteenth-century leisure options. Between 1800 and 1850, the percentage of Americans living in cities of over 8,000 tripled. By even more narrow census definitions, the urban population of the United States increased from just 5 percent of the total in 1790 to more than 25 percent in 1870. Simultaneously, the seemingly boundless economic opportunities in the new republic conferred middle- and upper-middle-class status on larger numbers of the ambitious. Situated away from rural farmlands and privileged with time to spare, this urban, cramped, bored, and overworked populace began to concern itself with the question of how to spend its free hours satisfactorily. Two solutions appeared—new forms of in-city recreation and temporary escape to the pastoral hinterland. The latter possibility grew in popularity throughout the nineteenth century as canals, steamboats, and railways afforded relatively easy, cheap, and fast access to rural getaways.[2]

As *urban* places, resort towns uniquely satisfied the needs of an *urban* clientele, influenced by the Romantic movement, to reexperience the charms of a nearly forgotten yet sentimentalized countryside while avoiding its inconveniences. Nineteenth-century vacation travelers to the West, for example, often registered disappointment and anger at the starkness of the rocks, sand, and mountains forming the landscape. Promotional literature may have likened the Colorado Rockies to the Swiss Alps and southern California beaches to the Italian Riviera, but tourists who had no particular liking for the outdoors per se demanded "a specific and identifiable point whose impact was immediate and that could be represented in a paragraph or a picture frame." However bucolic, the wilderness must be tamed. Indeed, it was in the *towns* of Colorado and California, places bearing the unmistakable mark of civilization, that visitors lingered the longest.[3] The attractions of the typical nineteenth-century resort town, then, while ostensibly rural, were necessarily urbane.[4]

Promoters and boosters, ubiquitous in American urban history, were responsible for the transformation of rustic places of "inspiration" to pleasure centers. Drawing on European models, many such resorts experienced a quiet, early phase solely as religious and health retreats for the devout and infirm. Responding to an urban market, however, boosters arranged for mineral waters, sea-bathing, and sightseeing to be enjoyed in very small daily doses and only as part of brief excursions away from comfortable, if not luxurious, hotels. Thus, the Brooklynites patronizing Coney Island enjoyed solitude, salt air, and beautiful seaside vistas within the secure and domesticated confines of the Coney Island House. And Atlantic City, with its beaches, shoreline concessions, and teeming Boardwalk crowds, embodied "the extreme juxtaposition of urbanity and wilderness" that became the resort town's trademark.[5]

Throughout the nineteenth century, resort towns grew in number and flourished. Most were concentrated in the East, along the Atlantic shore, but by the latter quarter of the century, they were numerous enough to warrant two volumes of *Appleton's General Guide to the United States and Canada*—one containing the New England and Middle Atlantic states, the other the southern and western states. In the Northeast, resort towns included places like Saratoga Springs, New York; Newport, Rhode Island; Bar Harbor, Maine; Marblehead, Massachusetts; Niagara Falls, New York; and Oyster Bay, Long Island. In the South, there were Hot Springs, Virginia; Warm Springs, Georgia; Southern Pines, North Carolina; and Pensacola, Florida. Sunrise, Wisconsin, was a midwestern tourist stop; and in the West, Salt Lake Springs, Utah, and Pasadena, California, were among the health and resort centers.[6]

Saratoga Springs and Newport before 1870

The fame of the springs at Saratoga among North American whites dates back to 1767, when they were discovered by Sir William Johnson, British representative to the Iroquois Nation. Some twenty years later, Philip Schuyler, onetime commander of American troops in northern New York State during the Revolutionary War, established Saratoga as his country residence. General Schuyler cut a road from old Saratoga (present-day Schuylerville) to High Rock Spring (in present-day Saratoga Springs) in 1783. The Schuyler estate attracted many New York socialites curious about the spring waters' reputed medicinal value in relieving dyspepsia; George Washington was among the early distinguished visitors.[7]

The foresight and efforts of a local booster, Gideon Putnam, established Saratoga Springs as a true resort town. A native of Hartford, Connecticut, Putnam first ran a sawmill in Saratoga Springs; he floated staves, shingles, and lumber down the Hudson for the New York City market. In 1802, with capital borrowed from his father-in-law, he built a wooden, three-story structure to accommodate seventy guests beside Congress Spring that villagers jokingly labeled "Putnam's Folly." The last laugh went to the Yankee, however; within one year, the springs—which had rarely attracted seventy visitors in an entire summer—now required even more tourist accommodations. Putnam expanded Union Hall, his first guest house.[8]

In 1806, Putnam tubed Washington Spring and Columbian Spring by fitting them with piping to permit their consumption as drinking and bathing water by prospective guests. In 1811, he began construction of another hotel, Congress Hall, but never lived to see its completion in 1815. He died in 1812 from injuries sustained in a fall from the scaffolding for the new building. Before his death, though, Putnam engineered several significant aspects of the physical plan of the blossoming summer spa: the laying out of Broadway, the major thoroughfare; the opening and improvement of several other roads; the placement of Congress, Columbian, and Hamilton Springs on wide, public streets; and the erection of several buildings to facilitate visitors.[9]

Despite Putnam's efforts and the growing reputation of its many springs, Saratoga Springs's life as a lucrative resort community was threatened briefly during the first quarter of the nineteenth century. In 1808, Dr. Billy J. Clarke ran a highly successful evangelistic crusade in the area. As a direct consequence, Saratoga Springs soon claimed one of the nation's first temperance organizations, the Moreau and Northumberland Temperance Society. The influence of this religious element on everyday life at the spa was great. The daily routine consisted largely of hymn singing, buggy riding, and partaking of spring waters as baths or medicinal drinks. No card playing or dancing were permitted. Hotels began the day with prayer meetings and Bible study. Guests were forbidden to arrive or depart on Sunday. Saratoga Springs began to lose less-pious souls to nearby Ballston Spa, whose main hotel, the Sans Souci, was modeled after the palace of Versailles and, true to its name, indulged its guests' desires for pleasure. For this reason, 200 visitors per season flocked there.[10]

A secularization of life in Saratoga Springs was ultimately accomplished. In 1819, Saratoga Springs achieved designation as a special township with the right to govern itself. Then, in 1826, the smaller area of the town that developed around the springs was incorporated as a separate village. These legal maneuvers gave the village the authority and mandate to protect its particular commercial interest—the promotion of a tourist economy. Liquor options and a permissive attitude toward gambling and other forms of entertainment naturally resulted. Congress Hall then introduced billiard rooms and provided an orchestra. Dancing, unchaperoned rides to the countryside, and poker in private rooms soon followed. By 1830, the village also permitted faro, chuck-a-luck, and roulette in billiard halls and bowling alleys. A gambling house opened in 1842 in an alley near the United States Hotel.[11] During the sixty years encompassed by this study, Saratoga Springs's appeal as a gambling haven, however, stood in defiance of state legislation that declared all betting, except that at the racetrack, illegal—a largely rhetorical capitulation to the prevailing sentiment of nineteenth-century America that financial gain acquired by any means other than productive work undermined the fabric of the nation. Gambling was prohibited generally in New York State in 1819. But by becoming a special township in that year and a self-governing village seven years later, Saratoga Springs had secured an unofficial amnesty from serious enforcement of the act; local authorities winked at gambling because it contributed too significantly to the resort's success. Despite subsequent antigambling state legislation in 1851 and 1855 intended to strengthen the general prohibition, the practice continued in the spa.[12]

It was John Morrissey who introduced horse racing in Saratoga Springs. In 1861, the Irish Morrissey—a former boxer, ex-Tammanyite, and New York City gambling house proprietor—moved his gambling establishment to Matilda Street (later, Woodlawn Avenue) in Saratoga Springs. Concessions were made to the local reform element: women were not allowed in Morrissey's gambling rooms. Morrissey further neutralized potential opposition to his enterprise by contributing to local churches, benevolent associations, and charities. The voices of moral outrage thus silenced, Morrissey proceeded to build a thoroughbred horse racetrack in the village in 1863 and develop a program of four days of racing, two races per day, starting the third of August each summer. A racing association was formed that included among its members several of the nation's social leaders—for instance, William Travers, stockbroker and wit; John Hunter, sportsman; and Leonard Jerome, the lawyer whose daughter, Jenny, became Lady Randolph Churchill. The racing association promptly built a larger track in 1864. In 1865, the first Saratoga Cup Stakes was held, and Morrissey opened an even larger casino near Congress Park.[13]

As a result of these entertainment innovations, guests returned to the spa, slowly at first, but in force by midcentury. As early as 1825, when Dr. John Clarke, proprietor of New York City's first soda fountain and now a retiree in nearby Yorkshire, began bottling the water from Congress Spring and shipping it downstate, Saratoga Springs was listed in travel guides as a regular stop on the national summer vacation circuit that started in New York City in July and went on to Ballston Spa with excursions to the Catskills, Saratoga Springs, Glens Falls, and Lake George until September. The number of yearly visitors steadily grew from Putnam's projected 70 in 1802 to 8,000 in 1833 and 12,000 in 1859. These last two years, the permanent populations were only about 2,000 and 7,000, respectively. Moreover, the success of Morrissey's ventures was so phenomenal that by 1870, the daily attendance at the track alone reached 10,000.[14]

The 1833 arrival of the first railroad, the Saratoga and Schenectady, contributed directly to the gain in summer business. The line operated between Schenectady, New York, and Saratoga Springs, passing through Ballston Spa. The business of this route was so narrowly limited to summer guests during its early years that it often closed completely in the winter and offered horse and sleigh transportation instead to passengers during the cold season. The leasing of the Saratoga and Schenectady Railroad and the Albany, Vermont, and Canada Railroad by the Renssalaer (or Troy) and Saratoga Railroad in 1860 made it possible for the visitor from New York City to travel by rail to Saratoga Springs from either nearby Troy or Albany after passing up the Hudson River by steamboat or train. In 1871, this entire system was leased by the Delaware and Hudson Canal Railroad Company, which provided transportation service to Saratoga Springs for the period under study.[15]

For fifty years, then, from roughly 1820 to 1870, Saratoga Springs reigned as "the cynosure of the Nation's resort society."[16] Several similar ventures on the part of hopeful entrepreneurs followed Putnam's successful lead in the erection of Union Hall (later, the Grand Union Hotel). The Columbian Hotel opened its doors in 1809. The Pavilion began business in 1819, and the United States was built in 1824. These grand hotels were joined by several other small guest-, rooming-, and boardinghouses in providing seasonal visitors elegant lodging, social exposure, and good times of the highest order. By 1869, there were thirty-three hotels and twenty-two boardinghouses in Saratoga Springs, a village of only 7,516.[17]

A typical vacation day at Saratoga Springs during the antebellum period consisted of breakfast at eight after a six o'clock trip to the springs; walking, sitting, or strolling along Broadway or on the hotel piazza; dinner at two; more walking or perhaps a drive to view the town's outskirts; supper at seven; and evening dancing and entertainment. This basic schedule could be supplemented with ventriloquist and comedic acts, magic shows, lectures, concerts, amusement rides, bowling, faro, poker, and other games of chance. Each of the town's several hotels generally offered a sampling of these activities. After 1863, a trip to the track to attend the horse races helped to complete the day's agenda.[18]

While Saratoga Springs practically was born a resort town, Newport, Rhode Island, experienced an early incarnation as a thriving port city during the colonial period. Three years of British occupation during the Revolutionary War, however, severely paralyzed its trading economy. The city's shipping business never recovered, especially after the War of 1812 delivered a second crippling blow, and only unprofitable attempts at small-scale industry followed.[19]

The transformation of Newport into a summer resort, then, followed the failure of other avenues of enterprise. From the 1750s, Newport had served as a summer haven for wealthy southern planters already familiar with the northern slave-trading center. For them, it functioned additionally as an escape from the malarial heat of southern swamps. These seasonal visitors usually stayed in boardinghouses or rented local farmhouses. Families from Philadelphia, New York, and Baltimore soon followed the example of the southerners. In 1825, the Brinley House was opened on Catherine Street as a hotel to accommodate the budding summer business; by 1830, several boardinghouses counted on a regular trade in summer vacationers.[20]

In the 1840s, Newport's pioneer summer visitors were joined by a group of mainly New England intellectuals who dominated the scene until roughly 1870. Among the more famous cultured Bostonians were Oliver Wendell Holmes, Julia Ward Howe, Henry Wadsworth Longfellow, Henry James, and George Bancroft. These literati sought creative and artistic inspiration in Newport's natural beauty and spent a good portion of their days there at the Redwood Library, Art Association, and Reading Room.[21]

It was not until after 1870 that Newport acquired an identity as a city of summer mansions built by the leaders of fashionable society. During the antebellum period, prominent visitors summered instead at boardinghouses like the Ocean House, which first opened in 1844 on Bellevue Avenue; it later expanded and changed its name to the Bellevue Hotel. By 1852, several other lodging places—including the Bateman Boardinghouse and Farm, the Atlantic Hotel on Bellevue Avenue, and the Fillmore Hotel on Catherine Street—could be found at the resort.[22]

By midcentury, the shape of Newport as a summer "cottage" colony emerged, largely owing to the efforts of Alfred Smith, a local tailor turned land speculator. In 1851, for only $22,700, Smith purchased 140 acres of farmland south of the town limits and later cajoled the town council into extending Bellevue Avenue, the major summer thoroughfare, through this property from Ocean House down to Bailey's Beach on the southern end of town. Smith also associated with Charles Hazard Russell, a wealthy Rhode Islander who had acquired 300 acres of land south and east of Touro Street in 1845. Reportedly, Smith rode about the streets of Newport in a leather chaise, reins in one hand and a map of the city in scroll form in the other. As he spotted "substantial men," he called them over, subjected them to a spirited sales pitch, only releasing them after a deal had been struck. So successful was this enterprise that by 1852, twelve cottages had been built for exclusive summer residence by four prosperous Bostonians and eight gentlemen from the South and the Middle Atlantic states.[23] George Mason, the editor of the local *Newport Mercury*, observed in 1854: "Here, those who come to pass a few weeks are so charmed with the climate and scenery of the island; a desire to build becomes irresistible, and the result is a lot with a commanding view is purchased, a neat cottage erected, and the happy household only leave for their winter quarters when the north winds and the falling leaves proclaim the warm season at an end. . . . Thousands now assemble at Newport every year."[24]

The Fall River steamship line, which began operating in 1847, supplied most of the transportation to Newport. Passengers from New York City steamed up Long Island Sound into Narragansett Bay to disembark at Newport. Those leaving Boston for Newport traveled by train and then switched to steamboat at Fall River, Massachusetts.[25]

For the midcentury hotel guest in Newport, the day's activities did not start until after dinner at two o'clock in the afternoon. A drive down Bellevue Avenue to Easton's Beach in a barouche rented from a livery stable followed. Guests took tea at six and then enjoyed a game of whist. Except for an occasional hop at one of the hotels, the evening ended at ten. The inauguration of regular evening dancing and receptions between 1860 and 1870 helped enliven the day's schedule.[26]

As social marketplaces, resort towns like Saratoga Springs and Newport throughout their history drew a diverse clientele of Americans at the more comfortable end of the economic scale. Con artist and gold digger, workers and farmers, business people and gentlefolk mingled and jockeyed for position as part of the American democratic experiment. An English visitor to Saratoga Springs in 1838, James Silk Buckingham, mused:

Saratoga affords perhaps the best opportunity that a stranger can enjoy for seeing American society on the largest scale, and embracing the greatest variety of classes at the same time; for except for the small shopkeeper and mere laborer, every other class has its representatives here. The rich merchant from New Orleans, the planter from Arkansas and Alabama, with the more haughty and polished landowner from the Carolinas and Virginia; the successful speculator in real estate from the West; the rich capitalist from Boston and New York; the official functionary from Washington, the learned professor from New Haven and Cambridge. The whole union is thus brought before the eye of the stranger at one view.

Hundreds who, in their own towns, could not find admittance into the circles of fashionable society . . . came to Saratoga, where at Congress Hall or the United States, by the moderate payment of two dollars a day, they may be seated at the same table and often side by side with the first families of the country; promenade in the same piazza, lounge on the sofas in the same drawing room and dance in the same quadrille with the most fashionable beaux and belles of the land; and thus for a week or month they may stay at Saratoga, they enjoy all the advantages which their position would make inaccessible to them at home.[27]

Similarly, on Coney Island during the nineteenth century, "middle and upper class men went 'slumming.' Gamblers and prostitutes were not infrequently seen on the back stairways of the lavish hotels. And middle class families trudged up the sandy beach for dinner at the Manhattan [Beach Hotel] and a chance to be temporarily part of the elite."[28] Likewise, nineteenth-century advertisements for Atlantic City "contained many touching examples of class mixing by the seaside."[29] Similar mixing occurred at New York State's Catskills during the midtwentieth century:

There were the elderly couples, sent to "the mountains" for the summer by prospering sons in a gesture that gave the sons a neat boost in status; there were stenographers and clothing industry girls who saved all year to be able to afford two weeks at hotels like the Flagler or Grossinger's where they hoped to lure a rich manufacturer or lawyer to the altar. . . . Young men who were doing well as doctors, lawyers, or businessmen and could afford it took their wives to the more expensive Sullivan [County] hotels as a visible proclamation of success. There they could meet richer, older men who might help them in their careers, and also they encountered aggressive young people on the make sexually or in business and learned to spot and avoid the bungalow people who crashed the big hotels at every opportunity as part of their endless obsession with moving upward.[30]

The fluid composition of resort-town clientele, however, belies an under-lying, distinct ranking of society in such places. Class divisions manifested themselves in a hierarchy among resort towns since Americans differed in income and in relaxation preferences. The working class opted for short, inexpensive forays out of the city: visits to amusement parks, day excursions, and beach trips. Atlantic City, for example, catered chiefly to this group. The middle class could afford one-week to monthlong vacations in hotels where they preoccupied themselves with society-watching and social climbing; or, simply as leisure consumers, they contented themselves with their own mate-rial success. Ocean City, New Jersey, for one, and Saratoga Springs served such types. The wealthy, possessing the most free time, sought privacy, exclusion from the masses, and frequently indulged in extravagant material displays in private homes and grand hotels. Newport and Long Branch on Long Island counted this crowd as their patrons.[31]

When several classes targeted the same resort, a sorting process often en-sued. In antebellum Saratoga Springs, the hotel clientele sifted itself among Congress Hall (for the staid, conservative, and established wealthy); the United States Hotel (for the newly rich businessman); the Grand Union Ho-tel (for the elderly, the religious, judges, and professors); and the Pavilion and Columbian hotels (for the middle class and transients). Similarly, on Coney Island during the late nineteenth century, the working class occupied the center-west section of amusements. The middle class patronized the Brigh-ton Beach Hotel in the center-east portion. Finally, the upper class monopo-lized the exclusive Manhattan Beach Hotel on the island's easternmost tip.[32]

Gambling practices supply additional evidence of the ways in which class awareness and class differentiation occurred in the new resorts. Historian Ann Fabian has documented several sources of organized national opposi-tion to games of chance in the 1820s and 1830s—one of many nineteenth-century reform movements prompted by the Second Great Awakening. Above all was the threat of disruption of the nation's tenuous social struc-ture; monied gentlemen might lose their fortunes to struggling workingmen in a single unlucky night. Americans therefore felt most comfortable when gambling took place among those of similar class backgrounds. Fabian explains that "clubs where rich card players dealt faro to wealthy merchants who played in luxurious surroundings and dined on fine food" were considered "honest" because "they isolated those who could afford to lose from those who might turn to crime."[33] Such establishments were easily tolerated by authorities throughout most of the nineteenth century and even into the twentieth. Thus, to the extent that the hotels of Saratoga Springs were class segregated, so too were their gaming rooms.[34]

African Americans in Resorts

Blacks figured in the social mixing and social sifting at resort towns both as tourists and as service workers. During the period of declining interracial amity at the turn of the century, Atlantic City "made no real attempt to exclude blacks from the beachfront." Black women were seen bathing at the seaside and a black Philadelphia church sponsored an outing to the resort.[35] Detroit's nineteenth-century black elite families—the Pelhams, Fergusons, and Barriers—regularly vacationed at Bois Blanc Island, a north Michigan retreat near Mackinaw Island. In fact, beginning in the nineteenth century, a national black "aristocracy" mirrored the "genteel performance" of white middle- and upper-class Americans in resort-based leisure consumption. In addition to white patrons, Saratoga Springs, Newport, and Cape May, New Jersey, for instance, all drew a black clientele as well.[36]

But in a segregationist era, black tourists suffered restrictions at mainstream resorts. In the 1930s, black vacationers in Ocean City faced bathing and lodging barriers. Special travel guides informed African-American vacationers of the extent of services and facilities available to them. *The Traveler's Green Book*, for example, began publication in 1936 and offered "assured protection for the Negro traveler" by listing motels, hotels, private homes, and inns open to black guests. Saratoga Springs and Newport were among those vacation spots regularly listing special black accommodations. As late as the mid-1960s, *The Green Book* was still printed.[37]

Beginning in the late nineteenth century, distinctly black resorts emerged as the most trouble-free vacation option for African Americans. For example, the Frederick Douglass family pioneered the development of Highland Beach, a Chesapeake Bay vacation community outside of Annapolis, Maryland. Similarly, Idlewild, Michigan (about seventy miles north of Grand Rapids), although more of a rustic retreat than a true resort town at first, began as a resort in 1912 for "urban, land-hungry" midwestern blacks. Middle-class African Americans from Chicago, Detroit, Cleveland, Fort Wayne, and Gary purchased small real estate parcels there on which they erected vacation cottages or tents. Black railroad workers who bought property from Henry Flagler's East Coast Railroad spearheaded the development of Florida's first African-American beach community, Manhattan Beach, which thrived roughly from 1900 to 1940, offering cottages, pavilions, and an amusement park to black church groups and day-trip excursionists. From 1926 to 1958, Butler's Beach near St. Augustine, Florida, served as a retreat for black beachfront cottagers. And in 1935, the Afro-American Life Insurance Company developed American Beach on Florida's Amelia Island as a black oceanside haven.[38]

Like their counterparts in black urban ghettos during the era of Jim Crow, African-American entrepreneurs in black resort towns found sheltered business opportunities. Several small black proprietorships thrived at Idlewild, for example. They included brickmaking, dry-cleaning, canning, and horse-renting establishments. Moreover, from the 1920s to 1950s, Idlewild functioned as a "summer Apollo," a showplace for black entertainers denied access to white audiences. And during the 1950s, eleven black businesses operated within Manhattan Beach's seventy-eight-acre tract.[39]

Black wage earners found resort towns attractive in their ample supply of unskilled and domestic service work—occupational categories to which blacks were increasingly relegated as the nineteenth century wore on. In 1930 Ocean City, African Americans were employed in "certain domestic occupations and . . . in hotels." In the town of Oak Bluffs on Martha's Vineyard, they worked as hotel service employees. And in Atlantic City, African Americans labored primarily as "waiters, cooks, porters, and nursegirls."[40]

Because of their service economies, resort towns of the Northeast may in fact have drawn greater proportions of blacks than did larger, industrialized cities in the late nineteenth century. For example, while Manhattan, Brooklyn, Chicago, Cleveland, and Detroit remained less than 2 percent black during this period, Atlantic City's African Americans constituted from 15 to 20 percent of the total population.[41]

African Americans in Saratoga Springs and Newport before 1870

Increases in the populations of black Saratoga and black Newport prior to 1870 attest to the attractiveness of job opportunities in the two resort towns.

After the formation of the village, the number of African Americans in Saratoga Springs grew from 88 in 1830, to 185 in 1840, to 192 in 1850. By 1860, the 239 blacks in the spa constituted 3 percent of the village population. Prior to the Revolutionary War, the black presence in Newport stemmed from that port's involvement in the slave trade, a commerce so lucrative that it placed Newport in direct competition with Boston and Salem for primacy among New England's colonial seaports. The first slave vessel to reach the shores of Rhode Island arrived in Newport in 1696 and sold four Africans from a shipload of forty-seven. In fact, until 1736, most Rhode Island slave trading was confined to Newport, the transactions usually taking place on the corners of Mill and Spring streets and North Baptist and Thames streets, both within easy walking distance of the docks. More than half of Rhode Island's black population in 1708 lived in Newport; they numbered 220. By 1755, Newport listed 1,234 blacks among its residents. A decrease in the black population resulted from the interruption of maritime trade during the American Revolution. Thus, in 1782, only 600 blacks dwelled in Newport, but these represented nearly 10 percent of the total population. As Newport passed into its new phase as a resort, the African-American population first declined and then slowly swelled. In 1830, the 445 blacks in the town were 5 percent of the total population, and by 1860, 693 black Newporters constituted 6 percent of the town's residents.[42]

Enmeshed in the tourist economies of both places before 1870, African Americans cooked, cleaned, chauffeured, entertained, and otherwise catered to summer guests, but one can reasonably guess this may have been especially true of Saratoga Springs, whose urban identity was completely and exclusively linked to seasonal vacationing. In 1860, 43 percent of black Saratogians were "gainfully employed." Seventy-six percent of black men listing an occupation in that year's census were service workers employed as waiters, cooks, stewards, or general servants and laborers. The remainder spread themselves among several occupations: farmer, barber, tanner, peddler, hack driver, stonecutter, and blacksmith. Half of the black population of Newport in 1860 was "gainfully employed." Hotels and boardinghouses provided jobs for 20 percent of the total African-American population in that year. Nearly 60 percent of the black working men and 30 percent of the black working women earned their living as employees of the Bateman House, Aquidneck House, Pelham House, Fillmore House, Park House, Atlantic House, Bellevue Hotel, and—before its destruction—the Sea Girt Hotel.

These men and women labored as washerwomen, maids, waiters, porters, dishwashers, bellboys, hallmen, and general servants. Outside of hotel work, 22 percent of black males were in service and unskilled positions. How many of these non-hotel workers in Newport could be found in year-round, non-resort related jobs is impossible to tell from the 1860 census, but one may safely speculate that a fair number worked in the small industries and maritime ventures that persisted even into the seaport's resort phase. Only about 10 percent of Afro-Newporter male wage-earners worked in skilled crafts, professions, or proprietary positions.[43]

Black women workers in both places were even more confined to service positions. In 1860, 96 percent of them in Saratoga Springs were either cooks, washerwomen, or servants. The residual 4 percent labored as tailoresses or seamstresses. Of all employed black females enumerated in Newport during the same year, 98 percent were engaged in service work.[44]

African-American wage earners in Saratoga Springs and Newport matched national and respective statewide patterns. After 1825, faced with competition from German and Irish immigrants, blacks progressively concentrated in domestic-service positions. In New York State and Rhode Island, this meant a reduced presence in skilled trades as barbers, carpenters, blacksmiths, printers, sawyers, and maritime employees with a concomitant limitation to work as porters, servants, laborers, laundresses, waiters, teamsters, sextons, gardeners, painters, hostlers, cooks, draymen, stevedores, and unskilled jobs of various types.[45]

Local legends and literary evidence support an antebellum profile of black laborers as largely service and/or unskilled workers in the two resorts—but in Saratoga Springs especially. In Newport, one "Cuffy Cockroach" cooked memorable turtle soup. In Saratoga Springs, a "Gingerbread Frank" worked at various odd jobs, while former slave "Susan" made a living housecleaning. Dolly Carey was employed as the first pastry cook at the United States Hotel. Thomas and Nancy Campbell, once owned by Saratogian Jacobus Barhyte, remained in their former master's employ when freed, probably as farm hands, house servants, and/or attendants in his tavern. James Stewart, a British visitor at the spa in 1828, reported that he and his wife were referred to a "*lady* of color" after requesting a laundress. And among the black hotel employees was Francis "Frank" Johnson, a pioneer black entertainer and musician of national reputation. When Congress Hall contracted with Johnson and his Cotillion Band in 1821, it became "the first hotel in America to employ a Band of Music, and to adopt a plan of Hops and Balls." With few exceptions, Johnson played at Congress Hall each season until 1843. So popular was his music that his contract was amended to include additional morning and afternoon performances in Congress Park and alternate evening engagements at the United States Hotel. Among those who enjoyed his tunes were some of the new nation's leading politicians—James Monroe, John Quincy Adams, Andrew Jackson, Martin Van Buren, William Henry Harrison, John Tyler, Henry Clay, and Daniel Webster.[46]

Service work for the year-round wage earner at a seasonal resort often involved a patchwork of temporary jobs, as the careers of Solomon and Anne Northup illustrate. Solomon Northup, whose experiences as a freedman kidnapped and sold into bondage are recounted in a compelling slave narrative, moved his family from Kingsbury, New York, to Saratoga Springs in 1834; he worked as a violinist during the winter season. During the summer, he was employed as a hack driver at Washington Hall, a boardinghouse on north Broadway. He also worked at the United States Hotel and as a laborer on the Troy and Saratoga Railroad while it was under construction. Anne, Northup's wife, enjoyed a local reputation as a fine cook; her services were called on regularly at the United States Hotel and "other public houses of the place." Permanent residents of Saratoga Springs, the Northups were among those blacks who persisted in the resort town long after the last of the summer visitors departed.[47]

Those blacks who managed to carve a place for themselves in the local economies of Saratoga Springs and Newport before 1870 as successful independent entrepreneurs were unique and noteworthy. George Crum was one. Visitors to Cary Moon's restaurant on Lake Saratoga in the 1850s were treated to Crum's culinary wizardry and that of his aunt, Catherine Weeks. Crum, the son of a mulatto jockey from Kentucky, is credited with the invention of the potato chip; there are dozens of stories explaining how the famed Saratoga chip came about. One favorite version is that a guest at Moon's Lake House in 1853 complained to a waiter about the preparation of the french-fried potatoes and requested a new serving of them. Intending to transfer his outrage to the customer, Crum then peeled some potatoes as thinly as possible, dumped them in fat for deep-frying, salted them heavily, and sent them back to the table. Encouraged by the unexpected praise he received for his creation, Crum eventually parlayed his culinary talent into a profitable career as an independent restaurateur. Among his clientele were

William Travers, William Vanderbilt, Thomas G. Nast, Pierre Lorillard, and Grover Cleveland.[48]

Isaac Rice, Benjamin Burton, and George Downing stand out as Newport's leading black entrepreneurs in this period. Rice began as a gardener, then successfully supplemented this work with a catering business. Benjamin Burton, a Connecticut native, first came to Newport in 1845 and worked as a teamster for Gifford and Devens, local coal dealers. In 1849, having caught "gold fever," he left for California, where he accumulated the capital that allowed him to launch an express business on his return to Newport in the early 1850s.[49]

George T. Downing was the most successful of Newport's antebellum businessmen. Downing's father, Thomas, ran a popular oyster house and catering service in New York City. George followed in his father's footsteps at the age of twenty-six by opening a firm, George T. Downing, Confectioner and Caterer, on New York's Broadway in 1845. His clientele included the Astors, the Schermerhorns, and other New York social elites. One year later, Downing established a summer business in Newport at Catherine and Fir streets after receiving "repeated overtures to do so," perhaps from friends in high society who were now summering in the growing resort community. He bought an old estate on the corner of Downing and Bellevue in Newport in 1849 and continued in business there until 1865. His additional restaurants in Providence and Washington, D.C., supplemented income from the Newport operation. Furthermore, in 1854, with capital borrowed from his father, Downing built the luxurious Sea Girt Hotel in Newport, "sumptuously furnished for a resort for the wealthy." Despite the fact that the hotel was destroyed suspiciously by fire in 1860, he immediately invested in another project, Downing Block, "the first block of stores in Newport for summer business."[50]

Black Saratoga Springs and black Newport were also mostly female communities in 1860. In the largest age cohort, that of young adults nineteen to forty-five years old, females outnumbered males by a ratio of 1.5 to 1 in Saratoga Springs and 1.4 to 1 in Newport.[51] The shortage of men probably precluded marriage for many and may be reflected in the relatively large number of white-headed households in which blacks lived as boarders or as servants in both places. In Saratoga Springs, roughly 41 percent of households containing blacks were headed by whites; the comparable figure for Newport was 46 percent.

Small in number, blacks in Saratoga Springs and Newport still formed distinct geographic enclaves in their towns. A map of Saratoga Springs in 1820 shows a "few houses of colored people" on West Congress Street, then called Johnny Cake Road (see map 1). Black Saratogians might have made this residential choice, hoping to achieve closest proximity to the town's first hotels, places of potential employment. Another possible explanation for this black pocket lies in the town's physical layout. It was customary in pedestrian, preindustrial towns for the poor to settle at the edge of the city, leaving to the wealthy convenient access to centrally located commercial, religious, and political institutions. This might have been the case in Saratoga Springs in 1820 because, until that date, it was a town in two sections separated by a thick pine forest. The older, more developed upper village had sprung up around High Rock Spring near Schuyler's colonial summer home. The newer, lower village consisted of Putnam's property around Congress Spring. Blacks might have been restricted, therefore, to settlement in the then-peripheral lower village.[52]

The two residential centers in antebellum Newport similarly reflected the preindustrial pattern whereby workers sought to live near their jobs, but they also resulted from cultural forces. Since hotel life in the 1840s and 1850s was concentrated in the Kay Street-Catherine Street-Old Beach Road neighborhood, some blacks resided in the backstreets and alleys—Liberty, Downing, Fir, Fillmore Court, Bowler Lane, and Bath Road—on which was built housing for hotel personnel and guests' servants. Here, African Americans lived among the livery stables and storage barns that were connected with the hotels. The presence of early black churches—the Colored Union Church organized in 1845 and the Shiloh Baptist Church established in 1864—probably lured African Americans to this area of the town as well. After 1850, an area of West Broadway known as "New Town" was developed especially for the growing working class, black and white, that was attracted by the prosperous summer colony. The location of Mt. Zion African Methodist Episcopal (A.M.E.) Church there in the 1850s on Johnson Court off Kingston Avenue helped define the new neighborhood as black (see map 2).[53]

Newport contained more southerners than did Saratoga Springs during the antebellum period. In 1860, most black Saratogians (70 percent) were indigenous New Yorkers. This figure reflects two facts: first, prior to the Civil War's end, no significant migration of blacks from the South occurred. Secondly, of those antebellum blacks living in the North, most concentrated

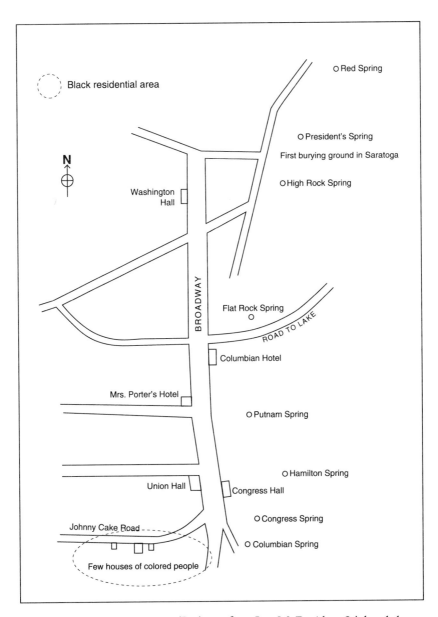

Map 1. Saratoga Springs, c. 1820. (Redrawn from Jno. M. Davidson Jr.'s hand-drawn map, 1890, Saratoga Springs Public Library, Saratoga Springs, N.Y.)

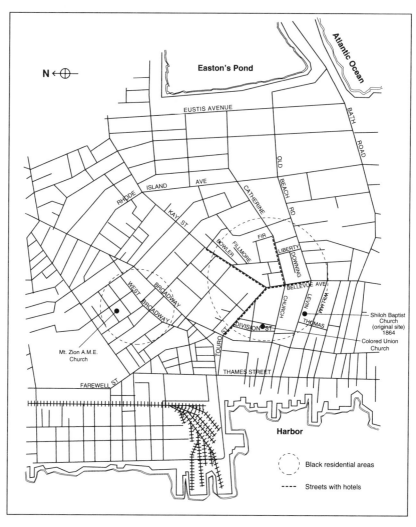

Map 2. Areas of Black Residential Clustering in Newport, prior to 1870. (Composite map based on Rhode Island Historical Preservation Committee, "The Kay Street–Catherine Street–Old Beach Road Neighborhood, Newport, Rhode Island" [Providence: Rhode Island Historical Preservation Committee, 1974], 14–16; Rhode Island Historical Preservation Committee, "The West Broadway Neighborhood, Newport, Rhode Island" [Providence, R.I., 1977], 17–19, 25; and William H. Boyd, *The Newport City Directory, 1856–57* [Newport, R.I.: A. J. Ward, 1863], 116, 229.)

in the states of Pennsylvania and New York. In contrast, more than 40 percent of black Newporters were not natives of Rhode Island in 1860; half of these were indigenous southerners, mainly from Maryland and Virginia. It is difficult to assess the meaning of these demographic patterns for Newport, but the presence of so many black Virginians and Marylanders might be partially explained by the fact that the two Chesapeake Bay states contained the largest number of free blacks in 1860. As a coastal town on a well-traveled water route, Newport, unlike Saratoga Springs, was in a better position to receive antebellum, free, northern-bound migrants—and perhaps even runaway slaves—from those states.[54]

As elsewhere in the antebellum North, racial prejudice marred the contours of black life in antebellum Saratoga Springs and Newport. Many legends of memorable African Americans in local histories reveal derogatory images belonging to an emerging national racialist ideology. Primus Budd and Mintus are mocked for their supposed pretensions. Budd, described in one account as "a princely mulatto," reputedly presided jealously over nothing less than a cannon kept in Saratoga Springs's Congress Park and fired every Fourth of July. Mintus, a black undertaker in Newport, drew attention for his "pompous conduct" and the "grotesque garments" in which he reportedly conducted funerals; these included a "long, blue, swallow-tail coat, with brass buttons." Others were simply buffoons. Gingerbread Frank curiously never wore shoes; he wrapped his feet in burlap instead. Susan ostentatiously paraded the streets in bright dresses and multicolored ribbons.[55] And Tom Campbell reserved a permanent place for himself in Saratoga Springs's collective memory by donning ladies' garb and riding into the town in a carriage behind Madame Jumel, Aaron Burr's infamous lover. The following version of this incident has been recorded:

> Plainly visible within the open carriage . . . sat "Tom" Camel, representing the veritable mistress of Aaron Burr! It was the custom of Madame Jumel, before going out of the village, to drive slowly through Broadway, that the unsophisticated inhabitants might have a proper sense of their own insignificance; and before it was discovered, Madame's carriage, followed by her counterfeit in "double" had paraded the entire length of the street—"Tom" Camel meanwhile fanning himself with a large fan, and bowing and curtseying to the crowds which had now gathered on every side! When the trick was at last discovered, Madame Jumel by turns threatened, and pleaded and

offered bribes. But "Brill" [perhaps another local black] and "Tom" were inexorable; and the two equipages actually went to the lake and back in the same order.[56]

Such popular renderings of African-American behavior reflect antebellum northern "romantic racialist" thought. Viewed through this local folklore, blacks in Saratoga Springs and Newport appear flamboyant and ridiculous at worst, fun-loving and comical at best, but always as a quizzical species of humanity. Indeed, in one memoir, the story of Tom Campbell is told in a chapter entitled "Queer People"; in another, Newport caterer Cuffy Cockroach is described as a "droll character." However exotic, they are a nonthreatening sort to be tolerated with good nature and condescension.[57]

Treated as "other" in local histories, black comportment is not presented in its own terms. Alleged presumptions are not seen as awkward attempts by a newly emancipated population to assimilate by emulating "respectable" white public performances or to possibly preserve African customs. Gingerbread Frank's burlap shoes are not even attributed to poverty. Rather, African Americans are judged by an unattainable Anglo-Saxon standard increasingly required in the antebellum America of full-fledged Americans.

A circle of discrimination accompanied prejudice. British visitor Stewart observed that blacks in Saratoga Springs were made to sit in a separate corner removed from the white worshipers during church services; the same practice existed in Newport. The operators of Saratoga Springs's Congress and Empire springs ignored pleas for redress in 1855 from a local black delegation protesting the reservation of "metallic goblets" for African-American patrons while whites were served in "glass tumblers." When Saratoga's racetrack first opened in 1863, a stipulation barring blacks from attending, almost certainly in deference to southern horse owners, was instituted. In Newport, the public-school system established in 1842 was segregated. And in both New York State and Rhode Island, property requirements remained for black male voters.[58]

Prior to 1870, African Americans in both resorts responded to unequal treatment locally and nationally by establishing separate institutions, engaging in abolitionist activity, and serving in the Civil War; in Newport, however, they engaged in even more strident efforts at race advancement. In the antebellum period, the building of separate black institutions simultaneously represented a reluctant accommodation to white exclusion and a positive

effort to replicate white models. The former case usually entailed specifically black social, economic, and political agendas. Both types of African-
American activism occurred in Saratoga Springs and Newport with the
appearance of black churches and voluntary associations.

Prior to 1870, formal black community life was limited to the religious
sphere in Saratoga Springs. The first black church, the African Methodist
Episcopal (A.M.E.) Zion Church, was organized in 1863, probably as a direct
consequence of discrimination in white congregations. The small body of
seven members met on Willow Walk, now Spring Street. Five years later, the
"most active religious types" founded a black section of the Sons of Temperance, the Abraham Lincoln Division. Members no doubt considered that, in
an evangelical age, participation in temperance work imparted a measure of
moral rectitude ordinarily denied by race.[59]

In Newport, the black community's formal agenda—as measured by
organizational life—was both religious and secular. In 1780, four years prior
to statewide manumission in Rhode Island, black Newporters organized a
self-help organization, the African Union Society, the first black association
in America, at the home of Abraham Casey, a carpenter and the father-in-law
of the entrepreneur Isaac Rice, on Levin Street. Most of the founding
members were native Africans wanting to return to their homeland. Accord-
ingly, the society regularly engaged in correspondence with antislavery societies in the Northeast, mainly on the issue of colonization.[60]

Newport Gardner led the colonization struggle. Born Occramer Mary-
coo, Gardner was brought to the New World at the age of fourteen in 1757
and sold to Caleb Gardner, a white Newport merchant. The African quickly
learned English and soon became a skilled musician. Newport Gardner was
freed after Caleb Gardner literally overheard his prayer for manumission; he
remained in Newport, working as a music instructor and attending the First
Congregational Church, where Dr. Samuel Hopkins, a strong opponent of
slavery, was pastor. Hopkins in fact devised a colonization plan for American
blacks that doubled as a missionary effort. This project directly involved
Newport Gardner.[61] In 1791, Hopkins wrote: "Bristol Yamma is the first
black on my list for a missionary; Salmar Nubia, alias Jack Mason, has been
thought of for another by Dr. [Ezra] Stiles and me. . . . Newport Gardner, is
in my view, next to Bristol and in some things excels him. He is a discerning,
judicious, steady, good man, and feels greatly interested in promoting a
Christian settlement in Africa, and promoting Christianity there."[62]

Gardner's departure exemplified the black colonizationist's despair over African-American prospects in the United States. On January 7, 1826, at the age of eighty, he, his son, and seventy-year-old Salmar Nubia set sail with sixteen others from Boston for Liberia. After a lifetime in America, Gardner poignantly declared, "I go to set an example for the youth of my race. I go to encourage the young. They can never be elevated here; I have tried for sixty years—it is vain."[63]

The African Union Society also focused on the immediate needs of the black community in Newport. Probably as a corrective to the disruptive impact of slavery on the family, it urged members "to have exact registers preserved of all the births and deaths which occur in your respective families." There was also a preoccupation with setting standards of individual conduct. Members agreed to "avoid frolicking and amusements" and exhorted other local blacks to have their marriages legalized.[64] The society's constitution reveals the motivation of the founders in stressing morality: "We beseech you to reflect that it is by your good conduct alone, that you can refute the objections which have been made against you as rational and moral creatures, and remove many of the difficulties which have occurred in the general emancipation of such of our brethren as are yet in bondage."[65] On the economic front, the society sought apprenticeships for black youths and maintained a sick benefit fund that provided for families and widows in the case of illness or death of heads of households.[66]

A new concern emerged for the society in the first decade of the nineteenth century. The payment of benefits to members and their families created discord within the association, especially after attendance at meetings and dues payments declined. Attempts to manage these problems involved two reorganizations with name changes for the society. Finally, in 1807, the association, now called the African Humane Society, merged with the recently established African Benevolent Society, an organization with the express purpose of founding and maintaining a black school. Despite constant financial worries, the African Benevolent Society and its school continued in existence until 1842, when the city of Newport assumed the task of educating children of all races.[67]

Newport's blacks also organized several churches during the antebellum period. The first, the Colored Union Church and Society, began in 1824 as a result of the efforts of twelve founders. These men were disgruntled with segregation in white churches. The new association preoccupied itself with

the general as well as the spiritual welfare of black Newporters. The ecclesiastical nature of this latest group was formalized in 1838, when the society's
members contemplated "some plan to organize ourselves into a church
covenant for the purpose of having the Lord's Supper administered to us as
an independent Christian church."[68] In 1845, the Colored Union Church of
Newport was incorporated; in 1859, it became the Union Congregational
Church.[69]

As a community church based on its members' shared experiences, beliefs,
and hopes as African Americans and Christians, the Colored Union Church
was short-lived. Theological differences within black Newport soon led to
the establishment of two additional, distinctly denominational churches.
The African Methodist Episcopal Church of Newport organized in 1845 and
incorporated in 1863 as the Mt. Zion A.M.E. Church. The Shiloh Baptist
Church formed in 1864.[70]

The persistence of slavery in the American South greatly troubled free
African Americans in Saratoga Springs and Newport. They learned of slavery's horrors from southern black servants who visited the towns each summer with their white masters; this knowledge fueled abolitionist sentiment
and activity. Comparing himself to the slaves of southerners who visited the
United States Hotel in Saratoga Springs between 1834 and 1841, slaves who
were "well dressed and well provided for, leading apparently an easy life, but
with few of its ordinary troubles to perplex them," Solomon Northup reflected: "Having all my life breathed the free air of the North, and conscious
that I possessed the same feelings and affectations that find a place in the
white man's breast; conscious, moreover, of an intelligence equal to that of
some men, at least with a fairer skin, I was too ignorant, perhaps too
independent, to conceive how anyone could be content to live in the abject
condition of a slave. . . . never once, I am proud to say, did I fail to counsel
any one who came to me, to watch his opportunity, and strike for freedom."[71]

Northup's disdain for slavery was shared by others in Saratoga Springs
and Newport. Both places hosted such prominent abolitionists as Frederick
Douglass, Harriet Beecher Stowe, and William Lloyd Garrison. Some slave-
holders in Saratoga Springs freed their slaves before 1827. Others supported
New York's repeal of its slave sojournment laws and enactment of personal
liberty laws after the passage of the federal Fugitive Slave Act of 1850. Reuben
Hyde Walworth, the last Chancellor of the Court of Chancellery in New
York State and an outspoken abolitionist, freed his southern wife's\slave,

Mary Dorothea "Dolly" Smith, when she joined his household as a servant in 1851.[72]

The story of the Underground Railroad in Saratoga Springs and Newport echoes the national legendary melodrama in which abolitionists rather than slaves are heroines and heroes. Local histories, more apocryphal than factual, hold that runaway slaves were sheltered at the Walworth homestead, the remotest residence on North Broadway. There, Dolly supposedly offered the fugitives warm bedding, good food, and safe passage with the chancellor's blessings. James Andrews Madison, a founding member and officer of the Saratoga Historical Society, allegedly provided another station stop in his wine cellar. The Isaac Rice homestead on William and Thomas streets in Newport also reportedly served as a layover point for fugitives.[73]

Legends notwithstanding, the reality of abolitionist sentiment in the antebellum resorts made them inhospitable milieux for southern visitors who toured the places with full companies of slaves, fanners and bootshiners included.[74] Indeed, at a town meeting in 1835, white Newporters drew up a petition addressed to the Rhode Island State Legislature requesting the passage of a gag law curtailing the first amendment rights of antislavery orators. This action prompted Garrison to remark that "it would be almost as hazardous to deliver an anti-slavery lecture in Newport as in Charleston or Richmond."[75] Given the depth and longevity of Newport's dependence on southern travelers, local merchants and hotel owners no doubt feared unfavorable repercussions should the coastal resort prove too unfriendly to the "peculiar institution."

Participation in the Civil War extended naturally from abolitionism for black Americans in Saratoga Springs and Newport. The former sent at least six volunteers who, along with those from Newport, served in the all-black Fifth Massachusetts Cavalry, the Fifty-fourth Massachusetts Infantry, and the Fourteenth Rhode Island Artillery, later the Eleventh United States Colored Artillery.[76]

Prior to 1870, a headlong press for civil rights occurred only in Newport. This effort targeted the matter of school desegregation and was spearheaded by George T. Downing. According to Downing's personal political philosophy, "racial amalgamation" through miscegenation represented the ideal route for complete acceptance of African Americans in America. He provided a model in his own family history. The son of a mulatto father, Downing married Serene de Grasse, half-white and half-East Indian. Until the day of perfect racial blending, however, he conceded that integration in civil affairs was an essential preliminary.[77]

According to Downing and his supporters, the segregated public schools in Newport must not stand. He dared to send his children to the local white school only to have them returned home. Downing then launched and financed a campaign of protest beginning in 1857. Joined by others in petition, he held public meetings and distributed pamphlets on the issue. Downing's argument was multilayered. He invoked the memory of the traditional alliance between Rhode Island blacks and the upper class. He documented the success of Boston's integrated school system. He cited the inferiority of black schools. In 1858, Downing testified before the Rhode Island House Committee on Education on behalf of statewide public-school integration. It was not until the 1866 legislative session, swayed by swelling radical Reconstructionist voices, that both state houses voted to ban public-school segregation in Rhode Island.[78]

It is on the issue of political development that black Saratoga Springs and black Newport differed most in the years prior to 1870. The Newport community evinced a stronger internal vitality in its more vigorous institutional life and varied approach to race progress, an approach that included colonization, self-help through secular benevolent associations, public morality, and integrationist efforts. In contrast, the Saratogian community cohered in just two small institutions.

Size is certainly one explanatory variable for this difference. In 1860, while African Americans comprised 3 and 6 percent of the populations of Saratoga Springs and Newport, respectively, the absolute number of blacks in Newport exceeded that for Saratoga by nearly three times. In Newport, then, blacks achieved the critical mass to sustain a more distinct identity.

Another consideration must be the presence of a leadership element. Newport possessed these in Gardner and Downing. Both men desired race advancement, strategized for it, and held the ears of influential, sympathetic whites. Downing's activism, moreover, reflected an additional, key aspect of Afro-Newporter politics—its connections to the wider and influential antebellum traditions of both Boston-based, New England abolitionism and northern, black abolitionism, the latter of which held central to its agenda the achievement of full civil rights for blacks as well as the termination of southern slavery.[79] No similar figures had yet appeared among black Saratogians, nor were Afro-Saratogians as consistently linked to similar political orbits, either nationally or regionally, prior to 1870. For the next sixty years, the African-American communities of Saratoga Springs and Newport would diverge in these two key aspects.

⟨✦⟩

Resorts such as Saratoga Springs and Newport, then, lured African Americans and the white middle and upper-middle classes from their earliest days. Wealthy whites sought escape from conventions of urban life yet insisted on the replication of its comforts, culture, and class-affirming rituals in resort towns. This involved the use of servants, among whom African Americans were included. Blacks, mainly drawn to the jobs created by the resort economy, experienced prejudice and discrimination of the type known generally in the nation and were faced with the task of developing responses to it. It is on this point that black Newporters and black Saratogians differed most. The seaport alone produced a deep, sustained, and clear record of African-American civil rights advocacy during the antebellum years, an important heritage that would partially explain the later diverging histories of the two black communities.

2

They Removed and Occupied a House

CHANGING PATTERNS IN POPULATION SIZE, RESIDENCE, SOUTHERN MI-
gration levels, and household arrangements all helped shape the contours of
the black community in Saratoga Springs and Newport between 1870 and
1930. African Americans favored or shunned living in these resorts in relationship to the vitality of the towns' economies and/or the promise of more
lucrative work opportunities elsewhere. The healthier state of Newport's
economy compared to that of Saratoga Springs dictated a larger black presence in the seaport than in the spa. In both places, African Americans
resided in neighborhoods close to their job sites and churches and in those
spaces that were remote from or deemed aesthetically undesirable by whites.
Southern blacks migrated to these resort towns in substantial proportions
even before World War I, attracted by familiar jobs and facilitated by increasingly easy transportation routes and expanding personal networks; this
was especially true in Newport. Owing to the often seasonal, temporary
nature of their stay in the towns, many African Americans in resorts could be
found in extended or augmented households as boarders, lodgers, relatives,
friends, or live-in help rather than replicating the more common national
pattern as members of a nuclear household.

Population Size

Determining the true size of the black population of the resort towns is a technically difficult enterprise. As summer resorts, Saratoga Springs and Newport possessed triple African-American communities consisting of permanent or year-round residents, seasonal workers, and tourists. The demographic profile of these communities undertaken here is based almost exclusively on census counts, generally taken during June, that *should* include all permanent residents, some seasonal workers, and no tourists.[1] There are, of course, important limitations on this expectation. First of all, the census traditionally has undercounted black populations.[2] Secondly, African Americans often maintained two or more residences as seasonal workers. Which residence to consider the principal home is difficult, seemingly arbitrary census business—subjectively determined by both enumerator and worker. Emma Waite, for example, worked as a cook and domestic throughout the winter, spring, and summer of 1870 in Saratoga Springs and in the fall of that year in New York City. Another black seasonal worker, Robert Jackson, worked as a headwaiter at Saratoga's Congress Hall in the summer of 1872 and operated a catering establishment in New York City during the winter months. Waite does not appear in the 1870 roster of Saratogians; Jackson does. True, Waite was a single woman possessing no real estate in Saratoga Springs, while Jackson was a married man who lived with his wife and son at the spa in a home he owned. However, scores of propertyless black staff of unknown marital status, working at several Newport hotels as seasonal employees, are listed in the 1860 census of the seaport.[3] Finally, vacationing African Americans might just as easily escape the census taker's tally as not. Discriminatory hotel practices limited black tourists to brief, one-day trips or to black lodging accommodations, where they were not included in population enumerations. At the same time, other black visitors who owned summer homes during this period were probably included in the census.[4]

Since the census was generally taken in warm-weather months—once the touring season had commenced in the two resorts—it provides an especially revealing picture of the impact of the resort economy and setting on the African-American communities they contained. This claim clearly depends on the exact timing of the various census counts consulted. Exceptions that might be alleged include the federal census enumerations of 1910, 1920, and

1930—taken in April, January, and April, respectively—and the 1925 Rhode Island state census—also taken in April. The relatively early timing of the April counts, however, probably had little impact on the size of the black Newporter population, since workers there often were involved in warm-weather, seasonal work that commenced before June. This included steam-boat jobs and work as farmhands in nearby Middletown, Rhode Island. And in the case of Newport, the April 1925 state enumeration helps compensate for the problems created by the very early federal count in January 1920. Preparatory work for the Saratoga season, however, began in June for the July and August rush. Still, use here of the manuscripts of both the 1900 federal census and the 1925 New York state census, both taken in June, aids in the construction of an adequate demographic profile of twentieth-century black Saratogian wage earners. Because of its reliance on the census, then, this study extends to most African-American wage earners in Newport and Saratoga Springs in both black- and white-headed households and to the other African-American members of the mostly black-headed households in which they lived.

Census records reveal that the start of summer swelled the size of the black community of Saratoga Springs. A good indication of the numerical significance of the summer crowd is revealed by the atypical New York state census of 1892, taken in February of that year. Then, the African-American population of Saratoga Springs consisted of 397 people.[5] Yet two years earlier during June, African-American Saratogians numbered 538—nearly one-and-one-half times as many (see table 1).

A critical gauge of the size and growth rates of the African-American population of Saratoga Springs was the degree of freedom accorded gambling activities, always an attraction for the village but one that gained in importance with the onset of the Gilded Age. While the spring waters continued to lure visitors, health seekers were far less numerous after 1870 than they had been in Gideon Putnam's day. In fact, "as a Spa, Saratoga sagged year by year into dilapidation and neglect."[6] Certainly, the hotels drew outsiders until their demolition after World War II. But it was gambling, horse racing, and horse-race betting—never interrupted by the Civil War and enticing even southern tourists to return in full force during the postbellum years—that became the central popular attraction for the village and over-shadowed even more severely the appeal of the spa's waters. The wealth-

Table 1. Black Population Size in Newport and Saratoga Springs, 1870–1930

Year	Black Population		Total Population		Percent Black		Percent Change in Black Population		Percent Change in Total Population	
	N	S	N	S	N	S	N	S	N	S
1870	786	301	12,521	7,516	6.2	4.0	—	—	—	—
1880	982	473	15,693	8,421	6.2	5.6	+24.9	+57.1	+25.3	+12.0
1890	1,410	538	19,457	11,975	7.2	4.5	+43.6	+13.7	+23.9	+42.2
1900	1,600	651	22,035	12,409	7.3	5.2	+13.4	+21.0	+13.2	+3.6
1910	1,631	589	27,149	12,693	6.0	4.6	+1.9	-9.5	+23.2	+2.3
1920	1,607	480	30,255	13,181	5.3	3.6	-1.5	-18.5	+11.4	+3.8
1930	1,554	442	27,612	13,169	5.6	3.3	-3.2	-7.9	-8.7	-0.1

Sources: U.S. Department of the Interior, Census Office, Ninth Census of the United States, 1870: Population Statistics (Washington, D.C.: GPO, 1872), 217, 257; idem, Tenth Census of the United States, 1880: Population Statistics (Washington, D.C.: GPO, 1883), 270, 326; idem, Eleventh Census of the United States, 1890: Population Statistics, vol. I (Washington, D.C.: GPO, 1897), 251, 305, 472, 480; U.S. Census Bureau, Twelfth Census of the United States, 1900: Population Statistics, vol. I (Washington, D.C.: GPO, 1901), 465. 474, 670; U.S. Department of Commerce, Bureau of the Census, Thirteenth Census of the United States, 1910: Population Statistics, vol. 3 (Washington, D.C.: GPO, 1913), 209, 246, 618, 626; idem, Fourteenth Census of the United States, 1920: Population Statistics, vol. 3 (Washington, D.C.: GPO, 1922), 683, 914; idem, Fifteenth Census of the United States, 1930: Population Statistics, vol. 3 (Washington, D.C.: GPO, 1932), 320, 765; Ninth Census of the United States, 1870 (ms.), microfilm reels 1088, 1089, 1472, National Archives, Washington, D.C.; Tenth Census of the United States, 1880 (ms.), microfilm reels 928, 929, 1210, National Archives, Washington, D.C.; Twelfth Census of the United States, 1900 (ms.), microfilm reels 1158, 1159, 1505, National Archives, Washington, D.C.; Thirteenth Census of the United States, 1910 (ms.), microfilm reels 1076, 1077, 1437, National Archives, Washington, D.C. Where discrepancies were found in the size of the black population between the published aggregate census statistics for a given year and the manuscript census data for the same year, the figure obtained from the manuscript is cited.

making possibilities in gambling well matched the materialistic, acquisitive spirit of the time. Gambling became "the magnet which drew most visitors to the Springs."[7] Indeed, it "placed an almost indelible stamp on the village."[8]

The growth of the black population of Saratoga Springs varied in relationship to the health of the increasingly gambling-centered economy for two reasons. First, gambling brought tourists, and tourists generated service-related jobs. Secondly, some African Americans were directly involved in gambling, even if only for peripheral income, as proprietors of permissive, "back room"-equipped bars, clubs, and restaurants on Congress Street, the black business thoroughfare running west of lower Broadway. During the last third of the nineteenth century, the deciduous climb in numbers among black Saratogians reflected the "wide-open" nature of the village. For example, the greatest surge in black population occurred between 1870 and 1880 (see table 1), a decade that began just one year after the opening of the John Morrissey Club House, best known as the "Casino," a tremendously successful and lush gaming establishment for wealthy whites modeled after European casinos, which probably sparked both a local construction boom beginning in 1870 and the operation of twelve gambling houses in the town by 1873.[9]

A downward slide in the growth rate among black Saratogians during the first third of the twentieth century followed the late-nineteenth-century spurt. This diminution can be traced, in part, to the success of a newly invigorated campaign to suppress gambling as a recreational option at the spa. As early as 1886, Anthony Comstock, secretary of the New York Society for the Suppression of Vice, had visited the spa, thus prompting twenty of Saratoga's houses of chance to close down during his few days' visit and rallying a rich minority of discomfited, reform-minded Saratogians to a sustained campaign that viewed gambling as "a disgrace and a detriment to the community's progress."[10] Another state antigambling law passed in 1889; this one targeted for misdemeanor charges all keepers of gambling establishments.[11] During the 1890s, Spencer Trask, an influential New York banker, broker, and Saratoga Springs estate owner, delivered another blow to the local gambling industry by publicly blasting racetrack gambling in the Saratoga newspaper he controlled. In 1894, Nellie Bly, the famed exposé reporter for the *New York World*, leveled additional attacks against dishonesty at the track. The Progressive Era "good government" movement, moreover, resulted in the removal from office of an elected village president, Cale Mitchell, owner himself of a Broadway gambling house, when state legislation in 1895 amended Saratoga's charter to require the appointment rather than the election of the village president. That same year, evangelist Dwight L. Moody led a series of revival services in Saratoga, adding fuel to the reform movement.[12]

This mounting pressure on gaming no doubt weakened the lure of the village to black seasonal workers and tourists, especially after the closing of the chief gambling center, the Casino. At first, Richard Canfield, Morrissey's last successor as owner, carried on, seemingly undaunted by occasional forced closings and constant public malignment. In 1903, he even enlarged the Casino with a new cafeteria wing and remodeled the surrounding park despite the fact that one year earlier, Comstock had arrested thirty-four Saratogian gamblers. But in 1904, in a precipitous move perhaps reflecting weariness from the incessant barrage of criticism, Canfield shut down the Casino.[13] Reopening it two years later, he announced that after the 1907 season, the Casino would be up for sale. The village bought it in 1911 but never again used it as a gambling establishment.[14] Today, it houses the very respectable Historical Society of Saratoga Springs.

Reform legislation of the early twentieth century hampered the resort's vitality as a racing center as well. New York State enacted the Agnew-Hart Bill in June 1908, less than one year after the Casino's final closing. The new law made it illegal to quote betting odds openly and for bookmakers to solicit business or to stand in a stationary place recording bets. Track attendance promptly declined, although bookmakers continued to work from their hotel rooms. After the 1910 season, reformers succeeded in securing the shutdown of all tracks within the vicinity of New York City, including tracks in Saratoga. Discouraged stable owners relocated to Europe. Thus, in the spring of 1911, the Saratoga Racing Association was compelled to announce the track's closing. After 1911 and until the track's reopening in 1913, the village's tourist economy lagged; and, as a consequence, the size of the local African-American population fell (see table 1).[15]

While Saratoga's appeal as a gambling center did continue into the twentieth century, that appeal lessened as the spa faced competition from new fashionable summer places—such as Bar Harbor, Maine; Lenox, Massachusetts; Southampton, New York; Long Branch, New York; and Narragansett, Rhode Island—many of which began to draw blacks as workers.[16] The purchase of Congress Hall by the city in 1913 underscored the decline. The sale of this once-grand and popular hotel marked a new era in Saratoga

Table 2. Black Population Change in Selected Northeastern Cities, 1910 and 1920

City	Population		Change (percent)
	1910	1920	
Albany	1,037	1,239	+19.5
Schenectady	274	388	+41.6
New York	91,709	152,467	+66.3
Providence	5,316	5,655	+6.4
New Bedford	2,885	4,998	+73.2
Boston	13,564	16,350	+20.5

Source: U.S. Department of Commerce, Bureau of the Census, *Fourteenth Census of the United States Taken in the Year 1920,* vol. 2: *Population, 1920* (Washington, D.C.: GPO, 1922), 47–48, 70, 77–78; idem, *Thirteenth Census of the United States, 1910: Population Statistics,* vol. 3 (Washington, D.C.: GPO, 1913), 238, 240, 628, 890; idem, *Fourteenth Census of the United States, 1920: Population Statistics,* vol. 3 (Washington, D.C.: GPO, 1922), 438, 680–81, 914; idem, *Fifteenth Census of the United States, 1930: Population Statistics,* vol. 3 (Washington, D.C.: GPO, 1932), 325–27, 767, 1083.

Springs during which tourists either traveled by automobile to visit the spa only for a day or two or summered in rented homes only during the August racing season.[17] Thus, as the hotel, track, and gambling businesses—all sources of African-American employment—faltered, so did black representation in the town.

As opportunities for blacks in the economically troubled resort town stagnated, other cities suddenly began to attract black workers with new industrial options. During World War I, jobs in industry that traditionally had been denied African Americans were made available to them for the first time as the manpower demands of warfare created labor shortages.[18] A look at the growth rates of the black populations of urban centers in relatively close proximity to Saratoga Springs and the mushrooming industrial sectors in their economies tells the story. As the black populations of Albany, Schenectady, and New York City, for example, generally grew between 1910 and 1920, that of Saratoga Springs declined (see tables 1 and 2).

In Newport also, the black population generally fluctuated in size as the tourist economy waxed and waned in vitality. While absolute and relative numerical expansion among black Newporters marked the last third of the nineteenth century, comparative retrenchment characterized the first third of the twentieth century (see table 1).

The nature of the postbellum and the early twentieth-century Newport tourist clienteles, however, differed considerably from that of the antebellum period. Hotels and their patrons—intellectuals, artists, and middle-class vacationers—were supplanted by a company of well-to-do industrialists of recent fortune who summered with their families in mammoth mansions, demurely called "cottages" by contemporaries, in the hopes of securing social position and recognition among America's monied aristocracy. This new seasonal crowd first appeared in Newport in the decade prior to the Civil War's onset but grew to dominate the summer scene in the town in the postbellum period.[19]

During the ten-year interval between 1880 and 1890, the black numerical presence in the seaport spurted at a rate higher than any other considered here (see table 1) once the seaport redefined itself as the summer vacation mecca of the wealthy. The opening of the Newport Casino in 1880 marked the opening of the decade. James Gordon Bennett Jr., the publisher of the *New York Herald*, built this entertainment center in hostile reaction to the stodginess of the Newport Reading Room, the established men's club. By 1885, the new building—which contained club rooms, tennis courts, a restaurant, and a theater for both plays and dances—had become "the center of Newport life." One historian argues that, more than any other development, the grand balls held at the Newport Casino "inaugurated the era of conspicuous and often outlandishly lavish spending in Newport" that came to define the town.[20] Some time shortly after 1888, when an alliance between the New York patrician Caroline Astor and the social arbiter Samuel Ward McAllister resulted in the publication of "The Four Hundred"—a roster of approximately 400 persons uniquely qualifying as the nation's social elite— McAllister persuaded Astor as "Queen of the Four Hundred" to establish a summer residence at Newport. Many other New York ladies and social hopefuls followed suit by settling in an assortment of marble villas each summer. Mindful of McAllister's dictum that Newport "was the place above others . . . to take social root in," the women contented themselves to sit "on the stool of social probation" for at least four seasons.[21] Blacks were not usually employed as house servants for this new crowd. Instead, African Americans readily found work aboard the steamers that transported the mushrooming number of visitors to and from Newport.[22]

The contracting growth rate among black Newporters during the first third of the twentieth century may be linked partially to the seaport's loss of glamour and appeal to New York society. The year 1914 has been described as Newport's "last golden summer." World War I may have had a negative impact on the seaport's high life. One Newport newspaper reported a scare regarding the possibility of enemy submarine attack on the Atlantic seaport. Or perhaps much of America's aristocracy, now linked by blood through late-nineteenth-century marriages to European nobility, preoccupied itself with political events overseas. The marked absence of key New York society leaders from the Newport scene, however, provides a more readily verifiable explanation for the seaport's waning attraction for the aristocracy at this time. Mrs. Stuyvesant Fish, one of an early twentieth-century triumvirate of successors to Caroline Astor's crown, died in early June, just before the commencement of the 1915 season. The passing of this Newport hostess contributed to a stewardship vacuum among socialites. Around the same time, moreover, several *grandes dames* turned their attention away from social arbitration and conspicuous consumption and toward the women's suffrage and peace movements. Most notable among these was Mrs. Oliver H. P. Belmont (formerly Mrs. William K. Vanderbilt), a second ruler in the triumvirate. In fact, in a significant departure from its normal use as an entertainment site, Marble House, Mrs. Belmont's Newport mansion, served as the location for the 1914 strategy meeting of the Congressional Union, forerunner of both the Woman's Party and the National Woman's Party. Throughout the 1920s, although living in France, Mrs. Belmont even served as president of the National Woman's Party.[23]

Newport also experienced a decline in the growth rate of its African-American population after 1900 because, like Saratoga Springs, the city could not compete with the new employment possibilities offered by industrialized urban areas during World War I. Nearby alternatives like Providence, Boston, and New Bedford experienced a rise in the size of their African-American populations (see table 2).

Residential Patterns

In both black Newport and black Saratoga Springs, the confines of recognizable African-American residential areas expanded as both communities grew numerically; but the sharpening, rigid separation typifying larger African-American urban neighborhoods never developed in the resort towns. In Saratoga Springs, the antebellum West Side cluster around Congress Street swelled to accommodate Irish and Italian newcomers. Irish settlement had

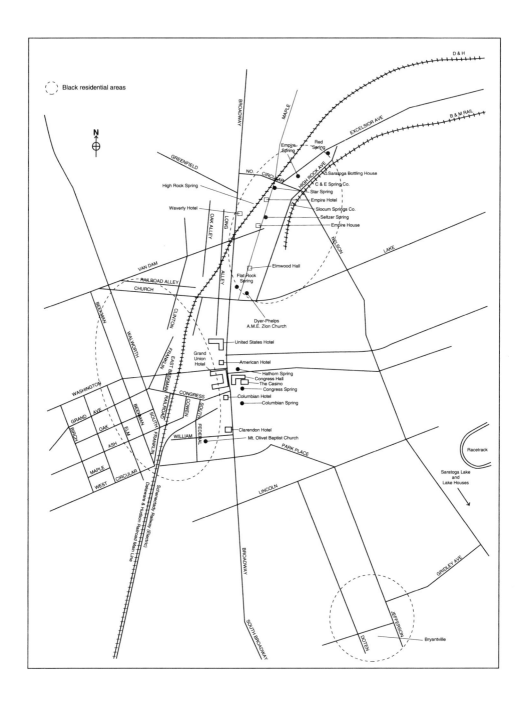

Black residential areas

N

GREENFIELD

BROADWAY

MAPLE

NO. CIRCULAR

HIGH ROCK AVE

EXCELSIOR AVE

D & H

B & M RAIL

Empire Spring

Red Spring

Saratoga Bottling House

C & E Spring Co.

High Rock Spring

Star Spring

Empire Hotel

Slocum Springs Co.

Waverly Hotel

Seltzer Spring

Empire House

OAK ALLEY

LONG

LAKE

NELSON

VAN DAM

RAILROAD ALLEY

Elmwood Hall

CHURCH

Flat Rock Spring

ALLEY

BEEMAN

CLINTON

Dyer-Phelps A.M.E. Zion Church

WALWORTH

United States Hotel

FRANKLIN

Grand Union Hotel

American Hotel

EAST BEEMAN RAILROAD

Hathorn Spring

Congress Hall

The Casino

WASHINGTON

CONGRESS

Congress Spring

Columbian Hotel

BEEMAN

COWEN

Columbian Spring

GRAND AVE

SOUTH

BIRCH

OAK

ELM

FEDERAL

Clarendon Hotel

ASH

WILLIAM

Mt. Olivet Baptist Church

MAPLE

PARK PLACE

Racetrack

WEST

CIRCULAR

Saratoga Lake and Lake Houses

Schenectady Railway (Electric)

LINCOLN

Delaware & Hudson Railroad Main Line

BROADWAY

GRIDLEY AVE

JEFFERSON

SOUTH BROADWAY

DOTEN

Bryantville

begun in 1832 with the construction of the Saratoga and Schenectady railroad. As railroad laborers, the Irish had taken up residence along the tracks
close to the rail yards in the West Circular Street area. By the midnineteenth
century, they had built neat, small homes on the newly laid streets named for
trees—Elm, Oak, Ash, Walnut, and Birch (see map 3). The preponderance of
Irish in this section of Saratoga Springs, particularly on Beekman Street, was
the reason for the area's popular name, "Dublin."[24]

By 1870, Italians began arriving in significant numbers, mostly to work on
the railroad; they moved into the lower part of Beekman Street, which
quickly became so thoroughly Italian that an 1893 city directory simply listed
the residents there as "Italian." Italians also succeeded the Irish on Ash, Oak,
and Elm south of Washington between 1920 and 1930 (see map 3). By 1930, in
fact, what was once called "Dublin" had been redesignated "Little Italy."[25]

A visible black presence on the West Side withstood the new ethnic
waves, however, for a combination of economic and cultural reasons. African
Americans remained because of the area's proximity to the several major
hotels that employed them. The Continental Hotel lay within the West
Side's borders, but not more than two blocks away from the eastern bound-
ary of the enclave stood the United States, American, Grand Union, Columbian, and Clarendon hotels (see map 3). An article in the *Saratoga Journal* in
1883 indicated the existence of employees' quarters on this side of town, for it
describes the plans for construction of similar staff accommodations by the
United States Hotel. Another news item notes the tenements on Beekman
Street as being occupied by "colored folks." Ernest Jackson, a lifelong black
Saratogian born in 1915, affirmed that the persistence of this West Side
concentration of African Americans lasted into the twentieth century. He
recalled that during his childhood, he lived on William Street, "right across

---

Map 3. Areas of Black Residential Clustering in Saratoga Springs, 1870–1925. (Com-
posite map based on F. W. Beers and Louis H. Cramer, *Combination Atlas of Saratoga and
Ballston* [New York: J. B. Beers and Co., 1876]; William L. Stone, *Reminiscences of
Saratoga and Ballston* [New York: R. Worthington, 1880], n.p.; Charles Newhall Tain-
tor, *Saratoga Illustrated: The Visitor's Guide of Saratoga Springs* [New York: Taintor Bros. and
Co., 1887], 8–31; and Council of Community Services of Northeastern New York,
Inc., "West Side Neighborhood Services of Northeastern New York, Inc." [1981], 3.
City directories for 1890, 1900, and 1910, as well as the federal and state manuscript
census schedules for 1880, 1900, and 1925 were also consulted.)

from the Grand Union's quarters where the [black] waiters and cooks all lived," and that blacks generally "lived on Congress Street, Cowen Street, Franklin Street, [and] William Street"—all on the West Side. Similarly, Edna Bailey Miller, an African-American woman who arrived in Saratoga Springs in 1924 as a young girl of twelve, remembered that when she was a youngster, most black Saratogians lived "on Congress Street, and then those streets called Franklin and Federal—over in that [West Side] area."[26] The presence of the largest black Baptist church, Mt. Olivet, is another factor accounting for the enduring concentration of Afro-Saratogians on the West Side (see map 3). Situated on the corner of William and Federal streets in 1910, the congregation helped confirm the definition of the area as black, just as churches in other burgeoning African-American communities provided a clear cultural identity to specific urban spaces.[27]

Cultural and economic forces also explain a smaller, late-nineteenth-century African-American enclave in the northeastern portion of the village enclosed by Broadway, Lake, Nelson, North Circular, and Maple avenues. Situated within these confines on Maple Avenue near Lake Avenue was Dyer-Phelps A.M.E. Zion Church.[28] Other economic clues—railroad tracks carving a corridor through the section as they left town; several spring sites with nearby bottling works; and the presence of at least three small hotels—suggest the possibility of places of black employment in this part of the spa (see map 3). Part of the work history of at least one black Saratogian family supports such an explanation: as a teenager, Edna Bailey Miller lived on High Rock Avenue near Dyer-Phelps, the church her father pastored for a time, and recalled working during the 1920s alongside her mother as kitchen help at Elmwood Hall while her brother collected spring water for guests at the Empire Hotel.[29] By 1925, 126 of the 577 African Americans in Saratoga Springs (just over one-fifth) still lived in this northeastern sector. Despite the continuing presence of the A.M.E. Church, the exhaustion of the vicinity's springs by the early twentieth century may have lessened employment options in this area for blacks.[30] Perhaps as a consequence, blacks had moved elsewhere in the village.

Another small area of black concentration appeared in the twentieth century on the southeastern fringe of Saratoga Springs. In 1925, only 79 of the 577 black Saratogians (about 12 percent) lived in this area east of Broadway and south of Circular Street and Park Place (see map 3). Yet one-quarter of all black homeowners in the city held property in this vicinity. One residential pocket within the section, Bryantville, focused on the area around Doten Avenue. Edna Bailey Miller recalled: "We used to call it Bryantville and there was a settlement of blacks [there]."[31]

Bryantville offered African Americans an affordable alternative to the inferior housing of the West Side. Edna Anderson remembered that her parents decided to locate in that section to escape the congestion and run-down housing of Ash Street. The Andersons bought their Bryantville plot inexpensively—three lots at $25 each—because the area was undeveloped. Wooded and beyond the reach of city utility lines, the region nonetheless represented opportunity and improvement for these pioneer families. Ms. Anderson proudly detailed the self-sufficient lifestyle available to Bryantville residents: "We grew our own vegetables. We had our own animals—cows, chickens, pigs. . . . We had everything. Had to worry about nothing."[32] African Americans in Bryantville, heedless of any notion that their area did not make the local list of prime real estate, took immense pride in their homesteads.

Despite the clustering of African Americans in some areas and streets during the sixty years studied here, in Saratoga Springs there were no strictly segregated black neighborhoods akin to the ghettos of larger urban areas. Rather, there was a pattern of dispersion of black Saratogians throughout the city marked by certain mixed neighborhoods in which blacks tended to concentrate. For example, in the experience of Joseph Jackson, an African American who arrived in Saratoga Springs from Vermont in 1910 at the age of seven, blacks "were scattered all over when I came here." He then listed his several residences in Saratoga Springs as a child: "Well, we lived in two or three places. . . . we lived . . . on Beekman. And then we moved from Beekman Street to Van Dam Street up by the el stop there, and then from there we went to Clinton Street. . . . My mother died on Clinton Street. My aunt and my grandmother died on Cowen Street. . . . I lived on Cowen Street when I was in school."[33] Beekman, Clinton, and Cowen were all in the West Side enclave. Van Dam and Greenfield were not; they were in the northwestern section of Saratoga Springs (see map 3).

Despite the lack of rigid segregation, however, the areas in which black Saratogians resided were often undesirable—near noisy, busy, and unsightly railroad tracks; in tight, narrow backstreets such as Oak Alley, Railroad Alley, and Long Alley; or in undeveloped sections lacking basic urban services.

African Americans living in Newport during the last third of the nine-

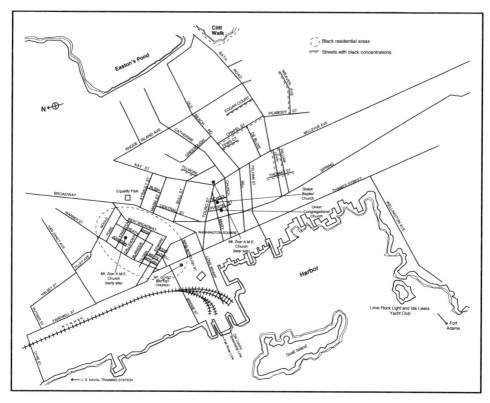

Map 4. Areas of Black Residential Clustering in Newport, 1870–1925. (Composite map based on *Map of the City of Newport, Rhode Island, with Principal Points of Interest and Summer Residences with Names of Owners* [Boston: Sampson and Murdock Co., 1930]. City directors for 1870, 100, and 1925, as well as federal and state manuscript census schedules for 1870, 1900, and 1925, were also consulted.)

teenth century continued to cluster in that seaport's westside sector, called "New Town." In the antebellum construction boom that had developed this area, several new streets that would provide residences for black Newporters—Burnside, Callender, Davis Court, Appleby, Covell, Edward, Feke, and White—were laid out. Between 1870 and 1900, as Newport's African-American population swelled, at least fifty more structures were erected in this westside enclave, now called "West Broadway" (see map 4). Conversely, the diminished growth rate of the African-American population after 1900 resulted in the building of fewer than a dozen new houses and tenements in the area between 1907 and 1921. Most West Broadway residences built between 1850 and 1920 were one- and two-family units. The structures were rectangular, simple, and most commonly 1½ or 2½ stories tall.[34]

Besides the availability of affordable housing developed for workers, West Broadway drew African Americans because of its proximity to the loading docks of the steamboats that accounted for much employment among black Newporters between 1870 and 1930 (see map 4). One local African American, William Bradford, lived on Kingston Street during the 1920s while working for a time on the Old Colony Steamship and Railroad Line. Similarly, Leonard Panaggio, a white Newporter, recalled that during the 1920s and 1930s, many local African Americans found employment as steamboat workers and that blacks mainly resided in West Broadway and often, more specifically, on Pond Avenue, in a housing structure called "The Blocks," a series of long, wooden buildings with rooms for rent at five dollars per month. Also within the West Broadway area were several alleys and backstreets—Johnson Court, Heath Street, and Spruce Street (later Kingston Street), for example—that furnished black housing (see map 4).[35]

The location of two black churches in West Broadway strengthened its appeal to African Americans. Until its relocation to Bellevue Avenue, Mt. Zion A.M.E. Church on Johnson Court stood in the area during this period as it had since the 1850s. And in 1897, the Mt. Olivet Baptist Church was situated on the northern end of Thames Street (see map 4).[36]

Throughout the period, African Americans resided with noticeable density in another area of Newport that flanked the northern end of Bellevue Avenue on both the east and west sides (see map 4); here again, black churches were powerful magnets. As it had during the antebellum period, Fillmore Street housed many black Newporters. Richard Berry, a white Newporter, recalled living with his family as a child on Greenough Place from 1913 to 1927, "back to back with a colored residential area called Filmore [sic]." Indeed, in 1925, the street contained some thirteen African-American households.[37] Similarly, Leonard Panaggio remembered black enclaves on Thomas Street, Weaver Avenue, and Chapel Street during the 1920s and 1930s.[38] Such backstreets, akin to alleys like Tews Court and Edgar Court, provided housing for black Newporters in this section (see map 4). George Turville, an African American who grew up in Newport during the 1920s, remembered some of the black residents of Edgar Court in 1925: "Families I remember on old Edgar Court are the Phillips family, the West family, the Tabb family, the Ross family, the Tate family, Miss Nellie Hayes, and the

CoaCoa family. Later, the Wiggintons lived there and we were one of several people who bought milk from the Wiggintons. They had cows and the milk was straight from the udder into your house."[39] Several black families lived on De Blois Street as well (see map 4). Turville recalled some of these: "De Blois Street no longer runs from Bellevue Avenue to Chapel Street, but old names still ring in my memory: the Yates family, the Green family, the Williams family, . . . the Warfields, the Major family, the Sutler family, Mrs. Leadbetter and last, but not least, Mrs. Harris."[40] The absence of occupational information in the 1925 Rhode Island state census makes it difficult to account for these black residences in economic terms. However, strong cultural imperatives—the continuing presence of the Union Congregational Church (formerly the Colored Union Church) on Division Street between Mary and Church streets, the relocation of Mt. Zion A.M.E. to Bellevue Avenue near Kay Street, and the 1868 relocation of Shiloh Baptist Church to the corner of Mary and School streets—help account for this later reshaping of the antebellum Kay Street-Catherine Street-Old Beach Road black cluster. Indeed, it was probably the tenacity of African-American concentration in this area that led Thomas Glover, a black landlord, to invest in rental property on De Blois and Fillmore.[41]

Migrants

Southern-born blacks constituted a noticeable portion of the African-American populations of both resort towns throughout the period reviewed here (see tables 3 and 4). The local presses of both Newport and Saratoga Springs took note of the influx of black southerners, especially those workers who came and went seasonally. In mid-June of 1888, for example, the *Saratogian* reported that local hotels were receiving "large consignments of colored help from the south." Similarly, in a story on the drowning of an African-American woman during the summer of 1901, the *Newport Mercury* explained that "she [had come] from the South in the spring to work on the island, in company with many other negroes, who come north for the summer."[42] This is especially true for Newport, where the larger numbers and ratios of migrants seem to indicate that the seaport possessed a more vibrant economy than did the spa. In 1870, southerners composed about one-tenth of all African Americans living in Saratoga Springs. By 1910, the year of the last

Table 3. Selected Places of Birth of Black Saratogians, 1870 and 1910

| | 1870 | | 1910 | |
	Number	Percent	Number	Percent
Northeast				
New York State	229	76.1	319	54.1
Elsewhere	26	8.6	64	10.9
	255	84.7	383	65.0
South				
Upper				
Maryland	6	2.0	28	4.7
Virginia	10	3.3	65	11.0
Other[a]	3	1.0	30	5.2
Elsewhere	17	5.6	63	10.7
	36	11.9	186	31.6
Total black population	301		589	

Sources: Ninth Census of the United States, 1870 (ms.), microfilm reels 1088, 1089, National Archives, Washington, D.C.; Thirteenth Census of the United States, 1910 (ms.), microfilm reels 1076, 1077, National Archives, Washington, D.C.

a. Includes Delaware, Washington, D.C., and North Carolina.

census consulted for Saratoga Springs in which nativity information is included,[43] northeasterners were still in the majority by accounting for two-thirds of the black population total. But those from the South in Saratoga now began to reach levels found four decades earlier in Newport by forming nearly the remaining one-third of all African Americans (see tables 3 and 4).

Meanwhile, Newport's appeal to black southerners increased during the last third of the nineteenth century and, while dropping in the first quarter of the twentieth century, remained strong. In 1870, southerners formed one-third of black Newport. The newcomers equaled almost one-half of all blacks in the town thirty years later. And in 1925, when other northeastern industrial centers more readily attracting southern migrants, one-third of African Americans in Newport still hailed from the South (see table 4).

Following traditional migration patterns of blacks to the Northeast, the states of the Upper South mostly along the eastern seaboard—that is, those due south and yet closest to New York and Rhode Island—supplied the greatest number of migrants.[44] While Virginia alone accounted for about one-third of all southern-born black Saratogians in both 1870 and 1910, a fairly wide range of southern states was represented in this group (see table 3). This was probably due to the nature of seasonal hotel work that

Table 4. Selected Places of Birth of Black Newporters, 1870, 1900, and 1925

	1870		1900		1925	
	Number	Percent	Number	Percent	Number	Percent
Northeast						
Rhode Island	281	35.7	496	31.0	719	43.4
Elsewhere	225	28.6	222	13.9	163	9.8
	506	64.4	718	44.9	882	53.2
South						
Upper						
Maryland	117	14.9	266	16.6	103	6.2
Virginia	84	10.7	319	19.9	290	17.5
Other[a]	48	6.0	117	7.4	82	4.9
Elsewhere	14	1.8	92	5.7	109	6.6
	263	33.4	794	49.6	584	35.2
Cape Verde Islands or Portugal	1	0.1	2	0.1	106	6.4
Total black population	786		1600		1657	

Sources: Ninth Census of the United States, 1870 (ms.), microfilm reel 1472, National Archives, Washington, D.C.; Twelfth Census of the United States, 1900 (ms.), microfilm reel 1505, National Archives, Washington, D.C.; Rhode Island State Census, 1925 (ms.), Rhode Island State Records Office, Providence.

a. Includes Delaware, Washington, D.C., and North Carolina.

often entailed the balancing of northern summer jobs with southern winter employment. In 1890, a black waiter, identified only as Codett, alternated between the Eastman Hotel in Hot Springs, Arkansas, and one of the Saratoga Springs hotels. Edna Miller recalled waiters at the Grand Union who regularly worked during the winter at the Royal Poinciana Hotel in Palm Beach, Florida. Also, as will be discussed more fully in the next chapter, the Saratoga hotels often used students attending the nation's black industrial schools and colleges as summer help—a workforce representing a variety of largely southern states.[45]

Virginia, along with a sizable contribution from Maryland, provided a plurality of southern migrants to Newport as well. Indeed, these two states alone supplied one-quarter of Newport's African-American population between 1870 and 1900. Even in 1925, some ten years into the Great Migration to the industrial North, nearly one-fifth of Newport's population consisted of blacks from Maryland and Virginia (see table 4).

The Virginia-to-Newport migration stream was facilitated by a well-established labor-recruitment chain and accessible transportation, two factors typical of the African-American migration experience.[46] Newport's Virginia labor-recruitment target area was seemingly quite particular: Culpeper County in northern Virginia. Situated in the northern piedmont region of Virginia, Culpeper had experienced great drops in its black population beginning in the 1860s, when freed African Americans fled the area because diversified small farms did not require large numbers of agricultural workers and because blacks, greatly outnumbered by whites, realized that they were not likely to gain control of local institutions on emancipation. As early as 1886, Armstead Hurley, a native of Culpeper County, had come to Newport at the age of thirty-two as a painter and glazier. He went on to establish a painting business that employed other Virginia natives—William Matthews and his cousin, Carl Butler, for example—as farmhouse painters.[47]

The Culpeper area connection to Newport continued into the twentieth century and duplicated national patterns of southern black seasonal migration from farms to towns and cities. Lindsay Walker, another native of the northern Virginia area near Culpeper who came to Newport in the nineteenth century for summer work, first appeared in the Newport census records in 1900 and was instrumental in bringing other Virginians to Newport in the early twentieth century. Walker worked through an established employment office in Washington, D.C., that "would recruit down there [in Virginia] on the basis of names he'd given them." Often, the recruits were laborers needed for the neighboring Middletown, Rhode Island, farms. In 1900, the Walker household contained nine boarders—all from Virginia and all working in the service field, generally as cooks and waiters. Ann Wilhoite came to Newport around 1900 from the region immediately outside Culpeper to work summers for the black restaurateur George Downing. After she and Harry B. Rice, a native Newporter, fell in love, they married and lived in the seaport.[48] In 1901, Lewis Phillips was brought to Newport from Culpeper County. He recalled:

> When I was a kid, these farmers would get in touch with somebody who knew somebody in the South and these people would migrate to Newport to work on the farms in the farming season, summertime, right out here in Middletown. And then at the end of the season, they'd . . . go back home again. . . . Then that would go on for a while and then after a while, somebody would drop off and decide they didn't want to go back to Culpeper, and stay here. And that's how my father got here. . . . Then, of

course, if they made out pretty good, then they'd write for a brother and he might come up here and not even go to the farm. He might get a job and go right to the city [Newport].[49]

Following the pattern outlined by Lewis Phillips, Amy Weston, born about nine miles from Culpeper, came to the Newport area around 1919. Her husband, Wheeler, had arrived first and worked on various local farms before sending for Amy and their children.[50]

The coastal location of Newport on steamboat lines also explains its relatively early, consistent, and potent draw to southern migrants. In fact, steamboats provided the cheapest, most direct form of transportation to the North for those traveling from southern coastal cities, especially if passengers opted to travel in steerage. Those journeying from Virginia could take the Old Dominion Line to New York. Those from Baltimore, Washington, D.C., and as far south as Florida had available the Baltimore, Chesapeake, and Atlantic Railway's steamers, which also ran to New York. From New York, the migrant transferred to the Fall River Line or the Old Colony Steamship Line and continued on to Newport.[51]

The most striking aspect of southern migration to Newport and Saratoga Springs is its relative volume in the years *prior to* the Great Migration. Surprisingly, the two resorts, even though they were *small* urban centers, drew southern blacks in proportions that matched those for their respective states as early as 1870. In that year, when the southern-born made up 16 and 28 percent of the African-American populations of New York State and Rhode Island, they comprised just over one-tenth and just over one-third of black Saratoga and black Newport, respectively. Also, between 1880 and 1910, when there was "no significant regional redistribution" of African Americans except for some movement to the West and to major northern metropolises, the percentage of southerners among Newport's black community climbed to almost half of the total.[52] Apparently, the enhanced social and political freedoms above the Mason-Dixon Line combined with the mainly service and unskilled jobs available in the two towns to pull these pioneering migrants to the northern resorts. Demographers Daniel M. Johnson and Rex R. Campbell have suggested that such early, relatively small, northward migration streams "developed pathways and linkages that served as mechanisms for facilitating and even encouraging later movements."[53]

The youthfulness of the populations of the two resort communities

Table 5. Age Distribution of Blacks in Newport and Saratoga Springs, 1870, 1900, and 1925

Age Group	1870		1900		1925	
	Number	Percent	Number	Percent[a]	Number	Percent
Newport						
0–18 years	195	24.8	437	27.3	547	33.0
19–45	418	53.2	849	53.1	695	41.9
46–65	143	18.2	253	15.8	341	20.6
65+	30	3.8	61	3.8	75	4.5
Saratoga Springs						
0–18 years	109	36.2	168	25.8	99	17.2
19–45	137	45.5	331	50.8	272	47.3
46–65	45	15.0	106	16.3	168	29.2
65+	10	3.3	27	4.2	36	6.3

Sources: Ninth Census of the United States, 1870 (ms.), microfilm reels 1088, 1089, 1472, National Archives, Washington, D.C.; Twelfth Census of the United States, 1900 (ms.), microfilm reels 1158, 1159, 1505, National Archives, Washington, D.C.; New York State Census, 1925 (ms.), Saratoga County Clerk's Office, Ballston Spa, N.Y.; Rhode Island State Census, 1925 (ms.), Rhode Island State Records Office, Providence.

a. For Saratoga Springs in 1900, there were nineteen individuals for whom no age is listed on the manuscript census schedules. The percentages listed do not include these individuals (2.9 percent of the total) and therefore do not add up to 100.

reflected the attractiveness of these places to migrants and seasonal workers. Between 1870 and 1930, at least a plurality and often a majority of African Americans living in Newport and Saratoga Springs fell within the nineteen- to forty-five-year-old age cohort. In 1870, this group accounted for 45.5 and 53.2 percent of black Saratoga Springs and Newport, respectively. In 1900, these figures were 50.8 for Saratoga Springs and 53.1 percent for Newport. Near the period's end in 1925, 47.3 percent of Afro-Saratogians and 41.9 percent of Afro-Newporters were between nineteen and forty-five years of age (see table 5).

In addition to southern-born migrants, the African-American populations of Saratoga Springs and Newport included foreign-born immigrants. From 1870 to 1900, these immigrant blacks constituted roughly 3 percent of the African-American populations of both towns. Most were from Canada or the Caribbean. In the twentieth century, even this small element proportionately decreased in Saratoga Springs where, by 1925, not even 2 percent of the black community was foreign-born and all in this group hailed from the Caribbean islands.[54]

Newport, however, presents a contrasting picture, since its foreign black population proportionately increased in the first quarter of the twentieth century. Almost all of these were from the Cape Verde Islands, an African country that was then a Portuguese colony, and/or from Portugal; Cape Verdeans in fact formed 6.4 percent of the black population in 1925 (see table 4). Like Hispanic immigrants to America, Cape Verdeans/Portuguese appeared in a wide range of complexion shades. Those recorded as black in the census were probably dark-skinned. Coming from a foreign country, they fostered among themselves a cultural identity distinct from that of black Americans. But once perceived as black in a racially segregated country, in many ways they were treated as other African Americans by the host society.[55]

Households

The seasonal nature of the resort economies of Newport and Saratoga Springs hampered the formation of nuclear households for blacks living in the two towns. Scholars of the black family have found that, in the latter part of the nineteenth century, nuclear-family arrangements—a father and/or mother with his/her children—represented from one-half to three-quarters of all black households. Yet in 1880, only one-third of households containing African Americans in the two resorts were nuclear (see tables 6 and 7). Elsewhere in the nation, not until 1925 did urbanization reduce the proportion of nuclear families to the 39 percent level as an adaptation to urban poverty and migration.[56]

In both Newport and Saratoga Springs, nuclear families gave way to augmented and extended arrangements to accommodate seasonal workers and migrants who labored at unskilled and personal-service jobs in the tourist economy. In 1880, augmented households—those in which black or white blood-related family members were joined by nonrelatives, sometimes servants to the family but generally boarders—in fact constituted one-half of all families in which blacks lived in Saratoga Springs and 41 percent of such families in Newport (see tables 6 and 7). The Woodrow household in Saratoga Springs was typical. Parents William and Rosa lived with their two children and Lucy Ware, a twenty-eight-year-old, unmarried migrant from Virginia; Lucy did domestic service work in the town. In the same year in Newport, widow Annie Brown lived with her two children and Louise Nall, a twenty-three-year-old, single boarder from Virginia who worked as a waitress. Nearing the end of the period in 1925, roughly one-third of blacks in

Table 6. Household Types Containing Blacks in Saratoga Springs, 1880 and 1925

	1880		1925	
	Number	Percent	Number	Percent
Nuclear	52	33.1	82	37.6
Augmented				
Live-in servants	41	26.1	13	6.0
Black-headed	38	24.2	62	28.4
	79	50.3	75	34.4
Extended	16	10.2	14	6.4
Single	7	4.4	47	21.5
Institutional	3[a]	1.9	0	—
Totals	157		218	

Source: Tenth Census of the United States, 1880 (ms.), microfilm reels 928, 929, National Archives, Washington, D.C.; New York State Census, 1925 (ms.), Saratoga County Clerk's Office, Ballston Spa, N.Y.

a. Includes blacks living in hotel employee quarters.

Newport and Saratoga Springs still lived in augmented households (see tables 6 and 7).[57]

No doubt, blacks in the resorts frequently chose to reside in those augmented households headed by African Americans because of the benefits they derived from this arrangement. Nationally, boarding was often a migrant experience, with lodgers frequently sharing the same place of origin as the household head. African-American boarders in the two resort towns fit this pattern in many cases. For example, the nine boarders living with Lindsay Walker in 1900 shared the Newporter's Virginia birthplace. And although William Woodrow hailed from Maryland, his wife, like their boarder Lucy Ware, had been born in Virginia. No doubt the protection and conviviality flowing from shared backgrounds and offered by the hosting family helped make the augmented household attractive to the boarder.[58] Thus, the black-headed, augmented household drew more black seasonal workers and migrants than did such institutional living arrangements as hotel employee residences (see tables 6 and 7). In 1880, for example, Maryland-born John Lucas, headwaiter at the United States Hotel, preferred to live with another young waiter, Ohio-born William Adams, and Adams's wife than to reside in the United States Hotel's employee quarters. In fact, only three such workers lived in those residences that year.[59]

Table 7. Household Types Containing Blacks in Newport, 1880 and 1925

	1880		1925	
	Number	Percent	Number	Percent
Nuclear	111	33.3	196	41.4
Augmented				
Live-in servants	88	26.4	27	5.7
Black-headed	50	15.0	106	22.4
	138	41.4	133	28.1
Extended	36	10.8	76	16.1
Single	42	12.6	61	12.9
Institutional	6[a]	1.8	7[b]	1.5
Totals	333		473	

Source: Tenth Census of the United States, 1880 (ms.), microfilm reel 1210, National Archives, Washington, D.C.; Rhode Island State Census, 1925 (ms.), Rhode Island State Records Office, Providence.

a. Includes blacks living in hotels or hotel employee quarters and those living in the City Asylum.

b. Includes blacks in the Home for the Aged, Mercy Home, and the City Asylum, as well as those living and/or working in the naval hospital, the naval training station, and the naval torpedo station.

Boarders and guests brought needed extra income to many American families in the nineteenth and the early twentieth centuries. This was especially true in resort towns, whose seasonal economies meant regular unemployment during the winter months for many families. The boarders/roomers also might be seasonal workers or black tourists barred by racial discrimination from hotels. Ernest Jackson recalled that during the racing season especially, black families often rented space in their homes in order to cash in on the summer bonanza. Such families, he declared, "would make enough money to last them for winter until next year." Similarly, the income from Lindsay Walker's nine boarders no doubt helped him support his wife and six children.[60]

Also included among the augmented households here are white-headed households in which blacks worked as live-in servants, but these declined in frequency over time. In 1880, one-half or more of African Americans living in augmented arrangements in Newport and Saratoga Springs found themselves in this situation (see tables 6 and 7). Maryland-born Cora Hunter worked and resided in Saratoga Springs as a servant in the home of a white physician, Elisha Rockwood. In Newport, coachmen George Thomas and

Wallace Murray—from Maryland and Washington, D.C., respectively—labored and lived in the household of the American historian George Bancroft.[61] By 1925, however, far fewer African Americans in both places lived in white households as servants; by then, only about 20 percent of blacks living in augmented households in the towns were live-in servants for whites (see tables 6 and 7). The reasons for the declining frequency of households with black live-in servants lie in the nature of both service work and this particular type of living arrangement. Domestic work in general was exceedingly strenuous labor, as attested by Saratoga Springs's Emma Waite. Again and again, she complained to her diary: "I am head over heels into the house cleaning[,] papering[,] and painting. . . . I am so sore and tired that I don't know hardly what to do. . . . I am getting played out on house cleaning. . . . I feel so sore and tired out . . . I hardly know which bone in my body aches the hardest. . . . I am almost dead, working from five o'clock this morning until nine at night."[62] The often poor treatment of *live-in* servants especially, both white and black, by the families for whom they worked throughout the nation was notorious. One black woman, for example, employed as a maid in a white household in Saratoga Springs during the summer of 1888, found her living quarters impossibly small. Her room was so narrow that she felt it necessary to keep her trunk outside the door. Trouble ensued from this arrangement, and the maid was fired. However, she refused to leave the home of her employer without full pay for the time she had worked. The mistress objected to doling out the four dollars and countered by reserving the money as a storage fee for the trunk! In a final, hysterical power move, the employer set the maid's dress afire.[63] Live-in servants, then, were generally overworked, underpaid, helpless against the whims of their employers, and severely restricted in freedoms. These negative features of domestic work largely explain the chronic and familiar national shortage of household service workers. Moreover, the flow of female servants from the South, where living-out was established practice for African-American domestics, may also have contributed to this decline.[64]

Boarding generally decreased in frequency throughout America in the early twentieth century as domestic migration and immigration dropped and as new types of urban housing provided alternatives for single workers.[65] While extended households, those in which immediate family members were joined by other relatives, provided an alternative to the augmented arrangement throughout the period, boarding in Saratoga Springs—whether with relatives, friends, or strangers—followed the national pattern of decline (see table 6). Since migration to the spa did not abate in the twentieth century, the decline in boarding may be explained by new housing arrangements for singles; indeed, the proportion of blacks living alone increased to become one-fifth of all African-American households in Saratoga Springs in 1925 (see table 6). For Newport, however, only boarding with *nonrelatives* as live-in servants decreased in the new century. Black-headed, augmented households and extended households—that is, boarding with relatives—as well as nuclear households proportionately grew, however slightly (see table 7). In this case, the strength and intimacy of the Culpeper network may be the explanatory factor. Settled migrants provided a base secure enough to encourage friends, spouses, children, and relatives from this Virginia area to join the northern households. Lewis Phillips recalled "a sense of togetherness" among Culpeper migrants. Because of their common origins, many "found distant relations in Newport."[66]

⁂

The structural dynamics of a resort-town setting in part determined the demographic dimensions of the history of Afro-Newporters and Afro-Saratogians. During the six decades following the Civil War, the popularity of Newport and Saratoga Springs as summer leisure spots persisted, but with modulations that in turn affected the size and growth rates of their African-American populations. As the resorts' appeal to tourists strengthened, their black denizens usually swelled numerically. African-American neighborhoods formed in close proximity to resort-related employers. Employment opportunities in the resorts resulted in the presence of a southern-born black element that was earlier and more salient than its counterparts in other contemporary African-American communities of the urban North. Finally, the seasonal nature of resort work dictated that the households in which blacks lived would be mainly of the augmented and extended type at the time when most African Americans lived with their immediate family members.

Simultaneously, African Americans were agents who helped arrange the demographic patterns of their existence. Some opted for work and life in Newport and Saratoga Springs even after new industrial work opportunities for blacks appeared elsewhere in the country after World War I. Afro-Newporters and Afro-Saratogians decided where to reside in efforts to be near their churches and redefined undeveloped borderlands as desirable locations for their homes. They shared their knowledge of employment possibilities in the resorts with friends and relatives in the South and facilitated the assimilation of newcomers in their midst by offering them lodging within their households. Others increasingly chose single households rather than live-in service with whites to preserve a measure of independence. Their numbers, neighborhoods, migration levels, and household arrangements resulted from their decisions, which—although hemmed in always by racial proscription and constrained by structural realities—were present nonetheless.

⚜ 3 ⚜

Common Labors

WAGE EARNING BECAME AN INCREASINGLY RACIALIZED EXPERIENCE FOR African Americans in resort towns during the period studied here. The types of jobs that blacks held in the towns were determined by the towns' economies. Newport's more diversified economy offered blacks a wider range of employment opportunities than did Saratoga Springs's more limited job base. But over time, largely on the basis of racial discrimination, both Afro-Newporters and Afro-Saratogians lost representation in certain previous occupational strongholds and were limited to the least lucrative jobs, jobs from which they were often not permitted advancement and in which they were either totally segregated from white workers or segregated in task assignments. These dynamics of work racialization generally applied to both black women and men. This fact combined with the generally heavier participation of black women in the paid workforce in comparison to their white counterparts such that, within the institutional apparatus of organized workers, gender differences between black female and male workers *seemed* to matter less than or were masked by common racial grievances. At the same time, however, proactive responses on the part of the African-American community to racial proscription in certain key occupations prevented and modified the depth of occupational decline. Moreover, within the insular world of racialized work—a world that, with rare exception, denied blacks a subjective experience of working-class identity in Marxian terms—African Americans developed their own social hierarchy, a hierarchy set apart from generally held notions of class and status.

The Structure of Opportunity

The summer brought the year's maximal financial opportunity to the black workers of Saratoga Springs and Newport, but employment possibilities were not limited to these seasonal openings. Between 1870 and 1930, African Americans in both resorts found regular employment opportunities in a variety of positions related to the tourists' needs across all occupational categories but particularly in the areas of domestic and personal-service work and/or unskilled labor. During this time period, 70.5 to 85.8 percent of Afro-Saratogians earned wages from this type of work; corresponding figures for Afro-Newporters were between 73.6 and 87.3 percent (see tables 8 and 9). In Saratoga Springs, these jobs mainly consisted of hotel, boarding-house, restaurant, lake house, and racetrack work. In Newport, blacks staffed hotels, boardinghouses, and restaurants, too, but also worked aboard the steamboats that carried visitors to and from the town.

While employment opportunities in the resorts were not limited to seasonal openings, clearly the unique abundance of tourism-related service jobs in Newport and Saratoga Springs explains the fact that African Americans were somewhat more densely concentrated in domestic and personal-service jobs in the two towns than they were in other cities of the United States. National census figures for 1910, for instance, show that 72.3 percent of all African-American males and 75.2 percent of all African-American females over the age of sixteen worked in domestic/personal-service, transportation, and/or general labor jobs.[1]

Saratoga Springs's hotels offered African Americans employment as ushers, porters, hallmen, bellmen, kitchen help, laundry staff, and waiters. Joseph Smith, the chief usher and self-described hotel manager at the United States Hotel in the late nineteenth century, wrote in 1897: "The waiters employed at the Spa are usually colored men, the [United] States [Hotel] never having had any other." Into the twentieth century, the predominance of blacks as hotel waiters in Saratoga continued. "At the Grand Union and

Table 8. Occupational Distribution of Black Workers in Saratoga Springs and Newport, 1870, 1880, and 1892

| | 1870 | | | | 1880 | | | | 1892 | |
| | Saratoga | | Newport | | Saratoga | | Newport | | Saratoga | |
	No.	%	No.	%	No.	%	No.	%	No.	%
Professional[a]										
Male	3	3.1	4	1.7	2	1.2	5	1.8	1	1.1
Female	1	2.7	1	0.4	0	—	4	1.7	2	4.3
	4	3.0	5	1.1	2	0.7	9	1.8	3	2.2
Proprietary[b]										
Male	2	2.1	3	1.2	4	2.3	20	7.3	2	2.2
Female	0	—	0	—	3	2.7	0	—	2	4.3
	2	1.5	3	0.6	7	2.5	20	4.0	4	2.9
Managerial sales/clerical[c]										
Male	2	2.1	5	2.1	7	4.1	14	5.1	3	3.3
Female	0	—	0	—	0	—	1	0.4	0	—
	2	1.5	5	1.0	7	2.5	15	2.9	3	2.2
Skilled/semiskilled[d]										
Male	23	23.9	18	7.5	29	17.0	41	15.0	12	13.0
Female	2	5.5	14	6.0	2	1.8	32	13.9	0	—
	25	18.9	32	6.8	31	11.1	73	14.5	12	8.7
Unskilled/service[e]										
Male	60	62.5	195	81.2	127	74.7	177	64.8	70	76.1
Female	33	91.7	218	93.6	104	95.4	193	83.9	42	91.3
	93	70.5	413	87.3	231	82.8	370	73.6	112	81.1
Agricultural[f]										
Male	6	6.2	1	0.4	1	0.6	8	2.9	4	4.3
Female	0	—	0	—	0	—	0	—	0	—
	6	4.5	1	0.2	1	0.3	8	1.6	4	2.9
Maritime[g]										
Male	0	—	14	5.8	0	—	7	2.6	0	—
Female	0	—	0	—	0	—	0	—	0	—
	0		14	2.9	0		7	1.4	0	
Military[h]										
Male	0	—	0	—	0	—	1	0.4	0	—
Female	0	—	0	—	0	—	0	—	0	—
	0		0		0		1	0.2	0	
Total workers										
Male	96	72.7	240	50.7	170	60.9	273	54.3	92	66.7
Female	36	27.3	233	49.3	109	39.1	230	45.7	46	33.3
	132		473		279		503		138	

Sources: Ninth Census of the United States, 1870 (ms.), microfilm reels 1088, 1089, 1472, National Archives, Washington, D.C.; Tenth Census of the United States, 1880 (ms.), microfilm reels 928, 929,

United States hotels," Ernie Jackson recalled, "all the waiters were black." Edna Miller concurred: "In the Grand Union Hotel, the head bellman and the headwaiters were all black men, and they had the whole charge of the hotels." Joe Jackson also recalled that "most of the colored men in Saratoga did hotel work. They were waiters and cooks."[2]

Like their Saratogian counterparts, black service workers in Newport also labored as waiters, porters, and cooks—although not so much in hotels, partly because postbellum Newport was no longer a "hotel town." Nor did African-American servants in Newport generally find employment opportunities in the great mansions along Cliff Walk. Lyle Matthews, a black

---

1210, National Archives, Washington, D.C.; New York State Census, 1892 (ms.), Saratoga County Clerk's Office, Ballston Spa, N.Y.

a. Includes actresses, artists, chiropodists, clergymen/ministers/preachers, college treasurers, dentists, doctors/physicians, lawyers, music teachers/musicians, teachers.

b. Includes barbers with own shops (hereafter w.o.s.), cab drivers with own vehicles (hereafter w.o.v.), bootblacks with own stands, caterers w.o.s., cooks with own businesses (hereafter w.o.b.), creamery merchants, expressmen w.o.v., druggists/pharmacists w.o.s., grocers/grocery-store owners, hat collectors w.o.b., horse dealers/traders, housepainters w.o.b., hucksters, intelligence/employment office operators, junk dealers, landlords/real-estate operators, lodging- or boardinghouse keepers, lunchroom proprietors, peanut peddlers/ vendors, restaurant owners, retail merchants/storekeepers, saloonkeepers.

c. Includes bookkeepers, coal-yard bosses, copy readers, foremen, headwaiters, hotel/ restaurant managers, jury keepers, letter carriers, messengers, newsboys, office boys, pages, proofreaders, railroad transfer men, salesmen/saleswomen, stable overseers, stenographers, stewards/clubhouse stewardesses, store clerks.

d. Includes auto repairmen, bakers, barbers (apprentices and journeymen), bicycle instructors, bicycle repairmen, drill runners, blacksmiths/wheelwrights, brass finishers/braziers, butchers, carpenters, caterers, chair caners/tub hoopers, chefs, cobblers/shoemakers, confectioners, coopers, dentist's assistants, dressmakers, electricians, embroidery/needle workers, engineers, firemen, gardeners, gas fitters, hairdressers, herb doctors, horse trainers, iron molders, jockeys, calciminers/painters/whitewashers, lathers, locomotive engineers, manicurists, masons, milliners, nurses, paning men, paperhangers, pastry chefs, plasterers, plumbers, policemen/patrolmen, print cleaners, printers, quarrymen, riggers, seamstresses, ship oilers, stonecutters, stone polishers, street pavers, tailors/tailoresses, tinsmiths, upholsterers, utility men, watchmakers.

e. Includes attendants, bartenders, bellboys/bellmen, boat cleaners, bootblacks, bottlers, busboys, butlers, cabdrivers/hackmen, caretakers, cartmen, carvers, chauffeurs, chimney sweeps, choreboys/choremen, clothes cleaners, coachmen, cooks, delivery men, dishwashers, domestics/house servants, drivers, errand boys, expressmen, grooms/horse rubbers/hostlers, hallboys/hallmen, hod carriers, (unspecified) hotel workers, janitors, kitchen helpers, laborers, laundresses/laundry workers/washerwomen, livery men, maids, office men, pantrymen, porters, railroad car cleaners, servants, sextons, teamsters, truckmen, ushers, valets, waiters/waitresses, wine receivers.

f. Includes farm laborers, farmers, tappers.

g. Includes boatmen/watermen, fishermen, sailors, seamen.

h. Includes army privates, acting stewards (navy), cabin or ship cooks (navy), cabin stewards (navy), engineers (navy), firemen (navy), gunner's mates (navy), mess attendants (navy), oilers (navy), seamen (navy).

Table 9. Occupational Distribution of Black Workers in Saratoga Springs and Newport, 1900, 1910, and 1925

| | 1900 | | | | 1910 | | | | 1925 | |
| | Saratoga | | Newport | | Saratoga | | Newport | | Saratoga | |
	No.	%	No.	%	No.	%	No.	%	No.	%
Professional[a]										
Male	2	0.9	8	1.7	6	3.0	12	2.3	8	3.7
Female	0	—	8	1.9	1	0.5	9	2.2	0	—
	2	0.5	16	1.8	7	1.8	21	2.2	8	1.8
Proprietary[b]										
Male	3	1.4	18	3.8	9	4.5	23	4.3	16	7.4
Female	3	1.9	5	1.2	6	3.1	10	2.4	4	1.8
	6	1.6	23	2.5	15	3.8	33	3.5	20	4.6
Managerial sales/clerical[c]										
Male	3	1.4	14	2.9	9	4.5	19	3.6	13	6.0
Female	0	—	0	—	2	1.0	4	1.0	5	2.3
	3	0.8	14	1.5	11	2.8	23	2.4	18	4.1
Skilled/semiskilled[d]										
Male	23	10.5	86	18.1	24	12.1	78	14.7	35	16.3
Female	8	5.2	36	8.5	6	3.1	37	9.0	12	5.5
	31	8.3	122	13.5	30	7.6	115	12.2	47	10.9
Unskilled/service[e]										
Male	177	80.8	326	68.5	146	73.4	363	68.6	134	62.3
Female	143	92.9	375	88.4	180	92.3	351	85.4	197	90.4
	320	85.8	701	77.9	326	82.7	714	76.0	331	76.4
Agricultural[f]										
Male	10	4.6	2	0.4	5	2.5	13	2.5	9	4.2
Female	0	—	0	—	0	—	0	—	0	—
	10	2.7	2	0.2	5	1.3	13	1.4	9	2.1
Maritime[g]										
Male	0	—	5	1.0	0	—	5	0.9	0	—
Female	0	—	0	—	0	—	0	—	0	—
	0		5	0.6	0		5	0.5	0	—
Military[h]										
Male	1	0.4	15	3.1	0	—	16	3.0	0	—
Female	0	—	0	—	0	—	0	—	0	—
	1	0.3	15	1.7	0		16	1.7	0	
Other[i]										
Male	0	—	2	0.4	0	—	0	—	0	—
Female	0	—	0	—	0	—	0	—	0	—
	0		2	0.2	0		0		0	
Total workers										
Male	219	58.7	476	52.9	199	50.5	529	56.3	215	49.9
Female	154	41.3	424	47.1	195	49.5	411	43.7	218	50.1
	373		900		394		940		433	

native Newporter, recalled that, during the 1920s, except for a handful of
gardeners and house painters, few African Americans worked in the seaport's
grand houses. "Not a lot of blacks were working on Bellevue Avenue," he
declared. "Most of that trade was Irish."[3]

The steamboats of the Fall River Line were in fact the major employers
of Newport's black service workers throughout the period. These steamers
were more than mere functional vehicles. They provided luxurious, hotel-like
accommodations for their passengers. An anonymous traveler in the 1870s
left the following description of them:

Sources: Twelfth Census of the United States, 1900 (ms.), microfilm reels 1158, 1159, 1505,
National Archives, Washington, D.C.; Thirteenth Census of the United States, 1910 (ms.), microfilm
reels 1076, 1077, 1437, National Archives, Washington, D.C.; New York State Census, 1925 (ms.),
Saratoga County Clerk's Office, Ballston Spa, N.Y.

a. Includes actresses, artists, chiropodists, clergymen/ministers/preachers, college treasurers, dentists, doctors/physicians, lawyers, music teachers/musicians, teachers.

b. Includes barbers with own shops (hereafter w.o.s.), cab drivers with own vehicles (hereafter w.o.v.),
bootblacks with own stands, caterers w.o.s., cooks with own businesses (hereafter w.o.b.), creamery merchants, expressmen w.o.v., druggists/pharmacists w.o.s., grocers/grocery-store owners, hat collectors
w.o.b., horse dealers/traders, housepainters w.o.b., hucksters, intelligence/employment office operators,
junk dealers, landlords/real-estate operators, lodging- or boardinghouse keepers, lunchroom proprietors, peanut peddlers/vendors, restaurant owners, retail merchants/storekeepers, saloonkeepers.

c. Includes bookkeepers, coal-yard bosses, copy readers, foremen, headwaiters, hotel/restaurant
managers, jury keepers, letter carriers, messengers, newsboys, office boys, pages, proofreaders, railroad
transfer men, salesmen/saleswomen, stable overseers, stenographers, stewards/clubhouse stewardesses,
store clerks.

d. Includes auto repairmen, bakers, barbers (apprentices and journeymen), bicycle instructors,
bicycle repairmen, drill runners, blacksmiths/wheelwrights, brass finishers/braziers, butchers, carpenters, caterers, chair caners/tub hoopers, chefs, cobblers/shoemakers, confectioners, coopers, dentist's
assistants, dressmakers, electricians, embroidery/needle workers, engineers, firemen, gardeners, gas
fitters, hairdressers, herb doctors, horse trainers, iron molders, jockeys, calciminers/painters/ white-
washers, lathers, locomotive engineers, manicurists, masons, milliners, nurses, paning men, paperhangers, pastry chefs, plasterers, plumbers, policemen/patrolmen, print cleaners, printers, quarrymen,
riggers, seamstresses, ship oilers, stonecutters, stone polishers, street pavers, tailors/tailoresses, tinsmiths, upholsterers, utility men, watchmakers.

e. Includes attendants, bartenders, bellboys/bellmen, boat cleaners, bootblacks, bottlers, busboys,
butlers, cabdrivers/hackmen, caretakers, cartmen, carvers, chauffeurs, chimney sweeps, choreboys/
choremen, clothes cleaners, coachmen, cooks, delivery men, dishwashers, domestics/house servants,
drivers, errand boys, expressmen, grooms/horse rubbers/hostlers, hallboys/hallmen, hod carriers,
(unspecified) hotel workers, janitors, kitchen helpers, laborers, laundresses/laundry workers/washer-
women, livery men, maids, office men, pantrymen, porters, railroad car cleaners, servants, sextons,
teamsters, truckmen, ushers, valets, waiters/waitresses, wine receivers.

f. Includes farm laborers, farmers, tappers.

g. Includes boatmen/watermen, fishermen, sailors, seamen.

h. Includes army privates, acting stewards (navy), cabin or ship cooks (navy), cabin stewards (navy),
engineers (navy), firemen (navy), gunner's mates (navy), mess attendants (navy), oilers (navy), seamen
(navy).

i. Includes collectors of grease, speculators.

They are floating hotels—with most of the modern improvements and accommodations that the best large city hotels now have. The staterooms, halls, parlors and saloons are costly carpeted; furnished with curtains, mirrors, and furniture harmonizing, and all lighted through with gas from elaborate chandeliers and tasty side-light fixtures. The stateroom we occupied had in it a full-sized mirror, walnut bedstead, stationary washstand, plate mirror, marble mantel, Brussels carpet, lace curtains, electric bell to summon servant, etc., and in all parts that can be seen—perfectly clean. They are four story hotels, room numbering up well into the hundreds; and with berths that are permanent in some saloons, mattresses temporarily placed on floors of parlors, they can accommodate 3,000 persons with lodgings.[4]

As "floating hotels," the steamboats required the same kinds of workers, with the exception of their nautical crews, as did conventional hotels. African Americans filled these slots. In *Priscilla of Fall River*, a historical novel depicting life aboard the steamboat *Priscilla*, first launched in 1894, the author described a boarding scene: "Scores of blue-uniformed, white-gloved, negro porters were lined up in orderly array to assist the several hundred travelers with their baggage."[5] The pages of the *Fall River Line Journal* regularly showed photographs of black crew members. Erick Taylor, a white native Newporter, concurred with this impression of black-run steamers. He recalled: "A great industry for black people . . . in Newport was the New York boats. They were the pursers and the workers on the boats. They'd be all the carriers and porters and things like that. And then they'd be the waiters in the dining room. The waiters were very well paid. In addition to being the waiters and being paid for that, they also were helping them load and do other things. The New York boats were frankly directed by black people. . . . The captains were always white people, but they [the blacks] would actually run the boat. They'd have three hundred or four hundred people on the boat and they had to feed and wash them, as it were."[6] Richard Berry, another white Newporter, whose memory of the Old Colony Line stretched back to 1916 and whose father was superintendent of the Newport-based repair yards of the New England Navigation Company, recalled that blacks "comprised the Steward's Department [of the steamships] from Head Waiter to Porters."[7] Ed Dunbaugh, whose grandfather owned a competing Long Island Sound steamship line, offered a corroborating memory of black-staffed steamboats, although for a later period, 1931 to 1942.

All of the stewards were black. . . . The chief steward[,] who was an officer, was white, and the assistant steward, who was an officer, was white. The black stewards were all of the same level. The stewards served two different functions: before the steamer sailed they would be in the dark uniform on the dock and as a passenger came in or purchased a ticket one of them would come along and take the passenger aboard the ship, make sure he got a key from the purser, carry his bags up to the room, and would expect a tip for that. Then, as soon as the boat sailed, they would put on white jackets and become dining room waiters in a sense, but they were called stewards.[8]

Apparently, Dunbaugh applied the label "steward" here very imprecisely and comprehensively to include *all* service workers on the steamers; in fact (and in stricter terms), the stewards' duties were supervisory and managerial with regard to culinary and dining operations. Dunbaugh, a professional historian, added, "I have done a good deal of research on the period between 1900 to 1910 and that's as far back as I can go, and I know the dining room stewards were black then."[9]

Similarly, the census reflects, albeit with numerical imprecision, African-American involvement in hotel and steamboat work throughout the period. Because the census manuscripts do not regularly specify the type of facility at which wage earners labored, it is often impossible to know where a person noted as a steward, waiter, cook, porter, or the like worked—whether in a restaurant, private home, clubhouse, lake house, hotel, or steamer. For instance, in 1870, the census *explicitly* indicates only fourteen blacks in hotel-, boardinghouse-, and restaurant-related service work in Saratoga Springs— certainly a very low figure since the two major hotels alone each employed a minimum of 150 to 250 dining-room helpers. For Newport in the same year, the federal enumeration clearly shows that 28 African Americans worked at the Atlantic House, 41 at the Ocean House, and 51 at the Aquidneck House. In 1880, at least 56 Afro-Saratogians were involved in hotel-, boardinghouse-, and restaurant-related service work. And in Newport during that year, hotel and steamboat workers were among the 42 cooks, 38 waiters, and 7 porters listed in the census. In 1900, the African-American wage-earning population in Saratoga Springs included 60 waiters/waitresses of all types, 13 cooks/ chefs of all types, 5 hotel bellmen/bellboys, 2 hotel hallmen, 2 stewards, 1 hotel busboy, 1 carver, and 1 hotel wine receiver. At the same time, Newport contained 96 cooks, 41 waiters, 10 porters, 5 stewards, 1 hotel messenger, and 1 hotel houseman. In 1910, 52 cooks, 32 waiters/waitresses, 7 hotel watch-men/housemen, 4 hotel bellmen, 3 hotel porters, and 1 hotel pantryman labored as members of the black population of Saratoga Springs. For New-port that year, 94 cooks (6 explicitly for ships or steamers), 22 unspecified waiters, 5 hotel waiters, 4 hotel bellmen, 2 hotel elevator operators, 2 pantry-men, 2 steamboat stewards, and 1 boardinghouse waiter were counted among black workers. Finally, in 1925, the census recorded 35 unspecified waiters, 31 cooks, 4 hotel bellmen/bellboys, 4 unspecified hotel workers, 3 hotel kitchen workers, 1 porter, and 1 hotel busboy in the African-American wage-earning population of Saratoga Springs.[10]

Although practically all steamboat and hotel workers were male, there were a few black wage-earning females working as cooks, waitresses, kitchen maids/girls, silver girls, pantry girls, chambermaids, laundry workers, and stewardesses. During the 1870 season in Saratoga Springs, Emma Waite "commenced work at the Congress Hall" on June 14, left that situation on July 11, and the next day "commenced work at the Continental Hotel," where she worked at some unspecified service position until September 14. This probably involved cooking; in her diary that year, she noted: "Mr. Hunter went to New York this morning and I have been Chief Cook." Likewise, one Mary Ann was a vegetable cook at the United States Hotel in 1874. Nancy Williams labored as a waitress in the chambermaids' dining room of the Grand Union Hotel in 1904. Geneive Epps worked as a hotel laun-dress in Saratoga Springs in 1910, perhaps for the Grand Union, which at that time maintained its own washing facility on Congress Street. In 1880, Rosebena Williams earned wages as a steamboat stewardess, a conve-nient post since her husband also worked as a steward on a steamer. And Ed Dunbaugh recalled the regular use of one or two stewardesses aboard each Newport-bound steamer "to attend to women passengers who might have a problem."[11]

These types of jobs for women reveal the operation of a gender-segregated system within the sphere of black hotel and steamboat labor that was compli-cated by systems of gender and race discrimination at large. The fact that black men rather than black women dominated service positions in the resorts' hotels and steamboats—as did men in the field of hotel work more generally during the period—suggests the ways in which the dominant con-temporary discourse regarding the innate suitability of women for domestic service work could be mutated or jettisoned entirely when financial remuneration was involved. Judging from the numbers, the same women who were fit to cook, clean, and serve the table in the home were deemed less fit to do so as paid hotel and steamboat employees. Also, when permitted to work in the hotels and on the steamboats, black women in the resorts dealt directly with the paying public less often than black men, another pattern with negative pecuniary consequences. As laundresses, kitchen girls, silver girls, pantry girls, or relief cooks, for instance, African-American women had no direct contact with hotel guests and therefore fewer opportunities for tips. Even in ostensibly similar positions—for example, waiting tables—black men were relatively advantaged. They held the more lucrative patrons' dining hall positions while black women served tables in the employees' dining room. A chambermaid's job, of course, was an exception, since it could involve both contact with the public and opportunities for tip receipts; but, significantly, only forty black chambermaids were clearly identified as such in the census during the period under study. Presumably, then, most hotel chambermaids in the two resorts were white. Thus, it would appear that in a job where sex segregation might have worked to the economic benefit of black women, white women instead were preferred. Finally, in other jobs where black women did communicate directly with the public, as in the case of steamboat stewardesses, they were restricted to serving a female clientele, a pattern that also may have resulted in less pay.[12]

Certainly, however, hotels and steamboats were not the sole providers of resort-related employment in the two towns. The racetrack in Saratoga Springs supplied African Americans with additional summer work as jockeys, stable hands, grooms, rubbers, and hostlers. The walls of the National Museum of Racing in Saratoga Springs, lined with photographs and paintings of famous horses—several being led by unnamed black stable workers—suggest the importance of African Americans in the Saratoga Springs racing world. A visitor in 1870 noticed the black horse trainers and observed several African-American jockeys as well. In fact, one historian found that most stable hands at the Saratoga track were black and included in his 1952 history of the resort a photograph of black hostlers posing near their "nigger shanties." A visitor in 1902 counted the "negro rubbers" among the frequenters of a local gambling establishment. And Edna Bailey Miller recalled her father's regular, early Sunday morning prayer meetings with black track workers during the racing seasons of the 1920s.[13] The census probably severely undercounted the number of African-American jockeys and stable workers in Saratoga

Springs, partly because the enumeration was done in June or earlier—before the start of the racing season in mid-July or August. In 1870, the census listed only five blacks in these occupations; in 1880, eighteen; in 1900, six; and in 1925, none. Yet the local press, which assiduously reported the alleged misdeeds of area blacks, often mentioned African-American hostlers: John Owens, a black jockey employed by a Colonel McDaniel, probably a white stable owner, was stabbed by another of McDaniel's African-American entourage; James Robinson, a black stable boy, shot a police detective who had attempted to interrogate him about shooting a stable dog that had barked at him the night before.[14]

Direct involvement in illegal gambling operations provided other money-making opportunities for a few black Saratogians. In 1902, two of the six gambling houses in Saratoga Springs catered expressly to black clienteles. Some waiters at the lake houses where gambling was especially notorious doubled as bagmen. Harvey William Reid, who lived in Saratoga Springs since 1900 (when he arrived at the age of 10), was a bagman for Newman's Lake House; he also worked there as a bartender, paying off authorities and delivering gambling receipts to the bank—probably during the 1920s. He recounted those days: "There used to be two guys out (by the bank) with big machine guns, one out near the top of the hill, and one across the street. Sometimes I would lay down in the car. . . . We'd go into town 125 miles an hour, used three cars, so (no one would) know which one had the money. The boss had the money all wrapped up in paper (all three cars got packages), one got the money, the others were fakes. Nobody knew, till we went to the bank, which was the real thing. That was $50,000 or more we used to bring to the bank every day!" Harvey and others also worked as numbers runners.[15]

Newspaper boys on the street corners of Saratoga Springs, some of them African American, hawked local journals containing the day's racing news and entries to passersby on their way to the racetrack. Ernie Jackson and Ed Pilkington remembered selling papers to summer guests when they were growing up in the town in the early twentieth century:

> We used to sell newspapers and racing forms. . . . You could always go down to the [newspaper] office and get thirty or forty papers and they would take your name. And then sometimes, you'd have to pay for them up front if you had any money. If you didn't, they would trust you until you sold them all

and came back and paid them. . . . We used to go down and get a bundle—maybe the *Saratogian*. . . . They had a pink sheet which came out after the races . . . which had all the entries for the next day. . . . The *Saratogian* was only two cents. . . . Some people knew the price and they'd only give you two cents, and some summer people—they always had a lot of money—. . . would give you a nickel or a dime or a quarter for the paper.[16]

I must have been about ten years old when I started hustling newspapers. I had my bicycle. . . . I'd be out there at six o'clock in the morning, pick up my papers, and by seven o'clock, I was rolling. Nine o'clock, I'd come in to settle up. With tips and everything, I could make fifteen dollars no sweat in those two hours every racing day.[17]

Saratoga's spring waters also provided moneymaking opportunities for blacks. In 1910, Alfred Franklin labored as a bottler while John Boardley worked as a teamster for a spring water plant. Charles Mann worked as a foreman in a spring water bottling plant in 1925. In the 1920s, when Ernie Jackson was a child, the black caretaker of the Grand Union Hotel's employee quarters walked approximately one mile every summer day to fill fifteen or twenty bottles with the Red Spring's waters, which he then sold to the waiters as a foot-soaking solution. As a teenager, Ed Pilkington worked the tables at the local drink hall, where guests could sample the Geyser, Hathorne I, Hathorne II, and Coesa spring waters. His job was to remove glasses and clean the tables after the customers had finished drinking.[18]

The summer vacation period in both towns created openings for several black businesses that were strictly seasonal operations. In 1916, for instance, Isaiah Jackson established Jack's Cabaret and Grill (later Jack's Harlem Club) on Saratoga Springs's Congress Street, an operation that remained a landmark through the 1920s and into the Great Depression. Jack's Cabaret opened for business only during the summer, since Jackson operated a similar establishment in Harlem during the winter months, but boasted a "packed house nightly." Popular among partying Saratogians, it did not open until after 10:00 P.M. and featured plenty of music, liquor, and nightclub acts. Louise Lillian Nelson, a local black, worked as a singer-dancer at Jack's in the early 1920s, and "Chick" Massey, an out-of-towner who settled in the spa in 1920, worked as a singing waiter there, although most of the entertainers were not year-round residents. Newport seamstress Ann Rice similarly operated a seasonal business; the wealthy Bellevue Avenue vacationers were her clientele.

Her grandson recalled that she worked from the family's William Street home, where "she had clothes pinned up in [the] front room, and would have people coming in all day in the summer." And, at the turn of the century, James T. Allen owned and managed the "Hygeia Spa," a summer café at Newport's Easton's Beach.[19]

Tourist traffic also presented many opportunities for African Americans to open businesses catering mainly to a summer clientele—sometimes black, sometimes white, sometimes mixed. African Americans in both towns operated boardinghouses for black seasonal workers and lodging houses for black tourists. The mother of the black poet William Stanley Beaumont Braithwaite moved to Newport in 1896 and opened a tourist home on De Blois. In June 1900, there were two additional such places in Newport. Mary Burrell ran a lodging house on Levin Street in Newport that she continued to operate at least until 1910, when she competed with three other similar businesses in the seaport. In 1910, six African Americans are listed in the census as boardinghouse/lodging house operators in Saratoga Springs. Another, William Alexander, is called a "hotel proprietor"; this establishment was probably a lodging house catering to black guests. In that year, Ella Holmes operated a rooming house for summer blacks on Walworth Street in Saratoga Springs and maintained this business throughout the period studied. She boasted a "capacity business" during the 1927 season, according to one source, who claimed at the time that "the 'States' or the Grand Union have nothing on her."[20]

Louise Lancko, Ella Holmes's daughter, eventually took over the family boardinghouse on Walworth Street and later added two more homes on Washington Street to the family's summer enterprise. The three operations catered to African-American workers and tourists separately, as Edna Miller explained: "Doctors and lawyers . . . lived in her big house. On the other side, . . . through the yard, she had another great big house, but [it was] for working people. . . . The doctors, the lawyers, the teachers want[ed] to sleep late . . . and the others . . . [had] taxis or their friends picking them up to go to their work or up to the track at 6:00 A.M. . . . they'd be blowing [car horns] and everything. . . . [The tourists] didn't want that."[21] The home-based location of the lodging house businesses accounts for the domination of women in this area of African-American employment.

Similarly, as home-based laundry work was a popular moneymaking option among black married women with children throughout the country during this period, black women in the resorts, Saratoga Springs especially, turned to this kind of work during the summer months. Florence Jackson of Saratoga Springs had six children and worked as a laundress from her home. Although her husband, James, was fortunate enough to have steady, year-round employment as a butler in a local white household, Florence helped supplement her family's income during the summer months by doing laundry. Her youngest son, Ernest, recalled helping his mother in this work: "We were really poor coming along and so my mother washed and ironed most of the summer to make extra money. I was always the one who had to deliver the clothes and pick up dirty laundry."[22] Mrs. Edna Bailey, who had two children, also opened a home laundry. Her daughter, Edna, explained its beginnings: "Paul Whiteman, Bing Crosby, and Rochester used to all have big houses here in Saratoga. . . . Bing Crosby was married to Dixie in those days and had a family. He had this great big house and his friends stayed there. They came to my mother's employment agency [described below] looking for help. They had very 'exclusive' underwear and shirts, and Bing wanted them done. My mother said, 'Well, we'll do them!' and so she and some women friends opened up a laundry, a hand laundry."[23] Similarly, Harvey Reid Sr. spoke of the laundry his mother, Ella Holmes, ran as a side industry—in addition to her boardinghouse—during the summer months. She did the wash for a white-run boardinghouse in Saratoga Springs.[24]

In both resorts, black businesses less discernibly and exclusively tied to the summer season no doubt garnered their greatest share of profits during the summer or warm-weather months, when the climate cooperated and/or an enlarged population demanded their services. This was especially true in Saratoga Springs. Using the 1925 city directory as a guide, for instance, a pedestrian traveling west from Broadway on the north side of the street would have passed Mrs. Georgia Jackson's boarding house, James Williams's second-hand goods store, Mrs. Mabel McFee's hair salon, Theodore E. Stanford's barbershop, Mrs. Laura Branch's lunchroom, and William A. Delesine's tailor shop. Continuing west under the Delaware and Hudson Railroad's overpass, the same stroller would have encountered on the right another boardinghouse—this one run by Mrs. Alverta Baker—and John W. Carter's shoemaking shop. Crossing the thoroughfare to return east along the south sidewalk, the traveler would also have seen Charles White's barbershop and Jack's

Cabaret and Grill. Finally proceeding again beneath the railroad overpass and gazing to the right, the walker would have passed Victoria Genz's dressmaking shop, Frank Jordan's barbershop, and John H. Stewart's restaurant.[25]

Year-round black-owned business operated in both resort towns, but far more frequently in Newport. In Saratoga Springs, only two regular, year-round black enterprises surfaced in the sources consulted for this investigation. The Pennington Pharmacy was one. In 1870, twenty-four-year-old Thomas H. Sands Pennington worked as a druggist/clerk, a job he had held for two years, probably for F. T. Hill and Company—a pharmacy owned by two white partners, F. T. Hill and John L. Perry, a medical doctor. Three years later, Dr. Perry ended his association with the business, thus allowing Pennington to replace him as coproprietor in early 1875. By March 1875, Pennington was sole proprietor. For two years, 1875 and 1876, Pennington is listed as manager of the pharmacy in city directories; but, according to R. G. Dun and Co. credit ledgers, he was out of business by July 1876. The financial assistance of Dr. Perry, however, enabled Pennington to reopen the pharmacy in 1880. For the next ten years, he ran the drugstore, which clearly catered to a mixed clientele. The local press even noted one capital investment in the business—a new cash register valued at $175, which provided a receipt tape for both owner and customer. The paper observed that the new adding machine was probably "the most expensive money drawer in town and most ingeniously constructed. . . . Mr. Pennington kindly exhibits it to all who apply."[26] Pennington also advertised his pharmacy in the local papers and business directories:

ORATORS use Pennington's Norwegian Troches.[27]

Use Pennington's Odontine for the teeth.[28]

H. Sands Pennington, Pharmacist, has in stock Dalmatian Insect Powder, Paris Green and White Hellebore, the well-known insecticides, also a general assortment of reliable drugs, patent medicines, and sick room requisites.[29]

Later, in the 1920s, Leonard Cochrane, with the help of his siblings, ran a creamery on Caroline Street, an avenue just south of Lake and running east of Broadway.[30]

Examples of such year-round operations, however, abound in Newport throughout the period. In the 1870s, these included the Burton Express

Company and the Downing restaurant, both of which had antebellum origins and continued at least through 1900. Downing had further investments in local real estate. In the 1880s, the Fayerweather blacksmith shop and the Hurley painting business appeared as new black enterprises. In 1880, Charles Fayerweather is first listed in the census as a blacksmith/wheelwright. His business was located on Spruce Street in the heart of the West Broadway neighborhood and remained open, although not consistently, until at least 1919. Armstead Hurley arrived in the seaport in 1886 as a painter and glazier at the age of thirty-two and continued in that line. In the memory of Lyle Matthews, Hurley's was "one of the two biggest painting businesses in the city." The Reverend Henry Jeter of Shiloh Baptist Church commented in 1910 that Hurley was "prepared to take as large a contract as any painter in the city. At his place of business [on Bridge Street], he is able to furnish you with all the painter's supplies, wall papers and everything in the line of business."[31]

More African-American businesses appeared in Newport during the last two decades of the nineteenth century, and others sprang up in the early decades of the twentieth century. James Allen opened a second restaurant with his brother, Henry, a baker and cook. David Allan, probably a relative of James and Henry Allen, operated a bakery and catering firm, first on Heath but later near Equality Park in the West Broadway area. Abraham Ash opened a restaurant and eventually created a specialty, "golden fingers—a type of sausage roll," that "he sold oft' times to sailors and people . . . at baseball games." William F. Robinson began a jewelry and watch repair service that ran through 1910. George Seaforth opened a saloon and, later, a restaurant on Thames Street that operated through 1910. Andrew Tabb ran a livery stable and express business on Edgar Court that "enjoyed the patronage of some of the wealthiest families coming to Newport" and continued as late as 1910. Cromwell West ran a drugstore on West Broadway from at least 1919. Louis Walker (Lindsay Walker's son) owned Paramount Coaches, a busline that competed with William K. Vanderbilt's Short Line, until 1933. Walker later started Walker's Taxi Service, a business that employed other local blacks like Oliver Burton as drivers, and teamed with another Afro-Newporter, B. F. Burton Jr., to operate the Broadway Garage. In addition to automobile parking and storage, this business provided a full array of auto maintenance and repair services.[32]

Newport's wider profile of year-round African-American businesses may be attributed to an economy that was more diversified than that of Saratoga Springs—a fact that also explained *non*tourist-related black employment in service and unskilled jobs in the seaport. Newport differed significantly from Saratoga Springs in the fact that, as a military training center, it offered African Americans nonseasonal, year-round employment opportunities in a relatively wide range. Sociologist J. Ellis Voss observed the importance of municipal and government employment for permanent residents of seasonal vacation spots in a study of another summer resort town—Ocean City, New Jersey.[33] Compared to black Saratogians, black Newporters were far better represented in these areas of work.

In contrast to Saratoga Springs, military-related employment opportunities existed through Fort Adams—a U.S. Army base located in the seaport since 1832. Those blacks taking advantage of these openings included one army private in 1880 and two unspecified army recruits in 1900. In addition, black civilians found jobs at or related to Fort Adams. In 1880, for example, Elizabeth Wyeth worked as a cook at Fort Adams while five other African Americans labored as live-in house servants for four army officers and an army surgeon. In 1900, two black cooks and one black groom were employed by army officers stationed at Fort Adams. Black wage earners in 1910 included one civilian army engineer and six servants for army families.[34]

In 1880, the U.S. Navy established a war college complex that included a naval training academy, torpedo station, and naval hospital—all providing especially attractive, rare wage-earning niches for African Americans, inasmuch as they were ostensibly racially egalitarian to all enlisted men before the onset of World War I. No such opportunity existed for black Saratogians.[35]

In addition, black civilians worked at the naval complex and as private servants for white naval personnel—entirely reproducing the type of wage-earning posts they held in other sectors of Newport's economy. In 1900, George Henderson was employed as a civilian laborer at the naval torpedo station. That same year, Sally Fowler, Lillie Woodland, and Wren Venner worked as cook, waitress, and housekeeper, respectively, at the naval hospital; two other African-American women labored as cook and waitress at the naval war college; Ephron King and Lewis Robinson earned wages as cooks for the navy; three black women worked as maid, nurse, and seamstress in the household of a white navy commander; and Patsy Westley and Emma Floyd were cook and unspecified servant, respectively, in the household of a navy surgeon. Black wage earners in 1910 included two navy cooks, one training station steward, one torpedo station steward, and two servants for navy families. Finally, in 1925, the census enumerated three African-American servants—one man and two women—in the households of an admiral and two commanders, respectively.[36]

As well as working for the military, African Americans in Newport held several other government-paid or government-related jobs on the city, county, state, and federal level; in Saratoga Springs, they apparently claimed far fewer of these positions. In the 1910 census of Saratoga Springs, a mere four blacks appear in government jobs; they were an attendant in an unspecified public office, a stenographer, a county laborer, and a village street laborer. In contrast, at the federal level in Newport, Charles Rice worked as a janitor at the post office in 1880, and H. Channing Rice was a special delivery man for the postal service in 1900. Ten years later, Herbert Williams and Arthur Townsend worked as letter carriers, and Edward Jackson worked as a janitor in a federal office building. State employees included statehouse janitor Robert Brooks in 1900 and statehouse page George Seaforth in 1910. In the same year, Robert Brooks found work with the Newport county government as a janitor in the courthouse.[37]

The city of Newport also offered government positions to African Americans. In 1880, Sarah Fizz cooked for the city asylum. In 1900, for example, five blacks working for the municipality in year-round jobs included two laborers, one police patrol driver, one policeman, one unspecified driver, one school janitor, and one city dump caretaker. The policeman was Oliver Dewick, who had worked for the department as a temporary worker from June 1890 to October 1896, when he was given a permanent position that he kept until his retirement in December 1922. That year, three other African Americans worked only summers for the city as water policeman, beach laborer, and beach clerk. In 1902, Louisa Van Horne was appointed to the teaching staff of the Newport city schools. Four years later, James Ray was appointed a special policeman. In 1910, black municipal employees included two police officers, one police patrol driver, one city wagoner, one city quarryman, two laborers for the street department, three unspecified laborers, one teamster, one cement finisher, two school janitors, one police station janitor, one school gardener, one cook at the asylum, and two new public-school teachers. Bernard Kay progressed within the city police department from an appointment as special policeman in 1914 to reserve policeman in 1918 to permanent policeman in 1920. In 1918, Frank P. Wheeler began permanent work as a police department chauffeur in May 1918. In April 1925, Frank H. C. Rice was elected to the office of special policeman at a town council meeting. And in July 1929, Oliver Burton was also named a special policeman (and would go on to become a reserve police officer in 1931 before receiving a permanent position in 1934).[38]

As a New England seaport, Newport might be expected to have offered wage-earning opportunities to blacks in other commercial maritime work that, as an inland spa, Saratoga Springs could not. In fact, the number of blacks involved in such labors was minuscule and declining throughout the period (as it had been since the midnineteenth century in other ports east of the Hudson River), partly because of a relatively depressed job market.[39] However, the steamship lines and shore-based maritime endeavors supplied a related work arena, especially since the New England Navigating Company (NENC)—owner of the Fall River Line during the early twentieth century—operated its mechanical and maintenance departments in Newport. Thus, in 1900, Newport's wage-earning pool included four boat cleaners and one boat keyman. In 1910, some African Americans filled the following occupations: fireman (1), dock stevedore (1), steamboat laborer (9), shipyard plumber (1), ferryboat engineer (1), steamboat company watchman (1), steamboat/boat cleaner-scrubber (1), NENC foreman (1), ship oiler (1), and unspecified dock laborer (5).[40]

Newport's larger black population supported a bigger and more enduring African-American professional and business element than that which existed in Saratoga Springs. Public-school teachers and black entrepreneurs in Newport have been noted above. In both towns, there were, of course, black ministers also. But throughout the late nineteenth century, in any given year, only one African-American pastor labored in Saratoga Springs because there was only one established black congregation, the Dyer-Phelps A.M.E. Zion Church; and, following denominational policy, these pastors were turned over every three years. Not until 1910 was a second black church established, thus adding a Baptist clergyman to the ranks of Saratoga's black professionals. In certain years, the pastors of these two churches were joined by a minister of an irregular, unestablished black congregation.[41]

On the other hand, during each year throughout the period, the three—and, after 1894, four—black churches in Newport supported at least a corresponding number of pastors. The tenures of two of these ministers were quite lengthy. Mahlon Van Horne, for instance, a graduate of New Jersey's Livingston College, pastored the Union Congregational Church from 1868 to 1897, when he left that position to assume a post as U.S. consul to the Danish West Indies, an appointment made by President McKinley. Henry Jeter, a graduate of Wayland Seminary in Washington, D.C., was ordained and installed as pastor of Shiloh Baptist Church in 1875 and manned the church's pulpit for forty-one years.[42]

Besides clergymen, African-American professionals and capitalists were scarce in Saratoga Springs. The more prominent black businesspersons there have been noted already. In addition, an occasional music teacher or artist appeared. Others—musicians or actresses—were probably not year-round wage earners since, in all likelihood, they supplied entertainment for the summer crowd. Edna Bailey Miller noticed this dearth of black businesses in Saratoga Springs immediately on relocating with her family to the spa in the 1920s from New Haven, Connecticut, where her family "went [to] everything black" because of the relatively wide array of African-American enterprises there. She expressed some slight, initial disappointment at her discovery of her new home's comparative lack of black business.[43]

In contrast to Saratoga Springs, Newport retained black medical doctors, a black dentist, a black chiropodist, a black lawyer, and at least fifteen different music teachers / musicians—many of whom persisted for at least a decade in the seaport. Marcus Wheatland, a medical doctor specializing in electro-therapeutics and radiology, married one of George Downing's granddaughters and practiced for at least one-quarter of a century, from 1900 to 1925, in Newport. His son Matthias (also called Alonzo) also worked in Newport, as a dentist, for at least as long. The pair's long years in the seaport were paralleled by those of chiropodist Edward Holloway. Sophia Rice taught music from at least 1880 to at least 1925. Ruth Chase did the same for at least ten years, 1900 through 1910. The physician Harriett Rice worked in the city in 1900. Ten years later, she was gone, but Eva A. Jones had arrived to practice medicine. And, by 1925, Dr. Rice had returned.[44]

Population persistence rates for the African-American community—in part a measure of its economic strength since, historically, the most transient populations have tended to be the most casually employed and the least financially secure—affirm the greater vitality of Newport's labor market over that of Saratoga Springs for most of the period. Black Saratogians quit their town more often than did black Newporters. Between 1870 and 1880, 23 percent of Saratoga's African Americans stayed on in the spa; one-third of Newport's African Americans remained in the seaport during the same period. Corresponding figures of the decade 1900–10 are 26 percent for Saratoga Springs and 35 percent for Newport. Only between 1910 and 1925 did persistence rates for the two resorts even out. During this period, 25 percent and 26 percent of the African Americans remained in Saratoga Springs and Newport, respectively. National economic changes wrought by World War I probably explain Newport's relatively declining appeal to African Americans during this fifteen-year period. As discussed earlier, blacks were drawn to industrial opportunities elsewhere.[45]

As in other urban places, the need for black women to work throughout the span of their lifetimes was greater than that for white women. During the early twentieth century, for instance, while white women often entered the workforce at the age of fifteen and sixteen, marriage and childbirth generally ended their involvement in the paying economy; their older children instead brought in wages to the household. African-American women, in contrast, continued to work after marriage and through their child-rearing years. Certainly, this was true of the two resorts. In 1910, over one-half (75 from a total of 133) of all married, black working women in Newport fell between the ages of 25 and 44, and another one-third (46 from a total of 133) were over 45. In the same year, 62.2 percent (46 from a total of 74) of the married, black female wage earners in Saratoga Springs were in the 25 to 44 age cohort, while one-fourth (19 from a total of 74) were over 45.[46] Driven by circumstances to work for pay in greater numbers, for longer periods of their lives, and in direct contradiction of normative gender-role prescriptions—as established through white women—black female wage earners in the resorts may have felt little class or gender solidarity with white working women of the time.

Labor force participation among married women in the two resorts confirmed the strength of Newport's economy in relation to that of Saratoga Springs. In 1880—when, elsewhere in the nation, 35.4 percent of black married women were working—corresponding figures for Saratoga Springs and Newport were 44.1 percent (30 from a total of 68) and 25 percent (32 from a total of 128), respectively. This suggests a relatively high level of financial security in black households in Newport at this time, and just the opposite for Saratoga Springs, since research elsewhere has shown that African-American wives tended to stay at home when their men had access to steady employment. Toward the end of the period in 1910, 53 percent (133 from a total of 251) of African-American wives were gainfully employed in Newport, while 65.3 percent (83 from a total of 127) worked in Saratoga Springs. Apparently, blacks wives in the spa especially needed to augment household income. Moreover, the employment rate of African-American married women in Saratoga Springs was almost exactly equal to the national figure, which was 64.2 percent in 1910, as based on a study of Boston, Buffalo, Chicago, Cleveland, Milwaukee, New York, and Philadelphia. Apparently, then, in contemporary terms, Newport's economy was not only stronger than that of Saratoga Springs; it also offered black families better options than several important northeastern cities.[47]

Discrimination

Negative racial attitudes toward blacks shaped, threatened, and, over time, worsened the structure of job opportunities available to African Americans in Newport and Saratoga Springs. The very fact that a majority of Afro-Newporter and Afro-Saratogian wage earners filled low-paying, seasonal jobs throughout the period—that is, experienced no advancement in occupational type—indicated a racially casted experience. However, race-based job discrimination, especially after 1890, was marked by additional features.

First, whites preempted work slots that blacks had previously monopolized or might be expected to dominate given antebellum labor practices. The absence of African Americans in the Cliff Walk mansions exemplified this trend in Newport. After the Civil War, the presence of northern and western European servants in the gilded households of the nouveaux riches made wealthy by industrial capitalism was thought to add an element of culture and refinement to the families to which they were attached. Hence, the Vanderbilt's Marble House engaged nine French chefs. The typical Newport mansion might require the regular use of over twenty servants; significantly, these often performed specialized tasks according to prevailing ethnicity-based social hierarchies and ethnic stereotypes. Many summer cottages included on their staffs, for instance, the "dignified" English butler and the "difficult," though indispensable, Irish maid. Newport was not alone in its preference for white domestic servants, for the practice of hiring immigrant domestics generally gained in frequency throughout the nineteenth century.[48]

Similarly, black hotel workers in the late nineteenth century faced mar-
ginalization as either new European immigrants replaced them entirely or
restricted them to only a few positions in an increasingly racially segmented
labor market. In 1889, for instance, white workers replaced what had been a
virtually all-black staff at San Francisco's Palace Hotel due to the protests of
an all-white cooks' and waiters' union. And Lorenzo Greene and Carter G.
Woodson found that, between 1890 and 1917, "throughout the entire North
and West most of the best hotels and restaurants replaced their Negro
waiters with whites." Certainly, the threat of displacement was real in Saratoga Springs. Emma Waite began work in 1870 at the Grand Union Hotel on
June 2, but she "was discharged . . . on account of their getting white help"
the very next day. And an 1892 guidebook distinguished the Windsor Hotel
for employing "white servants exclusively" and being "a strictly high class
house."[49]

Black jockeys lost ground in Saratoga Springs as a result of racial discrimination. Beginning in the late nineteenth century, they received fierce
(and frequently violent) competition, mainly from the Irish jockeys who
eventually replaced them. By the period's end, black racetrack workers in the
spa were relegated to groomsman positions.[50]

African-American navy workers experienced job slippage, too. Until
about 1915, U.S. Navy hiring practices were unusually egalitarian toward
blacks. The navy permitted integrated crews and offered blacks full eligibil-
ity for all ratings and equal pay. Thus, in 1900, the thirteen black naval personnel stationed in Newport held a wide range of posts, including those of
corporal's mate (1), coxswain (1), fireman (1), seaman (1), landsman (1), ap-
prentice (5), cabin steward (1), and mess attendant (2). Similarly, ten years
later, the sixteen black navy men worked as gunner's mate (1), oiler (1), fireman (2), engineer (1), warrant officer (1), seaman (2), steward (3), cook (2), or
mess attendant (3). During World War I and until 1932, however, a new naval
racial policy on paper restricted newly enlisted blacks to positions as mess
men (cooks, stewards, attendants); in practice, however, it filled these positions only with Filipinos. Consequently, in 1925, twelve of the fifteen black
navy recruits tended mess; the other three—two engine men and one water
tender—no doubt retained their positions as pre–World War I enlistees.[51]

In Newport's commercial maritime sector, increasingly unionized white
competition combined with a depressed job market to eliminate practically
all black-worker representation. Thus, in 1880, just three African Americans

were fishermen, a mere two were seamen, and only one a sailor. Ten years later, only two black fishermen and two sailors called the seaport home. And, in 1910, one fisherman and two watermen/boatmen earned wages from this seaport.[52]

In Saratoga Springs, the pervasive national pattern among black barbers of job loss to immigrant competition seemed to prevail during these years. Despite the growth of its black population, by 1925, there were only three African-American barbers in the spa—down from a total of ten in 1870.[53]

Another aspect of the pattern of racially driven job discrimination evidenced in both resorts was the barring of black access to new industrial-sector and many nonmanual jobs, especially in integrated labor markets. Josephine Silone (later Yates, the nationally prominent black clubwoman) graduated valedictorian of Newport's high school and returned with a normal school degree, hoping to obtain a position as a schoolteacher. Owing to color bias, she was spurned in her efforts. Similarly, Ed Pilkington explained that his contemporary Warren Cochrane (later the director of YMCAs in New York City and Atlanta) could not find a public-school teaching job in Saratoga Springs after graduating from Albany Normal School in the 1920s, simply because "the [white] community wasn't ready for it."[54]

The relative absence of black wage earners from managerial, clerical, and sales positions is yet another measure of the racialization of work opportunities. Historian Stuart Blumin has described how these new forms of nonmanual work—for example, store and office clerks, managers, foremen, bookkeepers, salespeople—functioned as the stuff of and path to an emergent social category in nineteenth-century America—that of the middle class. Certainly, in both resorts, an occasional African American gained access to this avenue to economic upward mobility. Thomas Pennington, for instance, began his career as a clerk in a white-run drugstore. Generally, however, blacks were absent from the managerial, clerical, and sales jobs in the resort towns. Even including headwaiters, head bellmen, and supervisory stewards in this job category does not yield impressive results. African-American representation here remained under 5 percent of the total black wage-earning population throughout the period. In Newport, no more than 3 percent of all black laborers were ever found in this occupational category (see tables 8 and 9). Writing in the 1880s, the Reverend Mahlon Van Horne referred to a rare, praiseworthy instance in which a black was hired as head clerk at a Newport establishment. He explained that this African-American worker obtained the position "under the rule of civil service, or fair play in exercise of commercial skill" after winning an employee competition sponsored by the proprietor—probably J. P. Aylesworth, a cooper—in which employees vied to bring in the greatest amount of new trade; still, the winner's white co-workers threatened to strike and were thwarted only with assurances from the owner's son that he would codirect the business with the African American.[55]

It may be expected that the small African-American professional and business classes in the resorts catered to increasingly segregated, all-black clienteles, since this was a developing pattern elsewhere in the nation at the time. However, the small size of the African-American populations of Newport and Saratoga Springs combined with their relatively high level of geographic dispersion seemingly to preclude a sharp separation of consumer markets along racial lines. The impression of most of the businesses listed above is that they catered to mixed, if sometimes largely black, clienteles. Certainly, this was true of establishments like Pennington's pharmacy, the Hygeia Spa, Jack's Cabaret, and the Cochrane creamery. However, grooming businesses—hair salons and barbershops—along with lodging houses, served racially distinct client pools.

The scope of these African-American enterprises in Saratoga Springs and especially in Newport does not deny their precariousness as black capitalist ventures. Most of the businesses may be categorized, according to Abram L. Harris's scheme, as amusement and recreational (e.g., Jack's Cabaret), real estate (e.g., Thomas Glover's operation described in chapter 2), retail trade (e.g., the Pennington pharmacy), or personal service (e.g., the Walker taxi business and Mabel McFee's beauty parlor). All such businesses produce rather small volumes of trade. Historically restricted to low-paying jobs, black business hopefuls were unable to accumulate the necessary monies to launch large-scale independent enterprises. Indeed, Benjamin Burton was able to begin his express business only with funds acquired in the California gold rush of 1849. And once established in business, these same entrepreneurs were hampered by their small and/or poor client pool in efforts to expand and even maintain operations. Typically, therefore, real estate holdings have served as the major financial resource of African-American entrepreneurs, but these are often extremely "unliquid" because of their location in black neighborhoods.[56]

Street corner in West Broadway, Newport. (Courtesy of the Newport Historical Society, P1813)

J. T. Allen and Co.'s Touro Dining Room, Newport. (Courtesy of the Newport Historical Society, P1822)

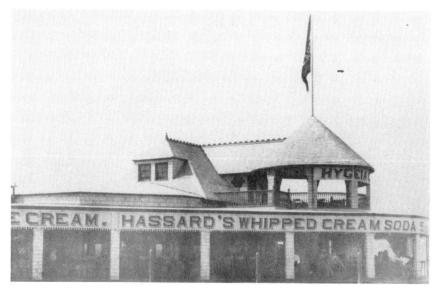

J. T. and D. B. Allen's Hygeia Spa, Easton's Beach, Newport. (Courtesy of the Newport Historical Society)

George Downing and family, Newport. (Courtesy of the Rhode Island Black Heritage Society. All rights reserved.)

James A. Ray, a Newport policeman, with his horse-drawn patrol wagon. (Courtesy of the Newport Historical Society, P288)

Employees of the William A. Jackson Moving Co. deliver an upright piano, Newport. (Courtesy of the Newport Historical Society, P1830)

Rev. Mahlon Van Horne (*left*) in his parlor, Newport. (Courtesy of the Rhode Island Black Heritage Society. All rights reserved.)

A morning workout at the Saratoga Racetrack, Saratoga Springs, 1913. (Courtesy of the George S. Bolster Collection of the Historical Society of Saratoga Springs)

Jockey George Smoot on Chuckle, c. 1923, at Saratoga Springs. (Courtesy of the Jane Rehl Collection)

An unidentified artist sketches the harbor at Newport while several youngsters look on.

A doorman (to the right of the entrance) awaits customers at Newman's Lake House, Saratoga Springs. (Courtesy of the George S. Bolster Collection of the Historical Society of Saratoga Springs)

Looking west on Congress Street, 1931. (Courtesy of the George S. Bolster Collection of the Historical Society of Saratoga Springs)

A nursemaid in Saratoga Springs watches her charges. (Courtesy of the George S. Bolster Collection of the Historical Society of Saratoga Springs)

The United States Hotel dining room, Saratoga Springs, c. 1890s. (Courtesy of Brookside, Saratoga County History Center)

George Crum in front of his restaurant at the south end of Saratoga Lake, Saratoga Springs, c. 1890. (Courtesy of the George S. Bolster Collection of the Historical Society of Saratoga Springs)

Workers take a break at the J. F. Hasenfuss Café, Congress and Federal Streets, Saratoga Springs, c. 1900. (Courtesy of the George S. Bolster Collection of the Historical Society of Saratoga Springs)

Broadway, opposite the United States Hotel, Saratoga Springs, 1907. (Courtesy of the George S. Bolster Collection of the Historical Society of Saratoga Springs)

R. G. Dun and Co. ledgers confirm the economic marginality of the African-American businesses in the two resorts—at least in the eyes of that firm's evaluators. In August 1870, "celebrated colored caterer" George Downing received the following rating: "very slow pay, in very poor credit and should be trusted with extreme caution." Still in business six years later, Downing was deemed a "very poor" credit risk in Newport despite his real estate holdings on Bellevue Avenue—the major tourist thoroughfare—which were valued at $8,000–10,000. Steward George Rice briefly attempted an unspecified business—perhaps a restaurant or catering outfit—some time after 1871, but failed in this by August 1874, only to return to the steamboats. Similarly, Charles Fayerweather suffered a business failure in 1886. And it was only the financial backing of John L. Perry, owner of the United States Hotel, that enabled Thomas Pennington to open his pharmacy. After nine years, however, he was reported in "close quarters" and no longer considered a good credit risk. Fourteen months later, his business failed.[57]

Ed Pilkington related a small personal example of how black and white workers holding identical jobs might perform different tasks—yet another index of the period's racialized labor market. He told how he was given more menial assignments than his white friend, Carl Baldwin, with whom he shared the job of table boy: "I had to mop up the floors. . . . I don't remember Carl mopping up."[58]

Black female wage earners especially reflected the new racialization of work as gender discrimination generally combined with race to keep their work profile particularly depressed. Female workers labored almost exclusively in the areas of unskilled and domestic/personal service, very much in keeping with national and northern trends, where "black women's work . . . was synonymous with domestic service."[59] Between 1870 and 1925 in Saratoga Springs, the figures for African-American women wage earners in these areas were between 90.4 and 95.4 percent; for Newport, figures for the years 1870 to 1910 regarding black female workers fell between 83.9 and 93.6 percent. The majority of these workers in the towns was compressed into two job slots: laundresses/washerwomen and domestic servants. A conservative estimate of 660 of 1,298 (51 percent) of the total female workers in Newport throughout the period and 472 of a total of 758 female workers in Saratoga Springs (62 percent) fell into these categories (see tables 8 and 9).

Surviving, Preserving, and Advocating

Given the circle of discrimination that black wage earners faced in Newport and Saratoga Springs, one may well wonder how black workers managed to connect at all, let alone successfully, to the occupational structure in the two towns. Yet in repeated demonstrations of human resilience, African Americans throughout the period found ways to avoid certain kinds of service work that they deemed undesirable, to survive irregular employment, to hold on to key service positions in the two resort towns, and to press for wider employment opportunities in both resorts despite the strictures they encountered from hostile external forces.

First, the absence of black workers from Newport's great mansions may have partially reflected black decision-making. The hardships of live-in domestic service and the kind of work offered by Cliff Walk employers have already been noted. Given this fact and the emerging tradition of day service among African-American domestic workers, it is entirely reasonable to suppose that Afro-Newporters may have spurned wage-earning opportunities in the homes of the seaport's wealthy white residents.[60]

Second, those African Americans who desired a permanent home in Newport and Saratoga Springs found ways to navigate the uncertainties of a seasonal income. Saratoga Springs differed from Newport in that the African-American wage-earning population in the spa was much more dependent on seasonal summer employment, and this in turn made off-season survival a harder issue for them. To be sure, in both resorts, employment opportunities dropped considerably in the winter. Lyle Matthews recalled that "the winter months were kind of skimpy" in Newport, and Ed Pilkington labeled Saratoga Springs a "tough town" during the off-season. But year-round Afro-Saratogian wage earners were pressed more severely to devise special income-stretching strategies than their Newport counterparts.[61]

Reliance on summer savings, winter credit, and/or seasonally rotating jobs helped African Americans with permanent residences in the resorts survive through the cold-weather months. This was especially true in Saratoga Springs. Tips and income from renting rooms to tourists and seasonal workers contributed to savings. Saratogian Robert Sims recalled: "You could make enough during the season to fairly well carry you for the three winter months." Annie Massey, whose husband worked as a spa waiter, further explained: "Regardless of what money he made, it was how [we] handled it.

Now his check he got from the waiting, they'd give it to him. I'd say, 'Just listen! Just give me them tips!'" And she put them aside for lean times. During the 1920s, housing rentals increased about 100 percent during the summer season in Saratoga Springs. Ernie Jackson recalled: "A lot of people had rooming houses . . . for the people that came up for the season. . . . They would make . . . money by selling drinks and food, and renting rooms. Because they could rent, say, ten rooms and [only] have one bathroom at that time." As one Saratogian explained it to a visitor: "We get ours in August!"[62]

A number of black Saratogians concurred that creditors conventionally permitted winter bills to accumulate until they could be paid the following summer. Some deemed this a kind practice. Edna Bailey Miller recalled almost wistfully that "people helped people. . . . If my mother's house got cold . . . because she didn't have money for [fuel], but would have it soon, she could call someone in charge and he'd tell the . . . men, 'Mrs. Bailey doesn't have any heat and she's having a terrible time! . . . You go over and give her some. . . . I don't care if [she] doesn't have the money now. Do it!'" Others viewed this practice more critically. Ed Pilkington observed: "Many of the people would get behind. . . . And here's what.—They could go to the grocery store and tab. The owner would put it on the bill. The people weren't paying anything, see, because the storekeeper knew that when the money started coming in, they would pay. . . . The people would make their money in the summer months. . . . Then they'd have to pay back the stores. There would be the tab on coal and fuel (they sold pinewood for the coal stoves), groceries, and clothing for the kids. . . . Then they're broke again."[63]

When linked with the absence of a consistent cash flow, the reliance on credit from whites among Afro-Saratogians is reminiscent of black family budgetary practices of the preindustrial and agricultural economies of the nineteenth-century South. As sharecroppers, many postbellum southern blacks were gravely enmeshed in such dependencies between 1870 and the start of the Great Migration. In this comparison, black Saratogian workers differed from southern, rural African Americans only in two respects. The former did not work the land; and, of critical importance, they enjoyed a greater degree of social and personal freedom than was possible in the Jim Crow South. Seen in this light, resort towns like Saratoga Springs offered familiar and new life choices to black peasants at the turn of the century.

Contrasting with the picture of black Saratoga, almost no evidence points to as deep a dependence on winter credit by Afro-Newporters. In fact, this research uncovered only one reference to the practice. In a poem lauding early twentieth-century black businesses in Newport, Mora E. Hammonds refers to the Addisons' corner grocery store, where "they'd give you credit willingly when there was lack of pay."[64] Significant here is not only the solitary nature of this example but also the fact that the creditors were African American.

No doubt, blacks in Newport relied on credit when unemployed or otherwise hard-pressed financially, but the presence of a larger number of year-round job options ensured a greater likelihood of a steady income flow— from black and white sources—than was true in the spa. In Saratoga Springs, African-American workers anxious for off-season employment sometimes advertised their need; these included the "colored man and wife"—he, a hostler; she, a cook—who sought a "permanent situation" in 1879. On the other hand, laborers and service workers in Newport more regularly found work at a variety of private enterprises—butcher shops, dry-goods stores, ice companies, lumberyards, ironworks, commercial laundries, department stores, coal yards, shipyards, liveries—and even churches. In these various places of business, they worked as errand runners, janitors, porters, drivers, teamsters, riggers, ironers, watchmen, stevedores, hostlers, and sextons. No similar picture emerges for Saratoga Springs, where it appears that the city sidewalks were rolled in on Labor Day, leaving jobs for mainly those scarce self-employed blacks or for the few African-American servants in year-round, white households; the latter included James Jackson, who worked as a butler in one such home in the early twentieth century.[65]

Another option for surviving the winter was illustrated by Emma Waite, who left Saratoga Springs in the fall of 1870, after finishing seasonal hotel work at the Continental Hotel there, to begin a job as day cook at the Apollo Hall in New York City. As in her example, one might shift residences to find employment outside of Saratoga during the winter and return to work in the town the following season. This was the course selected even by permanent residents. Joe Jackson, for instance, became a bellman in nearby Schenectady's Van Curler Hotel every September 15 after his summer stint as steward of the Help's Dining Room at the Grand Union Hotel ended with the hotel's seasonal closing. Similarly, Joseph Smith sometimes worked as the superintendent at the Kenmore Hotel in nearby Albany after the racing season had ended. And Robert Jackson ran a catering establishment in New

York City during the winter months.[66] In contrast to this pattern, a picture
of a winter job vacuum in Newport does not materialize in as drastic detail.

The black community of wage earners in the resort towns did more to
control their economic lives than reject unappealing jobs and survive the lean
winters. In both towns, but in Newport especially, they responded to racial
barriers to moneymaking options by turning inward for alternative financial
schemes. The historical period studied here coincides with the "Age of Washington," a time in African-American history when the teachings of Booker T.
Washington spurred black wage earners to look within the black community
itself as a source of income. Elsewhere in antebellum America, efforts to advance black enterprise and black capitalization through self-help had led to
the formation of separate black mutual aid associations, fraternal societies,
banks, and lending sources. These endeavors continued particularly between
1880 and 1915, and black Newport was included in this project. In fact,
African-American fraternal societies capable of providing insurance and capital to members—and thereby stimulating small black-owned businesses—
proliferated in the seaport. The first Masonic order, Boyer Lodge Number 8,
was chartered in 1873. By 1885, the Odd Fellows group was formed, and
Canonchet Lodge Number 2439 was functioning as well. Five years later, two
of these organizations had acquired women's auxiliaries—the Heroines of Jericho Number 3 (Masonic) and the Household of Ruth 501 (Odd Fellows). By
1895, three additional chapters had been formed—Stone Mill Lodge, Salem
Royal Arch Chapter Number 6, and B. F. Gardner Commandery Number 6.[67]

These lodges and their sister auxiliaries prospered in Newport during the
first three decades of the twentieth century. By 1900, yet another Masonic
lodge, Mt. Calvary Commandery, existed. (It would disappear by 1905.) In
1910, the Heroines of Jericho no longer existed; but by 1920, the Masons had
gained two new black women's auxiliaries—Sheba Court Number 3 and
Esther Lodge Number 11—and three additional men's affiliates—Mt. Olivet
Consistory Number 39, Aleppo Temple of the Mystic Shrine, and Watson's
Masonic Beneficial Association. In 1930, ten black Masonic chapters functioned in the seaport—six for men and four for women. Other non-Masonic
orders existed as well. By 1900, the Knights of Pythias had been represented
in the city for eight years by Hope Lodge Number 3. By 1920, black fraternal
life in Newport also included one lodge of Good Samaritans, a women's Elks
lodge, and a men's Elks chapter.[68]

In addition to the fraternal orders, another source of black capital existed in Newport. Some time in the first decade of the twentieth century, the Rhode Island Loan and Investment Company was organized. This outfit loaned money "on real and personal property, notes and bonds" and also bought and sold real estate on commission. The local black businessmen involved as officers and/or directors for the company in 1911 included Armstead Hurley; Thomas Glover; David Allan; Lindsay Walker, a gardener mentioned in the previous chapter; Louis Andrews's father, Marcus C. Andrews, a laborer for the New England Navigating Corporation in 1910; James H. Downes, an independent cab owner and driver in 1910; James W. Johnson, a coachman for a private family in 1910; and George Williams, a watchman for a private family in 1910.[69]

The existence of the Rhode Island Loan and Investment Company and of the several fraternal groups reflected black Newport's engagement in an entrepreneurial spirit advanced by national African-American leaders during the period. Atlanta University's John Hope and, most notably, Tuskegee Institute's Booker T. Washington were among those who encouraged the development of a class of African-American capitalist-employers that would provide jobs for the black masses. The Hurley enterprise was exemplary in this regard. It employed other African Americans related and unrelated to the Hurley family. In 1910, two of Hurley's sons were painters, and his daughter worked as a bookkeeper for the business. But Lyle Matthews recalled that his father, William—not a Hurley relation—and cousin, Carl Butler, also worked for a time with this outfit as farmhouse painters until the two formed their own painting partnership.[70]

Differing noticeably from Newport, Saratoga Springs claimed far fewer black fraternal orders that could offer financial assistance to local, aspiring entrepreneurs. The first black fraternal association in Saratoga Springs was Mt. Lebanon Lodge, a Masonic society organized in the 1870s. For many years, Mt. Lebanon Lodge Number 33 was the sole black Masonic chapter, although there were exceptions. In 1905, for instance, three separate black Masonic lodges—Mt. Lebanon Lodge, King Solomon's Commandery, and Saratoga Chapter Number 14—existed in the town. A black Odd Fellows group, organized in 1888, also functioned throughout the period. Not until 1934 did a branch of the Elks appear in black Saratoga; but, as early as the 1920s, some black Saratogians like Joseph Jackson joined affiliates in nearby Albany and Schenectady.[71] The relative dearth of black businesses in Saratoga Springs may be partially attributed to this small supply of indigenous lending sources of would-be proprietors.

Meanwhile, among Afro-Newporters, yet another sign of their receptivity to the philosophy of black self-help through entrepreneurship was their participation in the National Negro Business League, an organization founded by Booker T. Washington in 1900 to support the cause of black businesses. In August 1908, Charles Fayerweather attended the league's Baltimore convention as a delegate from the organization's Newport chapter. Fayerweather in fact delivered the opening address for the meeting; his talk was entitled "One Hundred Years of Blacksmithing."[72]

The perennial use of blacks as waiters in the resorts' hotels suggests the existence of strong job information and recruitment networks within the African-American communities of the two towns—yet another money-making possibility devised by local blacks. These networks were especially attractive to African-American students and teachers, for whom resort work offered financial opportunities during an otherwise lean time. An African-American bellman wrote the *Saratoga Journal* in 1882, noting that "many of the waiters and bellmen are teachers and students, and they are now utilizing their vacation by working here. Their object is to prepare for usefulness in life."[73] Into the twentieth century, black students throughout the nation continued to take advantage of the special summer job opportunities extended to them in the nation's resorts, particularly in Saratoga Springs. "Every servant comes to a resort to make a good season," explained an African-American student of Fisk University in 1904. He had spent the previous summer as a waiter at a New Jersey summer resort hotel; "making a good season" meant earning as much money as possible during the fleeting vacation period. The student further explained the special importance of hotel waitering for black students: "Every summer vacation I employ my time in waiting on table to earn means to pursue my education. In fact, almost all the colored young men who are thrown largely upon their own resources, either wait on tables or work for the Pullman Company for means to pay for their education. There is no remunerative work open to us in the South; and in the North we can hardly find anything to do except as waiters or railroad men. After the schools close all the young men who can secure transportation, go North to find employment in some of the numerous resorts, or on the railroads."[74] Edna Miller remembered that hotels "brought help from all of the black [colleges], like Wilberforce and Virginia State." Ed

Pilkington concurred: "The waiters would be going to the black colleges—Lincoln or Howard—and they'd come up here for the summer and make their money."[75]

In the spirit of entrepreneurial self-help, black networks in the form of intelligence offices or employment agencies, catering especially to southern migrants and/or summer workers, facilitated the placement of blacks in seasonal jobs in both resorts. Often natives of the South, many of the operators utilized personal networks to link wage earners with jobs. Usually, the intelligence office was a one-person operation, with profit deriving from the registration fee required of all job seekers and the service fee paid by employers. It has already been noted that Newport's Lindsay Walker assisted black migrants from his native Virginia in their northward trek, connecting them with the Middletown farms. In 1900, both of Newport's black residential clusters—West Broadway and the areas off Bellevue Avenue—contained intelligence offices. Mildred Winston, originally a Virginian, ran an intelligence operation from her home on Spruce Street; and Pennsylvania-born Susan Cradle operated another in her Spring Street residence. Ten years later, Mary Williams, a South Carolina native, supplied African Americans in West Broadway with employment services, while Georgia-born Sara Ellen Owens and Virginian Jonas Elias provided similar services on William Street and Levin Street, respectively.[76]

The job networking operation run by Edna Bailey Miller's mother, Edna Bailey, was typical of many such services connecting African-American women with domestic jobs during the early twentieth century in that it was accompanied by a lodging house service as well. In the late 1920s and beyond, Edna Bailey ran an employment office during the summer months in Saratoga Springs, mainly for black female wage earners. Edna Bailey Miller explained: "In the summertime, my mother had an employment agency. The [black] schools would write her and then some of our friends would write her and say, 'Edna, you want to bring some girls up [from the South]?' They would always stay at our house. We had a ball! It was like a dormitory. It was just a house, but they all came. Their mothers would say, 'If you're going to stay at Mrs. Bailey's, you can go,' and so they would come. We had a little garage that my brother and some boys built in the back [of the house]. The boys stayed there in the back and the girls stayed in the house. My mother was old-fashioned, you know. No boys and girls stayed together in those days!"[77] Clearly, the Bailey enterprise doubled as a boardinghouse as well.

The existence of these intelligence bureaus, with many exploiting specific regional bases, underscores the highly personalized manner in which most African Americans obtained wage-earning positions in the resort towns. Whether black or white, the links in the job-getting network generally involved direct ties to influential individuals. Edna Bailey, for instance, as the wife of an A.M.E. Zion minister, had church connections throughout the Northeast and South, since the denomination regularly turned over pastors every three years. Indeed, the Reverend Bailey had pastored in Buffalo, New York, and New Haven, Connecticut, before coming to Saratoga Springs, and he left his family in the spa to accept a post in Kentucky. Certainly, mothers of good A.M.E. Zion college women and men who had met Mrs. Bailey at church convocations might easily exploit the friendship to advance their children's careers.

In the absence of intelligence officers, workers in the two resort towns obtained positions through other black contacts. In June 1871, for example, William Henry Rogers wrote to Dolly Smith, a black servant in a prominent white Saratogian household, requesting her intervention on his behalf regarding summer employment as a house servant. He wrote:

> i have been in employment ever since i came from Saratoga with the exception of six weeks and was very sick and the family i was living with shut up their house in summer and so leaves me without any situation for awhile and i thought i would take the liberty of asking you if you would not ask madam to employ me this summer. Although i did not act so very nice when i was hear of corse i am more experienced and much older now and it would not be expected that i should act so[.] i have made an engagement to go and work in [the] Congress [Hotel] and my brother too so he has changed his mind and i am most afraid to go their alone[.] i much more prefer working in a boarding house or private family[.] try and see [if] you can arrange it and give me an ancer . . . for i am anxious to know and beside i have partely made an ingagement to go to Newport, but their is no place i want to go but to Saratoga.[78]

Often, ministers served as points of contact between workers and employers. In 1873, for example, potential employers in Saratoga Springs were notified that they might obtain "two first class cooks and laundresses" by contacting the pastor of the Zion Church. Similarly, Robert Sims landed his first position as a dishwasher at the Grand Union Hotel through his pastor, the Reverend Gibson of the black Mt. Olivet Baptist Church, who also worked at the hotel in the glass and crystal department.[79]

The black headwaiters and stewards, however, were the gatekeepers to the prize seasonal jobs. The Fisk University student who labored at a New Jersey resort explained that a newcomer secured a summer position only after a face-to-face interview with a headwaiter. For East Coast resorts, these occurred in May in New York City, "the rendezvous for head waiters of some of the leading hotels in that section of the country," where "waiters from all parts of the country . . . congregate . . . that they may book with these head waiters."[80]

Once hired, first-timers needed only to prove themselves capable and eager at their assigned tasks in order to be rehired the following season and begin the ascent to the coveted positions of side waiter (serving special side orders), second waiter (just under the headwaiter), and, ultimately, headwaiter. The majority of the staff of waiters and bellmen under J. R. Bishop of the United States Hotel in 1924, for example, was composed of men he had worked with for the previous twenty years and of whom he felt "justly proud." Often, like Congress Hall headwaiter George Curry, they began their careers as low-level hall men, porters, bellhops, hat checkers, ushers, or dish carriers; or, like Grand Union Hotel headwaiter Joseph Thornton Lee, they started at lesser hotels where waiting was broadly understood to include such menial tasks as cleaning boots and horse currying.[81]

Recognizing the important role of black headwaiters and stewards in preserving the black male stronghold in this type of service work, black workers organized to ensure a secure future for themselves in this area of employment. In a key defensive move with positive ramifications for Saratoga Springs and Newport male wage earners, they formed the Head and Second Waiters' National Benefit Association on September 20, 1899, in Chicago. Guild-like, the organization's purpose was "to train and educate the negro waiters up to the highest standard of efficiency" in view of "changes often made by some of the leading hotels from colored waiters (their old standby) to white." If the continued use of black headwaiters especially could be assured, it was reasoned, the African-American monopoly on dining-room and other service positions could be maintained, since headwaiters hired their own supporting staff. In this line of thinking, black service laborers demonstrated their participation in an emerging national work culture of professionalism—one in which successful wage earners evinced mastery of a "body of systematic knowledge, . . . competence, superior skill, and a high quality of performance." But unlike most white workers—for whom the determination to adopt new professional standards increased the likelihood of substantial rewards in the form of upward mobility within mainstream society—for blacks, such a decision was an attempt to hold ground.[82]

This strategy worked. National and local observers regularly noted the presence of black headwaiters in Saratoga Springs and Newport and stewards—in this case, dining-room superintendents—in Newport. Throughout the period, in fact, all the headwaiters at Saratoga's Grand Union, United States Hotel, and Congress Hall were African American. In 1870, Robert P. Jackson served as headwaiter at the Grand Union Hotel. In 1871, he made a lateral career move to Congress Hall, where he remained through 1890 at least. Also in 1870, George A. Rice worked as a steamboat steward and continued in that post in 1880. Sometime after the launching of the *Puritan* in 1889, he became its steward and remained in that capacity at least through 1892. In 1887, Joseph T. Lee became headwaiter at the Grand Union Hotel and occupied that position at least through 1904, displaying "an individuality" that made him "the ideal superintendent of the dining room." In 1887, John Stannard filled the headwaiter's position at Congress Hall. He was described as "an excellent manager of the 150 active waiters under his direction" and remained in this post for a minimum of three years. George Curry became headwaiter of Congress Hall in 1892, a job he occupied at least through 1904. Praised as the "leading head waiter in . . . [his] company's employ" in 1904, Marion M. Martin worked as dining-room superintendent for the *Pilgrim* on the Fall River Line. In the same year, Robert James Patterson worked as headwaiter on the *Priscilla*, while Edward Wilson Diggs labored as headwaiter for the *Plymouth*. And in 1910, George W. Griffith and Charles Ramsey, both living in Newport, were steamboat stewards.[83]

Organization also helped African Americans retain jobs in yet another instance. Black barbers in Newport avoided the occupational slide their counterparts in Saratoga Springs and other cities experienced, probably by participating in a citywide barbers' union with a racially integrated membership. In 1925, in fact, the president of the union was a black man, William H. Hilton, listed in the census as a barber since 1900. Union activism even preserved a white clientele for some of these barbers. Anthony Peer is illustrative. This Pennsylvania native first appeared on the existing federal census schedules for Newport in 1900, when he was thirty years old. Perhaps he had come to the city on the advice of a possible relation, Pusey Peer, also a barber and native of Pennsylvania who had first appeared on the census rolls for the seaport in 1880. In 1900, Anthony Peer lived on Spruce Street with his wife and two children. Through 1925 at least, he continued to shave, cut, and style hair. In the 1920s, he operated his own shop, which catered to whites only.[84] George Turville recollected: "No Newport Blacks frequented his shop because Mr. Peer was one of those skilled Blacks who had always applied his talents for the benefit of whites only, which we know had often been practiced in the south. I remember going by Mr. Peer's shop often and would always watch with awe as completing a customer's hair, Mr. Peer would ignite a rolled up piece of newspaper and conduct it slowly about his customer's head singeing the edges of the hair yet igniting not a single strand of hair. What skill it required! For the uninformed, it was thought to be good practice to singe all hair strand edges to hold in the scalp oil thus preventing encroachment of baldness and bleeding of hair roots as believed by men of that day and time."[85]

The number of African-American barbers in Newport actually increased from four in 1870 to twelve in 1910, probably as a result of their involvement in the union. This strong showing is remarkable given the more pervasive national pattern among black barbers of job loss to immigrant competition during these years. On the other hand, Saratoga Springs, with no barber's union, followed the national pattern by experiencing a decline in black barbers from ten in 1870 to three in 1925.[86]

Why did African-American women wage earners in the resorts not organize as did black male headwaiters and barbers? They certainly had grievances: low pay, backbreaking duties, arbitrarily shifting assignments. For one thing, the physical isolation of domestic workers from each other inhibited collective protest. Also, the high level of turnover among domestic laborers— as women left in search of better conditions and opportunities outside the field or moved laterally within the field to new households—was heightened by regular infusions of southern migrants. The inconstancy of a constituent base, then, blunted the formation of a steady worker consciousness, even in such work venues as hotel and commercial laundries, where women worked in groups. Most likely, following the national pattern, African-American domestics trusted in an ethic of individualism and personal resourcefulness as their best strategy.[87]

Afro-Newporters and African-American women, however, achieved a

major breakthrough—quite out of step with the racialized, segregated employment trends of the time—when Louisa Van Horne acquired a position
as a public-school teacher in 1902. Again, this victory was won through community action. In 1901, 162 petitioners argued: "We have been made to feel
that her application has been ignored on account of conditions over which
she has no control [her race], and perhaps too because of a lack of information on the part of the school board as to the extent of employment of colored teachers in the mixed schools of the northern part of our country, especially in some of New England, New York, Illinois, and other states, for since
her application was filed with [the] superintendent an appointment has been
made of a [white] teacher not a resident of Newport, thereby showing a va-
cancy, a scarcity of teachers and the intention to ignore Miss Van Horne."[88]
Since teaching by 1900 had become a female-dominated profession, one
might be tempted to interpret Van Horne's admission to the Rhode Island
schools as a gender gain. And, in fact, it was. However, in terms of historically
subjective reality, it is significant that she allied herself with the black community on the basis of shared racial discrimination. To local whites, local blacks,
and herself, Louisa Van Horne was an African-American job seeker, not a
female prospective employee. While it is true that the establishment of
national professional societies commenced among black females after 1870,
during the next sixty years, these organizations established new work standards with the goal of eliminating segregationist, *racial* disparities in job
access, assignments, pay, promotion, and the like. In other words, the persistence of racial discrimination primarily linked black female professionals
to—and caused them to identify with—the African-American community
rather than the circle of oppressed wage-earning women trapped in femi-
nized careers, especially since that circle was also racialized.[89]

Black networks, black organization, and black agitation were not the sole
job-getting avenues used by African-American wage earners in Newport and
Saratoga Springs. Blacks also used white benefactors to their advantage.
White patrons were especially useful in enhancing career paths and/or
opening and keeping open occupational doors, many of them closed or
closing to African Americans in the late nineteenth century. Headwaiter
Robert P. Jackson obtained his first position in Saratoga Springs's Grand
Union Hotel during the antebellum period through a white benefactor, Mrs.
Joseph C. Luther, who arranged the deal. Andrew Tabb, born the son of
Virginia slaves, came to Newport in 1881 from Baltimore as part of the staff

of a Madame C. O'Donnell. Tabb worked as a coachman for the wealthy white widow, who had obtained a summer residence in the seaport. On one of his summer visits to Newport, Tabb met and fell in love with Alice Smith, a local widow he married in 1886. With Newport now as Tabb's home, he opened a livery stable and express business on Edgar Court that benefited directly from the acquaintances and contacts its owner had made through O'Donnell.[90]

Recognition of the benefits of white patronage and assistance persisted into the twentieth century. Lacking both the capital and technical skills, monopolized by whites, to move into primary employment and the wealth-making sectors of their local economies, African Americans were quick to advantage themselves when given the opportunity in the two resort towns. Before he entered college in the early twentieth century, Saratogian Warren Cochrane worked summers for a Mrs. Moriarta, a white boardinghouse proprietor, who "took [him] under her wing and taught him how to handle the books" and generally gave him "a good exposure." Ed Pilkington was also aided by the mother of his white friend and co-worker Carl Baldwin. Through the efforts of Mrs. Baldwin, Pilkington acquired his job as a table clearer. He recalled the day he went to Carl's house to learn that his friend had gotten a summer job at the drink hall: "I said, 'Mrs. Baldwin, where's Carl?' She said, 'Pink, Carl's got a job. . . . [It's] about time you started thinking of getting a job. . . . You're getting too old to be selling papers. . . . some day, . . . you'll want a reference from a job. . . . That newspaper hustling . . . [will be] no good to you. . . . You go right over [to the drink hall] and tell them you want a job!' "[91] Fearing rejection on the basis of race, Pilkington reluctantly complied, only to have his worst fears realized. He continued: "As slow as I was in going over there, I was like a rocket getting back to [the Baldwin] house, bounding up those stairs and telling her, 'Mrs. Baldwin, they don't want to hire anybody. They're not hiring any more.' . . . I will never forget that little straw hat [Mrs. Baldwin] wore. She had mixed gray hair with a bun in the back and she grabbed that straw hat, slapped it on her head, grabbed me by the hand, and dragged me over [to the drink hall]. She said, 'You give this boy a job!' "[92] And Ed Pilkington got the job.

Newspaper advertisements provided alternative avenues to employment for African Americans. In Saratoga Springs, although racial qualifications often appeared in job descriptions so that advertisements appeared for "two colored chefs" or "two white waitresses," a curious racial ambivalence may be detected in other notices for "a colored girl or middle-aged white woman" or "chambermaids, laundresses, waitresses, and girls for general housework—white or colored." These publications bespeak both the generally heightened race consciousness of the era and race neutrality with regard to uncoveted types of service work. Noticeably, however, the major hotels did not regularly advertise for help. Apparently, then, only a minuscule proportion of African-American wage earners in the spa secured jobs through newspaper notices.[93] This fact again underscores the importance of personal and individual liaisons in the job-getting process.

Despite the fact that revisionist historians have reconfigured considerably the image of the self-made American to show instead the pervasive importance of personal connections and patronage in career advancement, the use of such ties by ambitious, job-seeking black wage earners in Saratoga Springs and Newport is noteworthy nonetheless for two reasons. First, the dependence on personal sponsorship required to obtain and advance in many of the jobs described above was particularly endemic to service work itself. Above all else, the successful servant must know how to please a guest, a customer, or an employer. Financial reward—whether in the form of tips, promotion, or continued employment—resulted from this precise attention to the needs of employers and potential benefactors. Mindful of this fact, Newport steward George Rice was careful to place a special market order for the First Lady, Mrs. Benjamin Harrison, when she traveled on his steamer. And Joseph Smith, after working for a decade as servant and butler in a couple of Hudson Valley, New York, households, decided to advance his career by traveling in Europe for a couple of years to equip himself with "general information to parties of Americans going to the Continent." In so doing, he followed the advice rendered to him by his father: "Make a confidante and friend of your employer. Consult him in your affairs; above all, I beseech you, do nothing to forfeit the confidence he has in you. Study his interests constantly." Clearly, Smith planned and prepared himself for employers wealthy and leisured enough to afford transatlantic vacations. His expectations were realized in his ascent to the position of head hallman at the spa's United States Hotel. Once in this position, Smith continued to approach his service to guests in a very personal way. During the 1889 stay of the Jay Gould family at the hotel, for instance, he decided to carry a revolver to safeguard these prominent visitors, explaining: "I meant to use every effective measure for the protection of the Gould party, if necessary, and I do not think that I was mistaken when I guarded against the sudden assaults of cranks on the lives of our wealthy citizens who were guests at our hostelry."[94]

Successful servants—especially waiters, who depended heavily on tips—entirely understood the necessity of deference to the whims and idiosyncrasies of patrons. They recognized the importance of familiarizing themselves with the personalities and biographies of the individuals they attended. Smith provided a glimpse into their thinking:

> The picture of a well-ordered dining room before the hungry boarders make an attack upon it is really impressive. The light is toned into a fashionable gloom, the tables are carefully furnished, and behind the row of napkins, arranged in war-like array in the goblets, and the tall celery glasses, stand the black-coated sentinels. Their faces are as destitute of expression as a store-box. That is not, however, because they do not think, but because they have the enviable faculty of simply appearing not to think. They can discharge every vestige of expression from their faces in a second's time. . . . Does the waiter think? Engage him in conversation on some subject near his heart, and you shall see. He knows everybody in the dining room. He is the best-posted man on personalities in any profession. He could tell highly interesting tales of the silent and awfully respectable looking man over there, if he would. He knows more about the woman with the resplendent diamonds and the captivating smile, than any two other individuals could ever dream of.[95]

These waiters clearly understood the commercial value of their knowledge. It was not to be used in idle gossip for, as Smith continued, these African-American waiters had "learned a lesson that would be very valuable to white employees—namely that a garrulous servant never keeps a situation." Rather, the waiters used their information to better serve, all the while looking to the pecuniary advantages that followed.

Secondly, the patron-client relationship that existed between black service workers and resort-town tourists harked back to paternalistic, preindustrial, antebellum relationships between workers and employers and between slaves and masters. While skill and competence quite naturally were valued under this system, the behavioral components of worker performance—deferential deportment, loyalty, amiability, and recognition of the superior status of one's employers—assumed perhaps an even greater importance. In contrast, the industrialized work relations that superseded the earlier system in the late nineteenth century and into the early twentieth century placed more emphasis on such rational, impersonal measures of employee suitability as technical expertise, scientific knowledge, training, and educational attainment. Realizing the strength of this shift at its 1901 convention, the Head, Second and Side Waiters' National Benefit Association even considered establishing a civil service examination to admit waiters to the vocation. Significantly, this measure was never adopted. Instead, many African-American waiters and wage earners laboring in positions tied to contact with tourists found themselves entrenched in a highly subjective, somewhat premodern order of employee-employer relations.[96]

Between 1870 and 1930, industrialization and urbanization contributed to an expanding upper middle class that looked nostalgically back—or, in the case of Newport, directly across the Atlantic—to fading European models of aristocracy. The growing middle class, in turn, mimicked the indigenous American nobility. Servants, ubiquitous in resorts, were critical in the process of affirming the ascent of this new monied element in the national social hierarchy. They provided social aspirants with public relief from menial and manual tasks and so helped define in a conspicuous manner their employers' exalted social rank. Servants, in other words, helped "en-leisure" that class of people gifted with the wealth and time to take vacations.[97] Ironically, resorts—as unique urban places that were themselves outgrowths of industrial *progress*—also stood as arenas for the display of an older, even ancient, order of social relations.

Class within Caste

Racial discrimination resulted in a racially contoured history for African-American wage earners in Newport and Saratoga Springs. The employment niches that blacks occupied and the ways in which they fought for position in the occupational hierarchy were largely dictated by societal racial codes. Yet within this experience of caste, hierarchies developed between elites and the rank-and-file workers. In other words, despite the fact that they formed and understood themselves to be a discernible caste as wage earners, African Americans in Newport and Saratoga Springs made distinctions among their gainfully employed. Racial codes reflecting a monolithic and debased view of black workers originated *outside* their community. In the eyes of Afro-Newport and Afro-Saratoga Springs, a stratified reality also existed for black wage earners. Internal class dynamics, assigning some workers exalted status, operated alongside the group dynamics described above.

The distinction between the elite and rank-and-file workers was determined by how close individual wage earners were in their jobs to the "average" or "normal" black work experience of low-paying, irregular, segregated, menial, and unskilled labor. Educational level was another important determinant of worker status in the black community. Also, for business owners, the racial distribution of one's customers could be an important factor dictating social standing. Elites, therefore, were relatively well-paid professionals, proprietors, or supervisors with an interracial clientele but, above all, relatively well-paid workers with permanent, year-round work. In fact, the regularity of work of any type—that is, a steady income—figured far more heavily in the elite-making equation within the black community than did job type.[98] Thus, headwaiters and stewards ranked high among the esteemed members of the black communities of Newport and Saratoga Springs.

Partially owing to the presence of college-educated individuals among the ranks of dining-room and kitchen superintendents, the black community—and often the white community—bestowed great esteem on hotel and steamboat workers in these supervisory roles. A nineteenth-century black contemporary commented that "while in years past the service was mostly filled by men untrained in intellect, but of great natural ability, it is, however, acquiring now a considerable addition of young men whose minds have been trained." He explained how racial discrimination accounted for the numbers of college-educated blacks among headwaiters and stewards: "This element is increasing more and more every year, for as the schools and colleges send forth their graduates in greater numbers every succeeding year, these graduates, finding the avenue of other industries congested to them, are turning their attention, to a great extent, to that calling which offers them the least resistance, and which years ago had been assigned by common consent to their forefathers." He continued, "it is also being recognized . . . that in the Republic of labor, honest toil for one's daily bread in any vocation, is honorable; and that no matter what the occupation may be, the calling is dignified, proportionately to the amount of intelligence required for the execution."[99]

The relatively good pay, especially, combined with the heavy responsibility and the obvious authority typifying these particular service jobs to add high status to headwaiters, stewards, and their families. George Bolster, a white clerk at Saratoga Springs's Worden Hotel during Prohibition, remembered that "the prestige for bell captains and head waiters was remarkable."[100] One nineteenth-century white visitor to Saratoga Springs admiringly observed that headwaiter Robert Jackson, his wife Jane, and son Winfield resided in the spa in a "beautiful, vine-clad cottage" and that Mrs. Jackson was "one of the [town's] neatest housekeepers"; he added that, having met "old Presidents, . . . scions of royalty, . . . and distinguished servants, poets, and historians," Robert Jackson had attained "perhaps one of the largest acquaintances of any one of Saratoga." Head usher Joseph Smith was not college trained. However, a practical education attained through extensive overseas travel and diverse life experiences earned him the respect of locals, who invited him during the summer of 1888 to lecture at Saratoga Springs's Grand Army Hall to a mostly white audience on the topic of "the genius and heroism of famous women."[101] Similarly, Newport steamboat steward George Rice was held in high esteem for the expertise with which he performed his extensive culinary duties. An entry in the *Fall River Line Journal* detailed his job: "The steward and chef of the hotel afloat [deal] with problems that do not confront the steward and chef ashore. On a [Long Island] Sound steamer like the 'Priscilla,' the steward must provide for all possible contingencies. . . . his supply of food must be ample enough for passengers and crew in the event of possible delays in the arrival at port. He must never run short."[102] One of Newport's newspapers reported favorably on Rice's skillful execution of these responsibilities during the summer of 1892: "Last night Mr. George A. Rice of this city resumed his old position as steward of the steamer Puritan of the Fall River line. . . . there is no question but that Mr. Rice had done very much to bring the reputation of the line in a culinary way up to its present high standard, and passengers of all classes unite in praising his uniform attention to every patron, whatever his social position."[103]

Sensitivity to social class—especially based on occupation—within the African-American communities of Newport and Saratoga Springs was reflected in the ranks of the local political leadership. Among the charter members of the National Association for the Advancement of Colored People (NAACP) chapters in both towns, a disproportionate share held relatively

Table 10. Profile of Black Charter Members of the Newport Branch of the NAACP, 1919

Name	Occupation	Name	Occupation
D. B. Allen	Caterer	J. W. Johnson	Sexton
Mrs. D. B. Allen	Not listed	W. J. Lucas (president)	Minister
H. B. Allston	Mechanic	Thomas Matthews	Plasterer
J. O. Banks	Janitor	G. Bradford Miller	Janitor
Charles Battle (secretary)	Mail Carrier	Mrs. Florence Miller	Laundress
William Bradford	Chauffeur	C. E. Miner	Sailor
George Brogden	Public Coachman	H. L. Robertson	Chauffeur
Ernest Burney	Laborer	William Robinson	Watchmaker
James Burney	Steward	T. R. Scott	Not listed
Samuel Burns	Steward	E. E. Stewart	Barber
C. F. Burton	Expressman	James Suggs	Cook
Carl Butler	Painter	Dorsey Suggs	Laborer
Lee Carter	Laborer	W. W. Tolbert	Janitor
Reymond Chase	Laborer	M. A. Van Horne	Dentist
Mrs. Norma Cross	Not listed	W. C. Walters	Laborer
James H. Derrick	Barber	Cromwell P. West	Druggist
Mrs. Alice Dinkins	Not listed	(vice president)	
E. J. Dinkins (treasurer)	Grocer	Theodore D. West	Barber
E. Harris	Not listed	Orville White	Mechanic
Mrs. Catherine Holmes	Not listed	Mrs. Ella Wiggington	Servant for
Armstead Hurley	Painter		private family
Mrs. Florence Jenkins	Not listed	Mrs. Florence Wiggington	Not listed
George Jenkins	Chauffeur	Frank Wiggington	Not listed
T. L. Jenkins	Chauffeur	L. Wiggington	Not listed
John Jennings	Plasterer	Hayward Williams	Not listed
W. S. Jennings	Insurance agent	George E. Williams	Caretaker
Lewis Johnson	Farmer		

Sources: NAACP Branch Files—Newport, R.I., group I, box G-195, Library of Congress, Washington, D.C.; Thirteenth Census of the United States, 1910 (ms.), microfilm reel 1437, National Archives, Washington, D.C.; Rhode Island State Census, 1925 (ms.), Rhode Island State Records Office, Providence; *Triangle* I (Mar. 1920): 1, 17, 20.

prestigious jobs. In 1919, the year the Newport branch was incorporated, when perhaps 20 percent of wage-earning Afro-Newporters were found in professional, proprietary, managerial/clerical, skilled or semi-skilled positions, more than twice that proportion—45 percent—of the founding members held such exceptional posts (see tables 10 and 11). Similarly, in 1921, when the Saratoga Springs branch came into being, when probably only 20 percent of laboring Afro-Saratogians earned incomes as professionals, business owners, supervisors, clerical workers, or skilled and semi-skilled workers, more than double that figure—46 percent—of the NAACP charter members claimed such distinction (see tables 10 and 11). Apparently, not only did the

Table 11. Profile of Black Charter Members of the Saratoga Springs Branch of the NAACP, 1921

Name	Occupation	Name	Occupation
John Branch	Barber	James M. Manigault	Hallman
Mrs. E. U. A. Brooks	Housekeeper	Leslie G. Manigault	Attendant of
Rev. E. U. A. Brooks	Minister		golf links
(treasurer)		Mrs. Leslie G. Manigault	Housekeeper
James Brown	Domestic[a]	Eve T. Marshall	Housekeeper
Mrs. James Brown	Chauffeur[a]	Oceana Marshall (secretary)	Housekeeper
Charles Carrington	Cook	Robert Marshall	Bank messenger
Florella Clayton	Student	Malinda McDonald	Cook
Gladys Clayton	Student	D. E. Nelson	Merchant
Leonard Cochrane	Merchant	Viola Pilkington	Domestic
Edith I. Coleman	Stenographer	D. J. Scott, Jr.	Tailor
Henry Coleman	Headwaiter	James P. Scott	Headwaiter
Mrs. Henry Coleman	Housekeeper	Mrs. James P. Scott	Housekeeper
Carrie Coon	Housekeeper	Perry Sloane	Waiter
Bessie Cousins	Laborer	Mrs. Perry Sloane	Dressmaker
Josephine DeFrest	Domestic	Josephine Spriggs	Cook
Alice Hailstork	Housekeeper	Albert Stewart	Chauffeur
James Hailstork	Waiter	Mary Stewart	Student
Hattie Heath	Housekeeper	Randall Stewart	Laborer
James W. Jackson	Butler	Etta Taylor	Domestic
Mrs. James W. Jackson	Housekeeper	Jack Taylor	Cook
William Jackson	Laborer	William Taylor	Carpenter
William Jones	Laborer	Amelia Walker	Maid
David King	Laborer	Ben Walker	Tailor
Edward Lancko	Laborer	Mrs. Ben Walker	Housekeeper
Carrie Long	Hotel keeper	H. A. Wayland (president)	Headwaiter
Charles Mack	Chef	Charles White	Barber
George Manigault	Newsdealer	James White	Housekeeper

Sources: NAACP Branch Files—Saratoga Springs, N.Y., group 1, box G-136, Library of Congress, Washington, D.C; Thirteenth Census of the United States, 1910 (ms.), microfilm reels 1076, 1077, National Archives, Washington, D.C.; New York State Census, 1925 (ms.), Saratoga County Clerk's Office, Ballston Spa, N.Y.

a. The occupations of Mr. and Mrs. James Brown were probably confused by the person collecting NAACP memberships.

general community, black and white, accord such workers special stature; these workers defined *themselves* as a high-ranking political vanguard and assumed the responsibilities for race advocacy that they associated with their class. By spearheading local civil-rights advances, NAACP members in Newport and Saratoga Springs simultaneously iterated a commitment to the democratic principle of "opportunity for the hard-working, the ambitious, and the meritorious" and affirmed the legitimacy of their status. In this, they mirrored contemporary members of the white bourgeoisie who assumed important public roles. The fact that their aggregate job profile lagged behind that of their white counterparts in no way impeded the currency of these race leaders within the African-American community.[104]

⦅⦆

Wage-earning African Americans in Newport and Saratoga Springs generally toiled at the kinds of jobs that in the late nineteenth and the early twentieth centuries became synonymous with black labor—unskilled, domestic, and personal-service work. Yet, had the song been written earlier, George Gershwin's "Summertime" might have served as the constant refrain of African-American wage earners in the two resort towns from 1870 to 1930 during the months of June, July, and August. For as the lyrics suggest, in the warm season, "the livin' [was] easy." For Saratoga Springs, with an economy singly focused on tourism from the beginning, this was especially true. For Newport, however, a coastal location and navy operations yielded a more diversified, year-round set of job options for black workers.

Race strongly limited the success and choices of black laborers, male and female. As was characteristic nationally for the period, they were pushed out of occupations in which they had previously enjoyed significant representation. Thus, Afro-Saratogian men experienced job displacement by whites as jockeys and barbers while Afro-Newporter men slowly disappeared from the rosters of commercial seamen and higher-ranking naval personnel. Also, in Saratoga Springs, black female hotel workers were sometimes replaced by white help. Blacks were denied regular access to nonmanual and professional jobs; men and women who wished to become public-school teachers in the towns, for example, usually were disappointed. Often confined to a segregated, relatively poor clientele, African-American businesses in both places were typically marginal ventures that frequently failed. And when found in interracial job settings, blacks worked at the most menial tasks—Afro-Saratogian males as drink-hall floor moppers, Afro-Saratogian women as hotel kitchen help, Afro-Newporter men as navy mess attendants.

Black female workers in Newport and Saratoga Springs, like women workers everywhere in the country, were restricted in job access and pay by the assumption that their primary commitment was to family and marriage—the household over which a man was the major breadwinner. But the fact of racial discrimination—which severely hampered income-earning efforts of black males—forced black women in the resorts (as elsewhere in the nation) to break gender codes to provide for themselves and their families. Despite the fact that, as women, they were not supposed to work, as blacks, they had to and did work. Moreover, as "renegade" female workers, they were doubly constricted to female work and to African-American female work.

Yet, African Americans in both places rallied as individuals and collectively to fight both the race-based prejudice and discriminatory practices common in the country's labor market at the time. Black male workers more than black female workers—and black Newporters more than black Saratogians—benefited from such efforts. In both places, African Americans devised strategies for surviving the "off" season through savings, credit, and job rotation. Newporters fought to hire a female teacher. Also in Newport, black barbers united with whites to prevent total racial segmentation in their vocation. In both towns, African-American headwaiters and stewards participated in a national organization that endeavored successfully to safeguard their positions. Women, however, forced into highly individualized work and tied to child-rearing responsibilities, relied on informal coping strategies to preserve incomes for themselves.

Within this racialized occupational profile and within the racial coping strategies, not surprisingly, black workers developed their own sense of class and status while not totally rejecting that of the mainstream culture. In a classic demonstration of Du Boisian double-consciousness, they evinced a dual-track understanding of hierarchy. The double-tiered system of boardinghouses in Saratoga Springs demonstrates the ways in which resort-dwelling African Americans shared in white society's high evaluation of professionals, business owners, and nonmanual workers. But in both towns, the racialized world in which they lived led blacks to esteem (head)waiters and stewards—those service workers in their midst whose income, education, and supervisory tasks placed them above the rank-and-file experience.

Conceptually, the work world of the resort-town laborers may be placed between the southern farm and the northern ghetto. Certainly, tourist and agricultural economies share seasonal rhythms of activity and dormancy. The credit system employed by year-round African-American residents of summer resorts paralleled that of tenant farmers and sharecroppers. The service work that engaged so many African Americans in the resorts required the kind of personal deference well understood by antebellum slaves and preindustrial workers. On the other hand, involvement in guild-like organizations and unions introduced the rationalized labor relations that typified the growing number of large urban industries and commercial enterprises of the period. Saratoga Springs and Newport, therefore, stood on opposite ends of the chronological and conceptual continuum of black work experiences linking the nineteenth and the twentieth centuries. The spa retained more of the earlier order; the seaport tended to herald the incoming system.

ᘓ 4 ᘓ

Common Hopes and Loves

THE DEMOGRAPHIC PATTERNS, NEIGHBORHOODS, AND WORK ROUTINES identified thus far only partially forged the racial identity of Afro-Newporters and Afro-Saratogians. That identity was completed by several additional factors: shared experiences of social discrimination, self-affirming social and cultural organizations, group-advancement efforts, and the summer passage itself. Each of these factors contributed its unique dynamic to the definition of black community in Newport and Saratoga Springs, but there was interplay among these elements as well. And while experience with discrimination, separate institutions, and race advocacy also typified black community life in other contemporary cities and towns in the nation, only in the resorts—especially Saratoga Springs—did a tourist season, with its yearly infusion of "outside" African-American perspectives, emerge as a distinct molder of black identity.

Discrimination Revisited

As elsewhere in the nation, a race-defined circle encompassed the range of social options shared by African Americans in the two resorts after the overthrow of Reconstruction. Located in northern centers, however, the African-American populations of Saratoga Springs and Newport largely escaped formal, pervasive de jure segregation. Rather, they negotiated their way through a tricky maze of "accommodationist racist" conceptualizations that merged a belief in an incalculably distant millennium of racial egalitarianism with contemporary assumptions of black inferiority.[1] The historical record suggests, though, that black Newporters may have fared somewhat better than black Saratogians in the way they were estimated and treated by local whites.

Prejudice on the part of white visitors and locals toward Afro-Saratogians reflected contemporary, nationally held stereotypes that pictured blacks as either childlike or bestial. Thus, one turn-of-the-century tourist disparagingly noted that two of the town's gambling houses were reserved for "negro [horse] rubbers and riff-raff." Similarly, the local press advanced contemporary stereotypes, often portraying African Americans as unlearned, brash, showy, and perennial sources of amusement. One item implicitly interpreted a local black woman's confusion of a federal census taker in 1890 with a town directory pollster as a kind of indigenous ignorance. Another column made sport of "an Italian and a colored man talking together understanding each in the language of the other." And readers were expected to guffaw heartily at the following report: " 'Darkgreen' is what a colored man who arrived in town the other day answers to. It appears that two occupying similar names are statesmen on the same job, and the water color distinguishes him from P. Green."[2] A newspaper cartoon feature, "Our Boarding House," had as one of its characters a simpleminded and comical black valet named Jason, ever effusing a dialect of southern, broken, "black" English: "Man, look at dem travel labels on dis yere suitcase of yours! . . . You sho' has been a walking glober! . . . Dat's whut ah lak about you. . . . You don't jes go hoofin' aroun' de corner. . . . No, suh, you export y'sef! . . . Ah totes his baggage pusonally all ovah de world!— Siam, Scotch, and 'Equator!' . . . Where I come fum, Mister Mango, they's a lake whut we all used to fish in—didn't use no poles or hooks—no, suh, we fished with tennis racquets!—th' fish would jump up out of the' watah, and we'd jes bat 'em with th' tennis racquet ovah on th' shore—dat's all!"[3] These relatively "benign," condescending attitudes could take an uglier, more aggressive turn, however, as during the spring of 1924, when a spate of Ku Klux Klan cross burnings occurred within the city.[4]

While the public schools in Saratoga Springs remained integrated throughout the period studied, de facto Jim Crow practices barred African Americans from certain amusements and reserved others "for blacks only." The racetrack, for instance, remained "officially closed" to black guests; an announcement for another facility read, "W. H. Frear will open the rink on the corner of Lake Avenue and Henry Street, for the use of respectable colored people."[5] African Americans were not welcome at the spa's hotels except as employees; and, as just noted, certain gambling houses were viewed as the exclusive preserve of blacks. In their 1916 report, the commissioners of the State Reservation at Saratoga Springs recommended segregated bath facilities for the few black tourists. They explained that "embarrassment has already been felt in affording an equal use of the bathing and other facilities to negroes. Many patrons strenuously object to using the same appliances and attendants generally refuse to draw baths for and administer treatments to patients of another race. Under these circumstances, it seems very necessary to provide separate and equal facilities for both races, but as the number of colored people applying for treatment is not over one per cent of the aggregate number of both races at present, it is not necessary to provide for the accommodation of a large number of colored people."[6] Occasionally, though, whites permitted blacks free access to certain entertainment facilities. A news article reported that Benjamin Sampson, an African American, won the sack race and that six blacks had run the hurdle race at Glen Mitchell, a local amusement park; presumably, whites attended the park that day, too.[7]

In contrast to Saratoga Springs, Newport's summer and year-round white populations seemingly harbored a more optimistic and inclusive attitude, however paternalistic, toward the local African-American population. May King Van Renssalaer, a "society" member, offered the following status report regarding Afro-Newporters in 1905: "The colored population of the twentieth century is a strong factor, and for the most part a very respectable portion of the inhabitants of Newport. The Negroes have their clubs, their societies, and their churches, but although rather apart from the mass of the populace, they are an integral part of it, commanding a certain respect accorded to their race in no other part of the country."[8] Lyle Matthews, who grew up in Newport in the early twentieth century, acknowledged the unusual "respect" accorded blacks in certain accommodations at a time when Jim Crow practices prevailed nationally: "Newport was different than the average town. . . . You could ride the streetcar without discrimination. You could go to the beach without discrimination. You could sit anywhere you wanted in the theater."[9] This white respect for blacks may also be inferred from the way in which white visitors took note of the town's African Americans: "Mill Street ran steeply down to the harbor and the Saunderstown ferry; voices from the street sounded clearly—the cheerful argument of a girl with her young man who was a sailor; sailors in pairs, boatswains and petty officers went talkatively by; Negroes addressed one another politely."[10] Here, the equanimity with which reference to blacks is made is remarkable for its time.

Even less sanguine white tourists acknowledged, albeit in a somewhat jaundiced manner, the relative evenness in Newport's race relations. One noted: "The 'old Newporter' is not above showing the place to a party of negro visitors whom he drives down the Avenue with conspicuous good-humour, but it is his good-humour that is the most striking element of the spectacle. . . . The colored population has increased after its prolific racial fashion, and the anomaly of a barouche full of dark dandies and dusky belles conducted by an Irish, or even . . . a native Newport driver is a frequent phenomenon."[11] Yet another observer supplied an illustration of Newport's racial tolerance in certain social interactions: "two interesting machines, together with an old, tumble-down hack, driven by a smiling negro, are to give you, perhaps a first example of Newport democracy; for having landed, three of your fellow passengers are rowed out to the fastest schooner in a tiny dinghy bearing her name; two are haled into the most expensive automobile . . . ; and another, a gentleman with forty or fifty millions . . . drives a hard and fast bargain with the driver of the tumble-down hack. . . . he is on a comfortable footing with the driver."[12]

Despite these somewhat unique illustrations of rhetorical and social acceptance accorded black Newporters, whites still held African Americans "apart from the mass of the populace" (as Van Renssalaer posited) and thus treated them as inferiors. In 1888, for instance, the esteemed clergyman Henry Jeter was prevented from waiting on the wharf with his team of horses for a friend arriving by steamer. A local newspaper apologetically admitted that the orders to Jeter to "drive off the wharf" were "arbitrary and outrageous." Lyle Matthews remembered that "restaurants would try to block you [from entering]" during the early twentieth century. A black couple, Edward and Elizabeth Simmons, complained that they were denied the right to dance in a dancehall at Easton's Beach during the summer of 1913. That same year, a black youth, suspected of firing into the air a bullet that killed a young white boy at Easton's Beach, was nearly mobbed and beaten to death by white spectators before the intervention of local police. Even then, the crowd threatened to storm the jail and lynch the alleged perpetrator.[13]

Self-Affirmation

Responding to racial discrimination, the black Americans in the resorts gathered in their own churches, lodges, and clubs for mutual support against a hostile world. In the process of maintaining this separate organizational life, they developed a parallel universe that mirrored the social world of contemporary whites. By the same token, however, this black universe was also an autonomous social and cultural space with an internal dynamic of its own where, much as Earl Lewis discovered in his historical investigation of early twentieth-century Norfolk, Virginia, "segregation became congregation."[14]

Institutional black religious life, the historical bedrock of the African-American community, had begun in the antebellum period in both Saratoga Springs and Newport, as we have seen, in response to discriminatory practices imposed by white churches. Moreover, in Newport, separate black churches had appeared as doctrinal differences appeared within the African-American Christian community. Thus, by 1870, Saratoga Springs claimed one black church—the A.M.E. Zion Church that eventually was renamed the Dyer-Phelps Memorial A.M.E. Zion Church—and Newport boasted three black churches—Union Congregational, Mt. Zion A.M.E. Church, and Shiloh Baptist. Only the towns' A.M.E. churches—Saratoga Springs's A.M.E. Zion (part of the New York State–originated African Methodist Episcopal *Zion* Church) and Newport's Mt. Zion (under the denominational banner of the Absalom Jones/Richard Allen-originated, Philadelphia-based African Methodist Episcopal Church)—stood as totally black churches in a formally separatist vein. The other two congregations, while entirely African American in membership, still affiliated with white-run denominations. Thus, Union Congregational associated with the Rhode Island Congregational Association, and Shiloh Baptist affiliated with the Rhode Island Baptist State Convention. Two new Baptist congregations, both named Mt. Olivet, appeared in the towns after 1870—a sporadic group in Saratoga Springs in 1883 that formally incorporated in 1910, and another flock in Newport in 1894.[15]

For black Saratogians and black Newporters, as for many Americans during the period, church membership and involvement represented a public endorsement of contemporary middle-class standards of decency and morality. Therefore, church events offered respectable opportunities for socializing and served as occasions for displaying and learning acceptable forms of public deportment and speech. African-American church social life, while clearly apart from white-attended activities, often paralleled the latter, whether self-consciously or not, thereby bespeaking black participants' middle-class sensibilities and aspirations. Throughout the period, for instance, Saratoga Springs's Mt. Olivet Baptist Church and Dyer-Phelps A.M.E. Zion Church hosted ice cream and strawberry festivals, ice cream and cake socials, picnics, fairs, bazaars, block parties, concerts, and lawn fetes. Newport's Union Congregational Church, Mt. Zion A.M.E. Church, Shiloh Baptist Church, and Mt. Olivet Baptist Church offered musical entertainments, strawberry festivals, annual excursions, picnics, outings, and patch parties. Churches also hosted lectures intended to have broad appeal; these included an illustrated presentation entitled "Around the World in Eighty Minutes" and another on "The Cultivation of the Intellect." While fund-raising needs often prompted many of these affairs, their significance here is the confirmation they provided of and for a legitimate, publicly approved social arena for African Americans.[16] In this sense, the black churches served simultaneously as "the major cultural brokers of the norms, values, and expectations of white society" and as places where African Americans in fact compensated for their "lack of access to mainstream society in their own institutions."[17]

At the same time, the black churches in Newport and Saratoga Springs sponsored lay discussion groups that considered topics of specific interest to African Americans. Thus, Dyer-Phelps invited Howard University sociologist Kelly Miller to deliver a critique of *The Leopard's Spots*, an early twentieth-century articulation of scientific racism authored by Thomas Dixon, who also wrote the novel *The Clansman*, the basis for the film *The Birth of a Nation*; the participants in the Saratoga Lyceum at Mt. Olivet Baptist Church learned about "The Life and Character of Paul Laurence Dunbar," the celebrated black poet; and the Union Congregational Church once featured a talk on "The Future of the Negro." In these ways, black churchgoers in the towns rejected racist depictions of themselves, celebrated their cultural heroes, and expressed optimism about their prospects in the nation.[18]

These artistic and intellectual forums also taught participants the formal rules of argumentation, self-presentation, and performance. In this vein, the Union Congregational Church once hosted readings by a Boston elocution-ist, and Dyer-Phelps's Frederick Douglass Literary Society once sponsored a debate on the esoteric subject "Resolved, That the captain, and not the lookout nor the doctor of a ship, was responsible for the saving of the shipwrecked sick woman taken off the desert island"—an event followed by a program of piano and vocal solos, recitations, and poetry readings.[19] Those in attendance at such events received expanded opportunities, otherwise limited in a racially segregated and hierarchized world, to sharpen their rhetorical, oratorical, and musical skills, either by participation or observa-tion. The fact that African Americans were generally denied chances to parade such talents in mainstream white society did not mar the attractive-ness of these accomplishments in the minds of the resort-town blacks. They were seeking refinement *for themselves.*

An overly romanticized view of church-based race solidarity in black Newport and black Saratoga Springs would be inaccurate, however. Church politics—interracial and intraracial—and differences in worship preferences and regional origins of parishioners were largely responsible for the forma-tion of the two additional black Baptist churches that organized in the re-sorts after 1870. Nationally, such ecclesiastical maneuverings eventuated the 1895 formation of the all-black National Baptist Convention, U.S.A., a devel-opment more or less coinciding with the founding of Newport's Mt. Olivet Baptist Church in October 1894 by a group of disgruntled parishioners be-longing to Shiloh Baptist Church. During the spring of 1894, Shiloh's over-worked pastor, the Reverend Henry Jeter, received orders from his doctor to take a vacation. Before leaving, and having to decide on a suitable replace-ment, Jeter conferred with the pastor of Providence's Congdon Street Baptist Church, who recommended an evangelist, one Joseph Murphy. Later revealed to be a confidence man and swindler, Murphy quickly proceeded during his brief stay at Shiloh to instigate and foment Jeter's ouster. After returning to Newport, Jeter successfully resisted the scheme by assembling condemnatory evidence regarding Murphy's character and past. However, the aggressiveness of Jeter's retaliatory action against Murphy—action backed by the Rhode Island Baptist State Convention—seems to have aggravated a latent tension between leadership and laity—or, more specifically, between the pastor and the deacon board. Such political struggles are common, even traditional, among black Baptists, owing to the congregational nature of church polity.

Lacking a centrally administered denominational hierarchy, local congregations are autonomous. The local pastor, deaconate, and membership jointly govern, sometimes with less than harmonious results. By the fall of 1894, Shiloh's dissenting faction announced its exodus with the explanation that its adherents "would have a church of their own, and no longer be under the white people." Thus, what probably began as an individually conceived, opportunistic attempt at self-promotion by a boozy, jackleg preacher conflated with local, internal power conflicts in a national atmosphere of African-American church separatism. The result was a second black Baptist congregation in Newport.[20] What is significant about this development is that it reveals the determination of individual black parishioners to create religious communities that reflected *their* sympathies. If they perceived that no such local communities existed, African Americans made them.

In this same spirit, Saratoga Springs's Mt. Olivet Baptist Church appeared seemingly as a consequence of a growing number of Afro-Baptists—many perhaps from the South, where the preponderance of black Baptists could be found and where most black Christians were Baptist. During the summer of 1883, a "colored Baptist mission" held Sunday services and Friday evening meetings in one of the assembly rooms of the town hall. By 1902, Afro-Baptists had organized informally, at first as the First Colored Baptist Church, with meetings on Congress Street. For the next seven years, beginning in 1903, black Baptists gathered strength—meeting at first in a house on Washington Street, then again at a site on Congress Street, and ultimately moving to a remodeled house at Federal and Washington streets in 1905. During these two years of relocations, consolidation, and renaming, the Colored Baptist Mission became the Union Baptist Church. By 1908, the black Baptist congregation had renamed itself—for a fourth and final time— the Mt. Olivet Baptist Church. A minimum of one-half (seven of a total of thirteen) of the members present at the church's incorporation in 1910 were southerners born in Virginia or Maryland. Similarly, at least one-half (three of a total of six) of the church trustees present at the same event were southerners by birth—Virginians, to be exact.[21] Thus, the members of the two Mt. Olivets bypassed existing alternatives, both black and white, to carve out worship arenas that expressed *their* understanding of themselves. In so doing, they explicitly countered white exclusion and implicitly negated white notions of black homogeneity.

African-American fraternal societies accomplished many of the same cultural and social functions as did the churches. Lodge proliferation in the two resorts (as elsewhere in the nation during the period) demonstrated the great extent to which resort-town blacks identified with mainstream bourgeois behaviors. Also, for beleaguered black men in particular, the lodges functioned as a comfortable, reassuring retreat, "an environment in which [they could] spend as much of their social life as possible among their own kind."[22] And because there was no prohibition against belonging simultaneously to several lodges and even several orders, black fraternal societies formed "complex cross-cutting structures" within the black world that fostered a sense of race solidarity.[23] Certainly, this was true in Newport and Saratoga Springs, where membership for each lodge included black "brethren" of diverse occupational, regional, age, and church backgrounds.[24]

The appearance of women's auxiliaries of black fraternal organizations was an indicator of the two black communities' acceptance of white middle-class patterns as well, since similar female auxiliaries were simultaneously appearing in the white orders. Women's branches of established male orders reflected the ways in which black women in Newport and Saratoga Springs, like contemporary white women, sought an autonomous public role. By participating in the auxiliaries' rituals, black women endorsed the domestic roles assigned to them by mainstream society. At the same time, the establishment of female auxiliaries took on a special racial meaning within the black community. For middle-class black aspirants, the female auxiliaries signified that black women had achieved a level of gentility otherwise denied them by their wage-earning activities.[25]

To the extent that they were parts of national organizations, African-American churches, fraternal societies, and women's auxiliaries yoked resort-town blacks to a wider national black culture.[26] They functioned to undermine strict parochialism among Afro-Saratogians and Afro-Newporters. Looking to the state grand lodge, church district meetings, and national conventions, black "joiners" in the towns could find enhanced sources of encouragement, enlarged social arenas, and ways of connecting to each other, whether country-bred or city-born, southerner or northerner, newcomer or old-timer, male or female, rich or poor, young or old, seasonal visitor or year-round resident.

Other clubs supplied outlets for "respectable" black socializing in Saratoga Springs. During the 1920s, the Dunbar Social Club served as a gathering place of local, achievement-oriented African Americans who proclaimed and reinforced their own middle-class, mainstream values through a program of shared social contact. The group met regularly from fall to spring at the homes of various members, although usually at the Edith Coleman house at Six Alger Street. There, the club planned hikes, sleigh rides, and other recreational activities. As self-styled elites, group members were somewhat apart from the black Saratogian rank and file. None of the Dunbar Club members resided in the West Side area. Most, in fact, lived east of Broadway, even if in modest dwellings. "They were the high mucky-mucks," reminisced Ernest Jackson.[27]

A profile of the known Dunbar Club participants during the 1920s reveals that a stable work history, ambition, and demonstrable middle-class sensibilities served as admission criteria. Club members therefore included the Mann family, one of perhaps two or three black Saratogian clans that attended the Episcopal Church—a perennial marker of elite status among blacks. Household head Charlie labored as a foreman in a spring-water bottling plant—a career achievement after a previous job as a hotel hallboy. Charlie's wife, Lena Mann, earned income as a cook after an earlier stint as a housemaid. Her son Robert attended college; her daughter Alice worked as a salesgirl in a candy store. The George "Jack" Wentworth family also participated in the Dunbar Club. George was a housepainter, a step up from his former job as paperhanger. Ursula Cochrane, a widow, and her sons also belonged. Robert Cochrane was a proofreader, presumably for a newspaper; Leonard and Marshall were coproprietors of the City Creamery, a dairy-products store. Percy served as clerk at the family store while Warren attended Albany State Normal School, a teacher's college. Henry Coleman, headwaiter at the Worden Hotel and a pillar at the Mt. Olivet Baptist Church, and his daughter Edith were members. Edith was a stenographer and was sometimes engaged in events at Dyer-Phelps. Teenagers like Edna Bailey and Edward Pilkington also participated. Pilkington guessed that he gained admission to the club because he was of a "certain type": "I was a goodie-goodie. I was in athletics in high school and a reporter for the yearbook . . . and I was known [favorably] in the town."[28] Similar clubs no doubt existed in Newport, although the written and oral historical records consulted for this study contain no mention of them. In the Dunbar Club—as in the churches and lodges—African Americans nurtured the highest aspirations for themselves and thereby cut against the grain of a social fabric in which they were often forgettable threads.

Political Strategizing

The African-American communities in the resorts generally approached race matters pragmatically. Moving with the times, they at first embraced the optimistic national civil rights and integrationist Republican agenda of the Reconstructionist era, remained hopefully loyal to the Republicans after the Compromise of 1877, and then slid into a more cautious accommodationist mode at the turn of the century. Only in the years following World War I did they begin a tentative push for social and political equality. Repeating national patterns elsewhere, African-American churches and their pastors in Newport and Saratoga Springs functioned as the major catalysts for race advancement. Other organizations, most notably the local National Association for the Advancement of Colored People (NAACP) chapters, devised group betterment plans as well. Throughout this period, black Newport evinced a more consistently militant and effective commitment to racial egalitarianism as an achievable goal than did black Saratoga Springs. Once again, the integrationist tradition and numerical edge possessed by the African-American seaporters may explain this difference.

Black people in both resorts began the period in an expectant mood regarding interracial amity under the guidance of the Republican Party, as did most African Americans, in the North and the South. In Saratoga Springs, for instance, A.M.E. Zion's pastor, the Reverend J. C. Gilbert, and T. H. S. Pennington were among a group of local "colored citizens" who sponsored a public lecture by Frederick Douglass in April 1870. Douglass, an ardent integrationist and the foremost black Republican spokesman of the day, delivered an address in support of the Fifteenth Amendment (extending voting rights to black men) that had passed the previous month. Douglass's speech expressed the loftiest, most patriotic contemporary visions of American democratic inclusiveness—citizenship and voting rights for Native Americans and Chinese immigrants, the future disappearance of ethnic and racial prejudice through education, the worthiness of African-American citizens as demonstrated by their performance as Civil War soldiers—and no doubt reflected the opinions of the event's black organizers and audience.[29]

Black Saratogians continued to demonstrate their confidence in a comprehensive civil rights agenda in the 1870s. Now possessing the franchise as provided in the Fifteenth Amendment, they allied themselves with the local Republican Party, whose leaders promised to represent their interests. Thus, after a parade in April 1871 commemorating the passage of the amendment, Captain J. P. Butler, a local, white Republican Party activist and village supervisor, addressed the largely black crowd. He reminded those assembled of "their duty as citizens . . . and impressed upon his hearers the sacredness of the ballot box, assuring them that if they desired good wholesome laws that they must elect good men to office [viz., Republicans]; if they did not, and should send their enemies [viz., Democrats] to the Assembly or to Congress to make laws for them in common with the rest of the community, that they would only be making slaves of themselves again and fastening the fetters upon their own hands and feet."[30] However, from the sources consulted for this study, there was no apparent payoff for Afro-Saratogian Republicanism on the *local* level, even in the types of patronage posts that blacks claimed as rewards for party fidelity elsewhere in the country.[31] Certainly, no municipal jobs for blacks resulted, and de facto segregation existed in the spa. Perhaps, given their tiny numbers, blacks in Saratoga Springs simply contented themselves with the knowledge that, as Republican voters, they were at least buttressing the party most responsive to their plight at the national level.

The following year, Afro-Saratogian dedication to the Republican civil-rights legacy stood unshaken despite the split in the national Republican Party. Throughout the summer months of 1872, a presidential election year, the Reverend M. H. Ross of the A.M.E. Zion Church encouraged such loyalties in defiance of the advice of longtime race sympathizer and former abolitionist Charles Sumner, who argued that African Americans should now back the new Liberal Republican Party. In early August, Ross chaired a committee of twenty-five that mounted a successful rally for presidential candidate Ulysses S. Grant at the town hall, where local blacks filled seats and squeezed into "spaces in both the aisles . . . and in and around the door." This was followed by an evening torchlight parade involving 100 Grant backers; they proceeded down Broadway to the United States Hotel, where a group of another 3,000 to 5,000 Grant supporters joined them. By late August, pro-Grant African Americans in the town organized a Grant and Wilson (Grant's running mate) Club with the Reverend Ross's participation. Seeking to guard the liberties guaranteed to blacks by the Thirteenth, Fourteenth, and Fifteenth Amendments and viewing Liberal Republicans as "enemies to [the] race," these organizers engaged some of the most eminent black civil-rights activists of the day as event speakers: Cincinnati-based Robert Harlan and Howard University law professor J. M. Langston.[32]

Similarly, in Newport, black integrationist voices—with clergymen prominent among them—sounded loudly in the postbellum years. But there, unlike Saratoga Springs, the historical record indicates that expedience rather than strict party loyalty determined black voting behavior and that measurable local results flowed from such strategy. George Downing, an outspoken integrationist of national repute, and the Reverend Mahlon Van Horne of Union Congregational Church were the leading civil-rights activists in the early years. Downing especially eschewed unbending Republican partisanship among blacks. During the 1880s, in fact, he gained a controversial reputation for promoting independent politics—by supporting a Democrat's (unsuccessful) bid for the Rhode Island state governorship and by running (unsuccessfully) for the state legislature on the Independent ticket—as the most self-interested course for African-American progress. Van Horne preached "fair play in all walks of life" for blacks. Having assumed his pastorate in 1869, for the next twenty-eight years, he participated in local and state government and in 1885 became the first African American elected to the House of Representatives of the Rhode Island General Assembly; he would serve three consecutive terms. During his lengthy tenure at the Union Congregational Church, Van Horne also served on the Newport School Committee from 1873 to 1892. This was a patronage post won in exchange for black backing of a Democratic candidate for mayor. Downing had spearheaded African-American support for this mayor's election with the understanding that black votes would be rewarded by appointments like Van Horne's.[33]

Concomitant with the general mood of the country, the last decade of the nineteenth century brought a more conservative approach to racial issues in Saratoga Springs and Newport that continued until roughly the end of World War I in 1918. In 1895, at the Atlanta Exposition, Tuskegee Institute principal Booker T. Washington first publicly urged blacks to forestall a full civil-rights agenda for an immediate focus on the uplift of the rural masses through vocational training, industrial employment, moral rectitude, self-help, and patience. The death of Frederick Douglass in the same year symbolized the passing of militant integrationism as the hegemonic philosophy among race advocates and their white allies. And one year later, the U.S. Supreme Court officially sanctioned segregationist laws and practices in its *Plessy v. Ferguson* decision. These national events were paralleled by the departure of local integrationists as race leaders in Saratoga Springs and Newport: Pennington in 1895 following the failure of his pharmacy; Van Horne in 1897 to take up a U.S. diplomatic post; and Downing in 1903 on his death. What then emerged in the resorts after 1890 was a comparatively restrained, carefully opportunistic, and less utopian strategy for race progress—a blueprint that received attention among a racially mixed group of adherents.[34]

Booker T. Washington's views were circulated in Saratoga Springs seemingly to the exclusion of all others during this period. During the summer of 1905, Washington visited the spa as part of a widely covered promotional and fund-raising tour for Tuskegee Institute. The jaunt to Saratoga Springs was probably one of many to other urban centers made from New York City, the northern headquarters that Washington established that year to be near millionaire philanthropists. While in Saratoga Springs, he spoke to white audiences at the First Presbyterian Church and the First Baptist Church and to a black audience at Dyer-Phelps A.M.E. Zion Church, to whom he revealed that he had once worked as a waiter in the spa. Declaring education and work to be the salvation of the black man, Washington articulated before the Saratogians his belief that agriculture and manual labor in particular were the strong suits of his people: "We place our emphasis on the agriculture, and the chemistry of the soil, because I believe that the negro is found at his best when he is out-of-doors. We must keep him on the soil until he gets the strength of mind that will enable him to live amid the temptations of your large cities of the north."[35] One year later, Bishop Alexander Walter of the A.M.E. Zion Church, in town to address the Western New York Conference of his denomination, aired similar ideas. While decrying recent disfranchisement measures against blacks, Walter echoed Washington's opinions by emphasizing that "all the negro asks is a fair chance," not social equality. Walter went on to recommend Washington as the best current leader of the black race, arguing that Washington was "entitled to the respect and confidence of negroes as a body" because of his "religious, financial, [and] educational influence" and because he had the "cooperation of the white people."[36]

Certainly, in Saratoga Springs, the bishop's claims regarding Washington's connections were reinforced before the local population by the latter's ties to philanthropist George Foster Peabody. Peabody's link to the resort was rooted in his business partnership with New York banker and spa estate owner Spencer Trask and in his affection for Trask's wife, Katrina, whom he had courted before her marriage. As a family friend, Peabody was among "a succession of famous guests" that the Trasks welcomed to their gothic

Saratoga Springs mansion, Yaddo, between 1893 (when the structure was built) and 1909, the year of Spencer Trask's untimely death. Moreover, Peabody maintained his own summer home in nearby Lake George through 1912, served as chairman of the New York State-authorized Saratoga Springs Mineral Springs Reservation Commission from 1909 to 1916, and kept a home in the spa on Circular Street from 1912 until 1921, when he eventually enjoyed a brief marital union with Katrina at the Yaddo estate. Peabody donated heavily to black education and especially favored Tuskegee Institute and Hampton Institute. The latter, Washington's alma mater, was an industrial school that served as a model for Tuskegee and the wellspring of Washington's educational philosophy. From 1900 to 1911, Peabody served as a board member for Hampton; and, during the early twentieth century, he was treasurer of both Hampton and Tuskegee. From 1908 to 1927, he served as treasurer of the Negro Rural School Fund, which was underwritten with monies supplied by Anna T. Jeanes, a Tuskegee/Hampton donor; from 1928 through 1931, he was the fund's vice president.[37]

Northern fund-raising tours—which provided the financial lifeblood for black colleges and technical schools—naturally targeted the monied patrons among the spa's seasonal crowd and were often scheduled for the summer, when student singers and speakers were available. Throughout the period examined here, Saratoga Springs audiences received financial solicitations from these institutions' representatives, sometimes with Peabody's assistance and sometimes with local African-American help (organized through Dyer-Phelps). In July 1920, for instance, Peabody presided over a meeting held at the Grand Union Hotel in support of Hampton Institute. Mrs. Spencer Trask was listed as one of the event's sponsors. A largely white audience of more than 300 people listened to students, graduates, and enthusiasts of Hampton, including four African-American singers, an Alaskan Indian graduate, and a native Mozambican alumnus who espoused the benefits of the school's vocational training. One of Hampton's white supporters explained the hope that industrial education offered to blacks and to American society: "Up to this point, in the race problem of the world three methods have been in use: the first, the extermination of the weaker by the stronger; the second, slavery; and the third, amalgamation. It is up to us to evolve a fourth method, which will be a real solution of the race problem. The fourth method will be to make it possible for each race, still living independently to contribute to the common welfare and common civilization." The evening event was a success, securing $657 in cash support and several full-scholarship checks and pledges. During the summer of 1926, Peabody sponsored a local concert featuring a quartet from Penn Normal and Agricultural School. During the same tourist season, the Reverend Dr. James Edward Mason, a promoter of African-American education who taught at Livingstone College and Industrial School, the A.M.E. Zion college in Salisbury, North Carolina, appealed for support of his institution before Dyer-Phelps parishioners. The church featured yet another black school quartet, this one from Voorhees Normal and Industrial School, during the 1930 season.[38]

The importance of white patronage-seeking as a black community-advancement strategy in Saratoga Springs—a strategy very much in line with Washington's own—is suggested also in the very name of the local A.M.E. Zion Church, Dyer-Phelps. Local records make it clear that the A.M.E. Zion Church was renamed Dyer Memorial A.M.E. Zion in 1888, when it moved to a new building purchased with money supplied by Mrs. Benjamin Dyer, a local hotel owner. In 1900, the church received a final name, Dyer-Phelps Memorial A.M.E. Zion Church, to mark a $500 gift from a summer cottager. This last donor was probably one of the descendants of Anson Greene Phelps, a deeply religious, wealthy, Manhattan-based, antebellum reformer-philanthropist and abolitionist who served as the president of the New York Colonization Society and on the boards of several evangelical organizations. In an effort to pass on a tradition of involvement in church causes, he left each of his grandchildren an inheritance of $5,000 to spend specifically on evangelical activities. Dyer-Phelps's patron in 1900 may well have been his granddaughter, Caroline Phelps Stokes, whose financial contribution established the Phelps-Stokes Fund for black education in 1911.[39]

As in Saratoga Springs, many of Newport's black population endorsed Washington's philosophies. Among African-American women, the 1896 formation of the Willing Women's League of Newport at the Union Congregational Church in part reflected their subscription to the black self-help component of Washington's ideology. This group must also be understood as a manifestation of the club movement among contemporary middle-class American women, who united in the spirit of Progressivism to provide myriad services to society's downtrodden—usually immigrants, urban dwellers, blacks, and/or other ethnic minorities. The result of this movement among black women was the creation in 1896 of the National Association of Colored Women (NACW), which merged the National League of Colored

Women and the National Federation of African-American Women. The
NACW motto was "Lifting as We Climb." Newport's Willing Women
Leaguers, then, were black women with middle-class sensibilities and aspirations who dedicated themselves to aiding the local black masses. In addition,
there existed a Newport chapter of the National Negro Business League, an
association of black entrepreneurs started by Washington in 1900; its activities were previously discussed.[40]

Newporter Dr. Marcus Wheatland, writing in 1908 for the *Colored Ameri-*
can, a publication edited by a Washington supporter, reiterated the Tuske-
geean's tenets regarding the need for character development and practical
education among African Americans. Like Washington, Wheatland had
risen from an obscure and disadvantaged youth and had financed his education with summer work at resorts. Not surprisingly, therefore, the article,
entitled "Getting Along under Difficulties," supplied a brief guide to the
contemporary African American seeking success in the face of "forces, ever-
present, ever-active, tending toward keeping him in the most inferior positions." Some of the advice is moralistic; for example: "No matter how much
you have, live moderately for the sake of your children. . . . Children are
greatly handicapped when they are brought up with their ideas centered
upon dress and show." Other advice is purely pragmatic, as when Wheatland
calls for black education oriented toward paying jobs: "When [children]
leave school it is a question of how much can they bring home now."[41]

The Reverend Henry Jeter, however, offered the most striking refraction
of Washington's thought among Afro-Newporters. On retiring from the
pastorate of Shiloh Baptist in 1916 after a forty-one-year tenure, Jeter announced his determination to pursue "a humane cause . . . wherein are
thousands [of African Americans] to be reached and saved." This effort,
known as the Jeter Movement, fell within the Washingtonian camp because
of its emphasis on black self-help through agricultural and industrial pursuits, which it recommended in moralistic tones. It specifically targeted
African-American urban youths and encouraged them to return to more
productive, healthful rural settings.[42]

Unlike the apparent Afro-Saratogian pattern, however, laboring in the
self-help spirit of the times for Afro-Newporters did not preclude attacking
the color line; in this respect, black Newport seemed very much in touch
with the eclectic program of the contemporary national Afro-American
League/Council (although this research unearthed no evidence of a local

chapter of this race-advancement organization in the seaport). When compared to black Saratogians, black Newporters during "the nadir" of race
relations were relatively tenacious in their pursuit of full equality, which they
combined with their self-help endeavors. Racial egalitarianism among Afro-
Newporters in the Jim Crow era drew on persistent ties to antebellum New
England abolitionism and was linked to a sympathetic Boston-based political orbit between 1895 and 1915. As chronicled in the previous chapter, black
petitioners in 1901 successfully rallied behind Louisa Van Horne to protest
the racism underlying her difficulty in securing a position as a public-school
teacher in Newport. Additionally, as early as 1905, the year of its inception,
W. E. B. Du Bois's Niagara Movement received support from Byron Gunner,
one of Mahlon Van Horne's successors as pastor of Union Congregational
Church. Gunner belonged to a Providence-based statewide group of Niagara
Movement sympathizers. In 1905—and again in 1912—Du Bois's Newport
followers arranged for him to lecture in their city.[43]

A second look at the public lives of Jeter and Wheatland reveals the ways
in which attacks on local, systemic racism were not compromised by black
Newport's commitment to self-help strategies. Perhaps it was their city's
experience as a naval base that prompted the Newport delegation to the 1911
meeting of the annual New England A.M.E. Convention, convening that
year in the seaport, to address "the prejudicial feelings alleged to exist in the
United States Navy against the colored sailor." The Reverend Jeter, in attendance at the convention, was especially vocal on this issue. As a result of the
Newport initiative, the convention formed a committee to investigate the
matter and prepare a report for presentation before "the proper national
authorities for redress."[44] This research did not explore the outcome of the
committee's action, which evidently did not prevent the navy's later discriminatory policies or improve the position of black sailors at the Newport
facilities, as we have seen. What *is* significant here, however, is the fact that
such an integrationist position was taken by Afro-Newporters like Jeter even
as they focused on achievement within a separate black sphere.

Dr. Wheatland similarly fostered integrationism by seeking to direct
mainstream, white-controlled institutions to include local African Americans among their beneficiaries. From 1910 to 1914, he was a member of the
Representative Council, Newport's city council, for Ward Four, an area
enveloping the black residential cluster east of Bellevue and south of Old
Beach Road. Between at least 1911 and 1918, Dr. Wheatland served as a

member of the Charity Organization Society, a private, municipal coalition of relief agencies. And, for a time, he participated on the Newport Committee on School Play Grounds.[45] No similar instances of integrationist activism on the part of African-American Saratoga Springs in the years between 1890 and the end of World War I surfaced in the historical sources consulted for this study.

After World War I, the African-American communities of both resorts, but Newport especially, returned to the strident devotion to racial egalitarianism that had typified the early postbellum period. This shift, of course, coincided with Du Bois's continuing ascent as a national civil-rights leader, Washington's death in 1915, and the postwar mood of agitation among blacks nationally. Using NAACP activism as one measure of the new, upbeat attitude of race advocates, it is clear that, between the two towns, Newport preceded and exceeded Saratoga Springs in such undertakings. The Reverend Clifford Miller of the Union Congregational Church, "authorized by a citizen's meeting," had first written the national NAACP office requesting instructions regarding the establishment of a local chapter in October 1913. Throughout 1914 and 1915, local attempts to establish a Newport chapter of the NAACP had persisted and been thwarted only by World War I itself (the financial depression brought on by the war had led to staff reductions at NAACP headquarters). Then, some time in 1919, allegations that a black female cook working at or near the naval training station of the war college had been slapped by her white male employer during an argument precipitated the final and successful attempt, spearheaded in part by the Reverend N. A. Marriott of Shiloh Baptist Church, to start a local NAACP branch.[46]

In the 1920s, the Newport NAACP grew numerically and in political influence. In August 1920, Mt. Zion A.M.E. Church hosted a Sunday mass meeting to kick off an NAACP membership drive that targeted 200 additional names. Notably, city mayor Jeremiah P. Mahoney attended the event and, in a speech before the gathering, spoke of the progress of African Americans since the Civil War, the patriotism of black soldiers in World War I, and his desire to join the organization. Twenty-five new members were secured that day. As the NAACP pursued its antilynching campaign, the Newport chapter participated by collecting money to contribute toward a national Anti-Lynching Fund and lobbying state legislators to support an antilynching bill. It also pursued a state civil-rights bill. As a result of these efforts, one state senator became an NAACP member and a backer of the proposed legislation, thus prompting the "local colored citizens" in 1923 to organize a testimonial banquet in honor of him and another elected sympathizer.[47]

Differing from Newport, the Saratoga Springs NAACP chapter began later and achieved no measurable results during this period. The spa's branch received its official charter in June 1921, but it seems to have followed this with no discernible impact on local race relations over the next nine years.[48]

Joining the NAACP branches, other signs of black protest emerged in the decade following World War I; but again, Newport outstripped Saratoga Springs in this regard. The *Triangle*, a "militant monthly of opinion," appeared briefly in Newport in 1920. The Reverend James Lucas, pastor of the Mt. Olivet Baptist Church and the first president of the local NAACP, published the periodical, which emphasized race pride, black achievement, and the need for full racial equality. National in its focus and shrill in tone, the *Triangle* provided information on race-related developments, preached integration, and urged its readers to advocate "liberty, justice, and equality" for African Americans. The magazine did not begrudge white sympathizers, but it aimed primarily at a black audience to promote indigenous activism. Several local black entrepreneurs responded favorably by funding the publication with advertisements. These included grocer E. J. Dinkins; caterer/restaurateur D. B. Allen; barber Sidney Shuford; and pharmacist Cromwell West. West congratulated the *Triangle* for "expressing the thoughts of the 'New Negro.'" Newport's black youth also probably embraced the ideas aired in the publication, since Lucas reportedly enjoyed an excellent rapport with them.[49] Cromwell West's post–World War I tenure as a councilman for Ward Two, which at that time included the West Broadway neighborhood, exemplifies again the relatively aggressive ways in which Newport's black community endeavored to advance itself.[50]

While postwar activism among blacks did not entirely bypass Saratoga Springs, only one instance of local black public defiance of prejudicial racial customs could be found. Edna Bailey Miller narrated the event, which probably occurred in the late 1920s and involved schoolchildren:

> One Friday, at school assembly, this [white] girl gave a reading. I can't remember what [the reading was] but it had the word "nigger" in it. "The niggers did this, the niggers did that." I looked at [my brother] Jimmy and I knew that as my brother, he'd stand by me, and I looked at [my friend] Florence and we got up. . . . All the black kids joined us and we walked out. I

said, ". . . Let's go to my house!" My father was there and we told him what
happened. My mother said, ". . . You don't have to feel bad because you're
not niggers, but even so, they didn't have to say it." We didn't go to school on
Monday until [after my father got back from some places he had to go]. All
the [black] kids came to my house [and] had breakfast. Then we went up to
the school. Together with my father, we straightened that out. We begged
our pardon, and the girl had to beg pardon, and the English teacher promised they would never have anything like that again—anything that embar-
rassed any race.[51]

Like the several black pastors in Newport, the Reverend Bailey here assumed
the role of race leader in Saratoga Springs. But unlike the African-American
clergy in Newport, the Reverend Bailey only acted in this single performance.

The school incident also highlights the fact that, unlike race advocates of
the period in Newport, African-American activists in the spa sidestepped
formal political structures. Linking the effectiveness of race strategies in the
seaport to engagement in party politics, Lyle Matthews recalled of the first
third of the twentieth century in Newport that if you were African American, "you could ride on the streetcar with no difficulties. You could sit in the
theater with any ticket when I was a child. People—ushers and usherettes—
would try tricks, but they wouldn't last long because the black folks were
Republicans and Republicans were in power."[52] Indeed, Newport's black
Republicans demonstrated their strength during the summer of 1908 when
the Republican Club for Ward Two sponsored an anniversary celebration.[53]
African Americans in Saratoga Springs also voted the Republican ticket
during this period, as did most black Americans in the pre–Depression era,
but their smaller numbers, higher levels of geographic mobility, limited
resources, and missing integrationist heritage combined to blunt any sustained, organized investment in formal political procedures in the spa. Instead, like African Americans in such other small towns as Oswego, New
York, they made personal appeals and turned to patronage networks that
had evolved over years of association with familiar local whites.[54] The fact
that Franklin Roosevelt, then governor of New York State, laid the corner-
stone for a new church edifice for Saratoga Springs's Mt. Olivet Baptist
Church in 1929 does seem to indicate that some spa-dwelling blacks considered courting the Democratic Party and/or vice versa, but the subsequent
departure of the church pastor under a cloud of suspicion regarding the

handling of congregational finances probably discredited the merits of such
political dealings.[55]

Summer: Socializing, Politicking, and Identifying

If the identities of the black communities of Newport and Saratoga Springs
crystallized in the several ways—formal and informal, social and political—
that have just been explored, the summer months intensified this process in
resort towns, especially in Saratoga Springs. Because they represented a dense,
seasonal menu of instructional models for Afro-Saratogians, the happenings
on Congress Street, Saratoga Springs's chief black commercial avenue, are
illustrative. The thoroughfare concentrated African-American nightlife in its
summer brothels, bars, clubs, and gambling spots until the 1950s, when
national crime hearings put a clamp on gambling life, and the 1960s, when
urban renewal mandated the destruction of most of the old buildings. During
the 1920s, though, especially when Harlem was in vogue, Congress Street
served as the spa's Harlem. There is no way to determine the exact racial
distribution of visitors to the avenue's establishments, but all the evidence
suggests that it was mixed. Robert Sims recalled: "There was Jack's Cabaret
and colored bars, but Congress Street wasn't necessarily the black section. It
was where just about everybody hung out."[56] Congress Street's after-hours
establishments permitted whites the opportunity to shed formal mannerisms
and participate without fear of disapprobation in a social world that was
designated sensual and exotic by mainstream culture. Prohibition was ignored
in the strip's speakeasies, and "at places like Jack's Harlem Club, bands played,
costumed women sang and danced, strippers stripped, comics joked, blues
singers broke hearts and female impersonators shocked the clientele."[57] In
addition, black prostitutes catered to an exclusively white clientele. Perhaps
precisely because Congress Street was off-limits to local Skidmore College
students, these privileged and curious white coeds flocked there in droves.
Whites, then, came seeking black music, black dancing, black food, or black
women.[58]

The fact that local white authorities winked at illegal activity on Congress caused many Afro-Saratogians to redouble their assertions of respectability. Preachers sermonized against the strip, neighbors called law officials
to inform them of questionable goings-on, and mothers warned their chil-

dren to keep off *that* street. The high times on Congress Street were definitely anathema to the dignified restraint prized by the upstanding among year-round African Americans, who feared both the stigma and possible results of association with the infamous area. The James Jacksons, for instance, lived on William Street, just a few blocks north of Congress. They were careful to enforce strict bedtimes on their children to keep them away from the trouble a few doors away.[59]

Other Afro-Saratogians, otherwise relatively isolated from the African-American mainstream, found that the explosion of segregated race-specific businesses on Congress Street supplied them with basic and rudimentary information about the web of restraints imposed on early twentieth-century black American life. Joseph Jackson, for instance, who arrived in Saratoga Springs in 1910 from rural Vermont at age seven, recalled, "I didn't know I was colored until I came to Saratoga, and I wanted to go to a barber shop as a kid. They had colored barber shops [on Congress Street]. We didn't have any in Vermont. So I saw there was a difference. . . . I guess you could go to a white shop but nobody would go if they were colored."[60]

On the other hand, by observing the habits and style of successful African-American tourists on Congress Street and elsewhere at the spa during the summer months, black Saratogians also gained an expanded view of black achievement and potential. "Hundreds of African-Americans from all parts of the country have gathered for the [1924] season's sports and are added features to the gaiety of the celebrated summer resort," screamed the *Inter-state Tattler*, a black "society" gossip newspaper.[61] This publication's logo, a radio transmitter receiving communications from Chicago, Washington, D.C., Havana, London, Paris, and *Saratoga Springs*, was in fact an indicator of the resort's appeal to leisured, successful African Americans during the 1920s for sure and even in earlier years. Former Louisiana acting lieutenant governor and U.S. senator P. B. S. Pinchback, for instance, frequented the spa during the prewar years. Charles Anderson, onetime supervisor of accounts for the New York Racing Commission and the recognized leader of black Republicans in New York State until his retirement in 1934, was yet another distinguished African American who visited the spa and even dropped by Jack's Cabaret. By their personal styles, such types exuded a level of prosperity and social achievement rare among blacks nationally but especially among year-round Afro-Saratogians. Pinchback appeared at the spa "draped in silks and tweeds, a shower of large bills falling in swank restaurants, on gaming tables, and at the race track." Similarly, Anderson was a cultured, bright figure, known for his Shakespearean allusions, familiarity with English poetry, and preference for talking politics "over a glass of champagne." It did not matter that Anderson was self-educated or that his most important official position was that of collector of internal revenue for New York. To Afro-Saratogians, he was affluent, cultured, and influential. Young, goal-oriented, local blacks who spent their summer watching such people from a distance were inspired by their example and presence to hope for more successes and fulfillments than those that normally came to local community members.[62]

A youthful Edna Bailey Miller was one of the watchers. She observed at night from her brother's parked car near Congress Park. She watched as a local correspondent for the *Inter-state Tattler*. And she watched from the church her father pastored. One of the summer parishioners at Dyer-Phelps was J. R. Bishop, head bellman at the Grand Union Hotel since roughly 1904, whose Hampton Institute training brought him into regular summer contact with Peabody while in Saratoga Springs. Miller recalled: "Mr. Bishop . . . was really a nice man. . . . He helped our church when he used to put on programs with [his] men. They could sing in quartets. And he had some connection . . . with Yaddo . . . in the days when George Foster Peabody was living. [Mr. Bishop] would have them give a program at our church." Edna Bailey Miller's contact with important, influential, trained African Americans surely helped shape her aspiration "to grow up to be like [them] one day." Watching the summer elites and absorbing the lessons they carried about a wider world of race possibilities, she declared: "Lord, please don't take me in August!"[63]

Summer workers also enhanced African-American church life in the spa. Edna Bailey Miller estimated that by the first Sunday of each August, nearly 500 people crowded into Dyer-Phelps (its normal enrollment figure stood at roughly 200 during the late 1920s). The overflow consisted largely of black tourists and seasonal workers who chose to attend Sunday evening services after leaving their jobs for the day. The church pastors even designed sermons and programs specifically for hotel and track workers. For what was its "largest service of the [1930] season," Dyer-Phelps divided its seating into two sections—the right side for United States Hotel employees and the left side for Grand Union Hotel employees. In other years, separate program days were arranged for United States Hotel employees, Grand Union Hotel employees, and racetrack employees. These special programs generally were held in August, as the season drew to a furious, fast-paced close. Thus, an apex in local church life coincided with the climax of summer activities.[64]

Saratoga's African-American summer hotel workers, moreover, organized their own social clubs and held their own social events. For hotel employees, these annual social rituals affirmed their inclusion and status within the guild of black service workers. Although the sphere of activities represented a separate world, local black permanent residents participated both directly— if they were hotel employees or invited to attend the affairs—and vicariously. In August 1874, the United States Hotel Social Circle, consisting of black staff members, sponsored a grand ball at the town hall. In August 1883, the United States Hotel Waiters' Club held its eighth annual reception at the town hall. In July 1888, a glee club of Columbian Hotel waiters gave an in-house concert for guests. During the summer of 1888, the Grand Union Invincibles, a black employees' group, organized several receptions and topped off the season with a big August event at the town hall. In August 1896, United States Hotel waiters held their annual cakewalk.[65]

In comparison, while Newport was not entirely lacking in special summer gaiety, young black Newporters were not as dependent on summer to supply a roster of inspirational role models. A perusal of the charter members of the NAACP branches in the two towns shows that although elites—those with skilled, nonmanual, and/or year-round employment—monopolized the political leadership in both towns, in Newport this group consisted of more indigenous black professionals (see tables 10 and 11 in chapter 3). Besides the usual ministers of the black churches, in Newport the elite included pharmacist Cromwell West and dentist Alonzo Van Horne. In addition, on any given day of the year, young black Newporters might catch a glimpse of one of *their own* elites, like Dr. Wheatland, in action. He was, in fact, "a familiar sight . . . carrying a box with X-ray equipment to and from the homes of the rich."[66] The relative dearth of year-round possibilities for professional and other well-paying, esteemed employment in the spa prompted Ed Pilkington to leave Saratoga Springs and resettle in New York City shortly after graduating high school in 1924. Yet for four years, he returned to his hometown during the annual three-month touring spell—and *not* necessarily for the work. He explained: "Saratoga in the summer, boy, had a magnetic effect! You were just drawn to it—the excitement of the community at that time!"[67] In contrast, it does not appear that summer occasioned as marked a metamorphosis in the richness of the social matrix for Newport's African-American community.

But summer did make this difference for both Afro-Newporters and Afro-Saratogians: it helped spark political activity. For instance, only nine of twenty-five members of the 1872 Rallying Committee that had supported incumbent President Grant were year-round Saratogians. Instead, the majority consisted of "colored waiters, a very respectable and influential class who came [to Saratoga] for a month in the summer."[68] In 1915, when Newport's Marcus Wheatland decided to engage Mrs. Butler Wilson—wife of the prominent black Boston attorney associated with the NAACP national president, Moorfield Storey—to speak before "a group of influential people in one of the houses in Newport" regarding the establishment of a local NAACP branch, he was planning in all likelihood to appeal to the affluent summer people for support.[69] This was similar to Washington's reliance on Saratoga Springs's tourists to underwrite his program. And the successful membership drive for the Newport NAACP in 1920 took place in August.[70]

The Saratoga Springs NAACP branch especially flourished during the summer and languished in winter as seasonal workers—many of them elites within the spa's black world—swelled and thinned the ranks of the organization with their arrival and exit. NAACP records, for example, reveal that one James Pride, an early member, listed Washington, D.C., as his permanent residence; he was obviously a seasonal worker. And in 1930, one H. J. McKinney, a United States Hotel employee, wrote to R. W. Bagnall, NAACP director of branches, requesting NAACP literature to address the entire black staff of the United States Hotel regarding the work of the organization. Apparently no local chapter was operative; and, significantly, McKinney was an Indiana resident.[71] Z. Marshall Cochrane, secretary of the Saratoga chapter in 1926, wrote to NAACP headquarters in the fall of that year, confirming the seasonal nature of NAACP work and black organizational life in general at the spa:

> In spite of the efforts of the officers of the local branch, we find it quite difficult to hold meetings now. Many of our members have gone away, while others do not seem to have much interest in racial pride to attend meetings regular. Our meetings have always been most interesting and of short duration, yet, strive as we may, we can't seem to interest the colored people here.

> We shall plan for a reception or get-together party in the near future and
> possibly this may help. Saratoga is a peculiar place insofar as in summer
> everyone is too busy to attend meetings while in winter a majority of the
> people are out of town, and it is difficult therefore to obtain even a quorum
> for meetings, . . . not only N.A.A.C.P. meetings but meetings of all local
> organizations—Masons, Odd Fellows, Elks, etc., etc. I am a Masonic officer
> and I think I know of what I speak.[72]

The crowded summer work schedules of Afro-Saratogians did not inhibit
black voluntarism in quite the manner Cochrane described, however. While
steady club attendance may have been difficult for many workers, and while
preoccupations with moneymaking may have precluded the *regular, ongoing*
pursuit of specific political programs, the fact is that African-American
associational life, formal and informal, was greatly enlivened during the
warm-weather months in the spa by the presence of white and black tourists
and by black seasonal hotel workers to a far greater extent than in Newport.

⟨⟨❦⟩⟩

Clubs, churches, fraternal orders, and their women's auxiliaries shaped the
contours of a normative social world and outlook for African Americans in
the resort towns. This perspective—decidedly bourgeois with its emphasis on respectable labor, female domesticity, and exemplary deportment as
membership requirements and as explicit messages and in its support of
black businesses—mirrored that of the white middle class. In this regard, the
black communities of Newport and Saratoga Springs repeated patterns
found among African Americans in other urban places of the period. At the
same time, the prescription offered by these organizations exceeded mere
imitation of white models. It represented separate, autonomous black sensibilities with regard to worship preferences, governance, proper estimation
of black women, and pressing political issues of the day. Race advancement
loomed large on the agendas of *all* of these organizations but especially for
the churches for whom pastors served as spokesmen, despite the country's
indifference to the civil liberties of African-American people.

Afro-Saratogians and Afro-Newporters alike shrewdly determined strategies with an eye to accessible resources and likely returns. Small in size and
possessing a comparatively transient leadership class, black Saratogians at
first rode the crest of Republican fervor regarding civil rights but then

retreated to a more measured emphasis on self-help as such fervor waned and as local philanthropists allied themselves directly with the Booker T. Washington formula. Afro-Saratogians turned instead to personalized requests for white benevolence. The appearance of an NAACP branch late in the period, while reflecting the militant ambience of the post–World War I period, seemed to be a largely symbolic development in view of the fact that so many of its supporters were seasonal workers. This political pattern resulted in sporadic, individualized achievements but no systemic gains for the black community in Saratoga Springs. Black Newporters also began the period optimistic about race progress. But blessed with an enduring core of politically sophisticated and connected integrationist leaders and larger in number than their Saratogian counterparts, Afro-Newporters pushed the race program on several fronts—through moralistic self-uplift efforts, the development of black business, marshaling the black electorate, representation in municipal posts, and pressure for civil-rights legislation. By the period's end, Newport's strategy proved more effective in carrying "the race" closer to an equal standing with local whites.

In both towns, the summer functioned as an important variable, supplying the resources for a heightened sense of group identity and political efficacy as African-American seasonal workers and tourists augmented their ranks and as white guests underwrote their cause. But Saratoga Springs felt the difference made by the tourist season more deeply than did Newport, which had more indigenous and persistent assets.

CONCLUSION

THE LIVES OF THE BLACK MEN AND WOMEN WHO PEOPLED NEWPORT and Saratoga Springs combine in a story that is at once American and uniquely African American. It is implicitly the story of how nineteenth- and early twentieth-century Americans, driven by economic imperatives and enlarged social aspirations, increasingly abandoned farming to participate in a complex urbanization process in which resort towns emerged as secondary urban places specializing in leisure as a commodity, a by-product of the wealth generated in larger, industrial cities. It is the story of how some of these Americans, the African Americans, figured in this process as mainly service and manual laborers deprived by prejudice and practice of more remunerative forms of employment and of equal civic engagement. It is the story of how the African Americans in the resort towns organized their rhythms, their routines, and their communities within the structures and limitations imposed on them from without to create a meaningful identity for themselves.

Solomon Northup's preenslavement years in New York State are illustrative in that they demonstrate the seemingly inescapable draw of the urban nexus and the more specific appeal of resort towns to African Americans.

Born in 1808 as a free black in upstate New York, Northup labored alongside his father, a farmworker. However, soon after his father's passing, a recently married Northup began his steady move away from rural industry to urban pursuits, initially as a response to family financial pressures. During the first winter months after his marriage, he busied himself helping to repair the Champlain Canal—significantly, an interurban transportation mode. He next secured contracts for the transport of timber by raft from Lake Champlain to Troy, New York—a regional commercial center. But Northup's growing contact with cities was not solely commercially driven during these years. Pleasure-seeking also prompted it, for he reported on a sightseeing trip to Montreal, where he "visited the cathedral and other places of interest in that city" and "from whence [he] continued [his] excursion to Kingston and other towns." Falling back on old habits two years after his marriage, he took a farm in Washington County, New York, where he "toiled laboriously in the field"; but, within three years, he and his wife could not resist the economic opportunities in nearby towns. Anne, a celebrated cook, found work in Sandy Hill (present-day Hudson Falls), the county seat, "during court weeks, and on public occasions . . . at high wages in the kitchen" at a local coffeehouse. During winters, musician Solomon "had numerous calls to play on the violin . . . throughout the surrounding villages [where his] fiddle was notorious." Recalling these urban engagements, Solomon remarked, "we always returned home from the performances of these services with money in our pockets." Ultimately, "the flattering anticipations" of city life "seduced" the Northups "from the quiet farm house, on the east side of the Hudson." Giving up agricultural employment altogether, they "removed to Saratoga Springs . . . and occupied a house" where Solomon not only found work but also regularly enjoyed the emerging urban routines of conspicuous consumption and display by strolling "through the streets and groves of Saratoga" with his children "clad in their best attire."[1] The city and the more specialized resort town thus offered ripe opportunities for Northup and his family in their version of the classic American quest for self-betterment broadly understood. As Northup was drawn to the spa in the antebellum years, so were other blacks lured to it and to Newport in the period following the Civil War and into the twentieth century.

To the extent that it repeated many contemporary patterns of African-American history, Northup's phase of life as a resident and servant to the enleisured in a resort town exemplifies still another theme in the narrative of the previous pages. Living and working in a small resort town in the North automatically classified Northup and the African Americans studied here as atypical against the larger backdrop of black American history. Yet, the everyday lives of Afro-Saratogians and Afro-Newporters duplicated the general black American experiences on several important counts—a fact that Northup rightly recognized when he described his life in the spa as presenting "nothing whatever unusual—nothing but the common hopes, and loves, and labors of an obscure colored man, making his humble progress in the world."[2] Poor, stigmatized by whites, and desiring proximity to workplaces and cultural establishments, African Americans in the two resorts clustered in mean, modest streets and in neighborhoods in which they represented a discernibly separate class of resident. They worked predominantly at unskilled and personal-service tasks as they did elsewhere in the nation. They participated in local race-segregated and race-oriented clubs, institutions, and activities, just as blacks did in other places. And inasmuch as a number of these associations—churches, lodges, guilds, and business organizations in particular—were organized nationally, the level of conscious connection and proud identification with a larger African-American world could be quite deep for black Saratogians and black Newporters. The summer season often intensified the race link as it swelled the black population with tourists and workers, and as the influx of influential, affluent, and sometimes sympathetic whites facilitated black political work.

At the same time, many unique details of black American life surfaced in this investigation of Newport and Saratoga Springs—details that may be related to structural aspects of the resort towns as urban places. The size, household structures, birthplace diversity, persistence, and wealth of the black communities varied directly with the health and relative importance of the tourist trade. As the resort economies prospered and suffered, the numbers of African Americans in both cities grew and declined, respectively. Fewer nuclear families were discovered among African Americans in the two vacation spots prior to 1925 than in other cities in the nation because household composition altered to accommodate seasonal workers—sometimes strangers and sometimes relatives. The supply of unskilled and personal service jobs available drew out-of-state and especially southern-born blacks to the resorts well before the Great Migration. This was especially true in

Newport, where ties to the South were enhanced by cheap sea transportation methods and personalized migration chains, and where the relatively diversified economy was more vibrant than that of Saratoga Springs.

An even more nuanced picture of African-American life results from comparison of the two resorts. Newport's stronger economy also served as a grounding force on the African-American residents, who were more likely to stay in their city from decade to decade than their Saratogian counterparts. Newport's more diversified economy supported a larger number of year-round, resident black professionals and elites than could be found in Saratoga Springs. The relative salience of black elites in the resorts in turn determined the quality of cultural, social, and political life in the seaport and the spa. Black life in Newport developed far richer dimensions than that in Saratoga Springs because of the larger number of African Americans privileged with the time, money, education, personal networks, and experience to devote to leadership and volunteer activities on a fairly consistent basis. Black Saratogians, on the other hand, tended to look to temporary summer role models and influences to inspire their community life. An integrationist tradition in Newport, moreover, permitted progressive race-advancement strategies to endure there throughout the period studied, even during the more conservative Washingtonian years, whereas black Saratogians appeared at that time to endorse the accommodationist program entirely.

In all of this, Afro-Saratogians and Afro-Newporters actively shaped their histories. They built neighborhoods and lived in streets close to their churches. The single among them affirmed a sense of racial community by choosing to live with family and other blacks rather than as live-in servants for whites. They rewarded the gainfully and steadily employed among them with high regard even when these workers were generally denigrated as menial laborers in the mainstream class system. They established churches that expressed their varied and special religious sensibilities. They developed social organizations that reflected and nurtured their own self-estimations of gentility and respectability. And, always, they lobbied for wider opportunities.

When viewed from 1870 to 1930 as relatively early receptors of southern migrants and as *small* northern towns, Saratoga Springs and Newport occupy a chronological and conceptual niche linking the agricultural South and the industrial North. In resort communities, seasonal fluctuations in life repeated the yearly vacillations in farm routines. This was especially true in Saratoga Springs, where the ebb and flow of wage-earning activity varied intensely. Southern migrants were well acquainted with the service and un-skilled work performed by most African Americans in the resorts as well. And certainly for those rural newcomers drawn to the farms surrounding Newport, the transition to northern life may have seemed especially easy. For those headed to the large metropolitan areas, Newport offered experiences with diverse (and even a few industrialized) employment options, organized labor, and group political protest. Thus, northward migration and urbanization in the African-American past held fewer discomfiting moments than the conventional narrative suggests.

Finally, there is ample indication from the history of African Americans in Newport and Saratoga Springs during the period explored here that some blacks may have chosen resort towns precisely because of their eclectic nature, especially during "the season." In resorts, black summer tourists did not need to sacrifice "culture" for small-town life. Black seasonal workers enjoyed the mix of profit-making, pastoralism, and a sophisticated social milieu. And when things got a little dull during the winter months for black permanent residents (who apparently preferred things that way), comfort could be taken in the knowledge that summer would return as it always did. During the season, these year-rounders could count on a fairly comprehensive exposure to the optimal range of contemporary African-American possibilities—good-paying service and manual labor, inspiration and leadership from a sprinkling of black elite workers or tourists, a rich separate cultural and social life, and vigorous political agitation. Blacks selected Newport and Saratoga Springs as residences because they offered a season—June, July, and August—that brought them, as African Americans, the closest they could get to achieving the American Dream.

NOTES

Introduction

1. Gilbert Osofsky, *Harlem: The Making of a Ghetto* (New York: Harper and Row, 1971), 12.

2. Edward L. Pilkington, interview by author, 25 June 1983; Edward L. Pilkington to the author, 12 Nov. 1983; Ninth Census of the United States, 1870 (ms.), microfilm reels 1088, 1089, National Archives, Washington, D.C.; Rhode Island State Census, 1925 (ms.), Rhode Island State Office Building, Providence.

3. See, for example, August Meier and Elliott Rudwick, *From Plantation to Ghetto: An Interpretive History of American Negroes* (New York: Hill and Wang, 1966), 1; Joe William Trotter Jr., ed., *The Great Migration in Historical Perspective: New Dimensions of Race, Class, and Gender* (Bloomington: Indiana University Press, 1991), 10–14.

4. On the disruptive impact of northern urbanization on African-American life, see: Osofsky, *Harlem*; Allan H. Spear, *Black Chicago: The Making of a Negro Ghetto, 1890–1920* (Chicago: University of Chicago Press, 1967); Harold X. Connolly, *A Ghetto Grows in Brooklyn* (New York: New York University Press, 1977); Kenneth L. Kusmer, *A Ghetto Takes Shape: Black Cleveland, 1870–1930* (Urbana: University of Illinois Press, 1978), 91–112; W. E. B. Du Bois, *The Philadelphia Negro: A Social Study* (1899; rpt., New York: Schocken Books, 1970); John Bodnar, Roger Simon, and Michael Weber, *Lives of Their Own: Blacks, Italians, and Poles in Pittsburgh, 1900–1915* (Urbana: University of

Illinois Press, 1983); Joe W. Trotter, "African Americans in the City: The Industrial Era, 1900–1950," *Journal of Urban History* 21 (May 1995): 440.

5. See John Blassingame, *The Slave Community: Plantation Life in the Antebellum South* (New York: Oxford University Press, 1979); Albert Raboteau, *Slave Religion: The "Invisible Institution" in the Antebellum South* (New York: Oxford University Press, 1978); Herbert Gutman, *The Black Family in Slavery and Freedom, 1750–1925* (New York: Vintage Books, 1976); Eugene D. Genovese, *Roll, Jordan, Roll: The World the Slaves Made* (New York: Vintage Books, 1976); Lawrence Levine, *Black Culture, Black Consciousness: African-American Folk Thought from Slavery to Freedom* (New York: Oxford University Press, 1977); Deborah Gray White, *Ar'n't I a Woman: Female Slaves in the Antebellum South* (New York: W. W. Norton, 1985).

6. See Elsa Barkley Brown and Gregg D. Kimball, "Mapping the Terrain of Black Richmond," *Journal of Urban History* 21 (Mar. 1995): 296–346; Earl Lewis, "Connecting Memory, Self, and the Power of Place in African American Urban History," *Journal of Urban History* 21 (Mar. 1995): 347–71; Kenneth W. Goings and Gerald L. Smith, " 'Unhidden' Transcripts: Memphis and African American Agency, 1862–1920," *Journal of Urban History* 21 (Mar. 1995): 372–94; Robin D. G. Kelley, " 'We Are Not What We Seem': Rethinking Black Working-Class Opposition in the Jim Crow South," *Journal of American History* 80 (June 1993): 75–112; Robin D. G. Kelley, *Race Rebels: Culture, Politics, and the Black Working Class* (New York: Free Press, 1994); Kenneth W. Goings and Raymond A. Mohl, "The Shifting Historiography of African American Urban History," *Journal of Urban History* 21 (May 1995): 435; Kenneth L. Kusmer, "African Americans in the City since World War II," *Journal of Urban History* 21 (May 1995): 491; Earl Lewis, *In Their Own Interests: Race, Class, and Power in Twentieth-Century Norfolk, Virginia* (Berkeley: University of California Press, 1991); James Borchert, *Alley Life in Washington: Family, Community, Religion, and Folklife in the City, 1850–1970* (Urbana: University of Illinois Press, 1980).

7. See Ira Berlin, *Slaves without Masters: The Free Negro in the Antebellum South* (New York: Oxford University Press, 1974); Joel Williamson, *New People: Miscegenation and Mulattoes in the United States* (New York: New York University Press, 1980); Willard B. Gatewood, *Aristocrats of Color: The Black Elite, 1880–1920* (Bloomington: Indiana University Press, 1990).

8. For the utility of indirect, personalized, psychologically complex, and often deceptive strategies by slaves addressing white owners, see Genovese, *Roll, Jordan, Roll;* Levine, *Black Culture, Black Consciousness.* On strategies in small northern towns, see James E. DeVries, *Race and Kinship in a Midwestern Town: The Black Experience in Monroe, Michigan, 1900–1915* (Urbana: University of Illinois Press, 1984) and Kathryn Grover, *Make a Way Somehow: African-American Life in a Northern Community, 1790–1965* (Syracuse, N.Y.: Syracuse University Press, 1994).

9. See, for example, David Katzman, *Seven Days a Week: Women and Domestic Service in Industrializing America* (New York: Oxford University Press, 1978), 237; Daniel Sutherland, *Americans and Their Servants: Domestic Service in the United States from 1800 to 1920* (Baton Rouge: Louisiana State University Press, 1981), 14–15, 26–34.

Chapter 1: Flattering Anticipations Had Seduced Them

1. Foster Rhea Dulles, *America Learns to Play: A History of Popular Recreation, 1607–1940* (New York: D. Appleton Century, 1940), 4, 16–17, 24, 26, 30, 36, 42–44, 66; Bruce C. Daniels, *Puritans at Play: Leisure and Recreation in Colonial New England* (New York: St. Martin's Press, 1995), esp. 3–26, 75–124, 141, 162, 215–22.

2. Dulles, *America Learns to Play*, 85, 148–49; David R. Goldfield and Blaine A. Brownell, *Urban America: A History* (Boston: Houghton Mifflin, 1990), 77. Goldfield and Brownell's urbanization statistics are based on the nineteenth-century U.S. Census classification of all places of over 2,500 inhabitants as urban. See Stuart M. Blumin, *The Emergence of the Middle Class: Social Experience in the American City, 1760–1900* (New York: Cambridge University Press, 1989), esp. 144–46, on the rise of new leisure institutions.

3. Earl Pomeroy, *In Search of the Golden West: The Tourist in Western Africa* (New York: Alfred A. Knopf, 1957), 32, 43, 47–48, 52, 54, 70.

4. Roderick Nash, *Wilderness and the American Mind* (New Haven, Conn.: Yale University Press, 1967), 44–66; James L. Machor, *Pastoral Cities: Urban Ideals and the Symbolic Landscape of America* (Madison: University of Wisconsin Press, 1987), 121–210. See Peter J. Schmitt, *Back to Nature: The Arcadian Myth in Urban America* (Baltimore: Johns Hopkins University Press, 1990), 20–32, for a treatment of the rural-urban synthesis among nature lovers during the Progressive Era.

5. J. A. R. Pimlott, *The Englishman's Holiday: A Social History* (Sussex, Eng.: Harvester Press, 1976), 22–119, provides a survey of English resort towns from Roman-patronized Bath to sixteenth-century Buxton and nineteenth-century Brighton in which boosters and secularization are critical catalytic forces. See also Rob Shields, *Places on the Margin: Alternative Geographies of Modernity* (London: Routledge, 1991), 75–78; Jeffrey Limerick, Nancy Ferguson, and Richard Oliver, *America's Grand Resort Hotels* (New York: Pantheon Books, 1979), 16; Robert E. Snow and David E. Wright, "Coney Island: A Case Study in Popular Culture," *Journal of Popular Culture* 9 (Spring 1976): 962–63; Charles Funnell, *By the Beautiful Sea: The Rise and High Times of That Great American Resort, Atlantic City* (New York: Alfred A. Knopf, 1975), 119. John F. Sears, *Sacred Places: American Tourist Attractions in the Nineteenth Century* (New York: Oxford University Press, 1989), esp. 3–11, 209–16, discusses the ways in which resorts reflected not only the secularization but also the continuing religious impulses of American society.

6. Dulles, *America Learns to Play*, 202; *Appleton's General Guide to the United States and Canada* (New York: D. Appleton and Co., 1879); *Appleton's Illustrated Handbook of American Winter Resorts* (New York: D. Appleton and Co., 1877), 7, 36, 89, 97; *Appleton's Illustrated Handbook of American Summer Resorts* (New York: D. Appleton and Co., 1886), 136, 138, 147, 177, 180, 184; *American Guidebook for 1859* (New York: H. Balliere, 1859), 30, 35, 37, 39, 52, 61; Charles Humphreys Sweetser, *Book of Summer Resorts* (New York: Evening Mail Office, 1868), 11; Bushrod Washington James, *American Resorts: With Notes upon Their Climate* (Philadelphia: F. A. Davis, 1889), 57–99, 127–45.

7. Nathaniel Bartlett Sylvester, *History of Saratoga County, New York* (Philadelphia: Everts and Ensign, 1878), 148–49; George Waller, *Saratoga: Saga of an Impious Age* (Englewood Cliffs, N.J.: Prentice-Hall, 1966), 29, 49–54; Limerick, Ferguson, and Oliver, *America's Grand Resort Hotels*, 23.

8. Sylvester, *History of Saratoga County*, 152; George Baker Anderson, *Our County and Its People: A Descriptive and Biographical Record of Saratoga County, New York* (Boston: Boston History Co., 1899), 134; Waller, *Saratoga*, 58; William L. Stone, *Reminiscences of Saratoga and Ballston* (New York: R. Worthington, 1880), 58; Limerick, Ferguson, and Oliver, *America's Grand Resort Hotels*, 23.

9. See Sylvester, *History of Saratoga County*, 152; Stone, *Reminiscences of Saratoga*, 63; Melville DeLancey Landon, *Saratoga, 1901* (New York: Sheldon and Co., 1872), 23.

10. Sylvester, *History of Saratoga County*, 152; Waller, *Saratoga*, 62–63; Hugh Francis Bradley, *Such Was Saratoga* (New York: Doubleday, Doran, and Co., 1940), 55, 57–59; Limerick, Ferguson, and Oliver, *America's Grand Resort Hotels*, 23.

11. Sylvester, *History of Saratoga County*, 154; Anderson, *Our County and Its People*, 133–34; Waller, *Saratoga*, 66–67; Bradley, *Such Was Saratoga*, 67; Limerick, Ferguson, and Oliver, *America's Grand Resort Hotels*, 24. For a summary of the historical connections between town incorporation and commercial concerns, see Jon C. Teaford, *The Municipal Revolution in America* (Chicago: University of Chicago Press, 1975), 3–34.

12. *Laws of the State of New York*, chap. 206, sec. 2 (1819), 258; ibid., chap. 504, secs. 1–2 (1851), 943; ibid., chap. 214, sec. 1 (1855), 323; ibid., chap. 428, sec. 1 (1889), 586; ibid., chap. 571, sec. 1 (1895), 378; New York State Constitutional Convention Commission, *New York State Constitution, Annotated*, pt. 1, art. 1, sec. 9 (1915), 7.

13. Waller, *Saratoga*, 81, 119, 126–27, 132.

14. Richmond Barrett, *Good Old Summer Days: Newport, Narragansett Pier, Saratoga, Long Branch, Bar Harbor* (Boston: Houghton Mifflin, 1952), 201, 204; Bradley, *Such Was Saratoga*, 70; Waller, *Saratoga*, 76; Melvin Leighton Heimer, *Fabulous Bawd: The City of Saratoga* (New York: Holt, 1952), 56; T. A. Richards, "Saratoga," *Knickerbocker* 54 (Sept. 1859): 241–56.

15. Anderson, *Our County and Its People*, 176–79; Sylvester, *History of Saratoga County*, 129–30.

16. "One Hundred and Sixty Years of the Music of Francis (Frank) Johnson (1792–1844)," booklet extracted from Charles G. Jones and Lorenzo K. Greenwich, *Leader of the Band* (Saratoga Springs, N.Y.: Historical Society of Saratoga Springs, n.d.), n.p.

17. Sylvester, *History of Saratoga County*, 165–69, 221; Anderson, *Our County and Its People*, 135–36, 185–87; Andrew Boyd, *Boyd's Saratoga Springs Directory for 1868–1869* (Albany, N.Y.: Andrew Boyd, 1868), n.p.

18. James Silk Buckingham, *America: Historical, Statistic, and Descriptive*, 3 vols. (London: Fisher, Son and Co., 1841), 2:441; Barrett, *Good Old Summer Days*, 166–74; Bradley, *Such Was Saratoga*, 77–79; Waller, *Saratoga*, 80–81.

19. Richard M. Bayles, ed., *History of Newport County, Rhode Island* (New York: L. E. Preston, 1888), 353–413, 488; William G. McLoughlin, *Rhode Island: A Bicentennial*

History (New York: W. W. Norton, 1978), 84–98, 100, 112–14; Carl Bridenbaugh, *Cities in Revolt: Urban Life in America, 1743–1776* (New York: Alfred A. Knopf, 1955), 166, 227, 257, 359, 368–70.

20. Bayles, *History of Newport County*, 488–89; McLoughlin, *Rhode Island*, 170.

21. McLoughlin, *Rhode Island*, 170.

22. Bayles, *History of Newport County*, 489; Rhode Island Historical Preservation Committee, "The Kay Street-Catherine Street-Old Beach Road Neighborhood, Newport, Rhode Island" (Providence: Rhode Island Historical Preservation Committee, 1974), 14; May King Van Rensselaer, *Newport: Our Social Capital* (Philadelphia: J. B. Lippincott, 1950), 30.

23. Bayles, *History of Newport County*, 489–90.

24. George Champlin Mason, *Newport Illustrated* (New York: Appleton and Co., 1854), 7.

25. Roger Williams McAdam, *Priscilla of Fall River* (New York: Stephen Daye Press, 1956); Roger Williams McAdam, *The Old Fall River Line* (New York: Stephen Daye Press, 1955); Edwin L. Dunbaugh, *The Era of the Joy River Line: A Saga of Steamboating on Long Island Sound* (New York: Greenwood Press, 1982), 4–15.

26. Van Rensselaer, *Our Social Capital*, 30–33.

27. Cited in Barrett, *Good Old Summer Days*, 165.

28. Snow and Wright, "Coney Island," 964. On "slumming" and the opportunities for flirtations in experimental, "liminal" experiences via resorts, see Shields, *Places on the Margin*, 83–101.

29. Funnell, *By the Beautiful Sea*, 53.

30. Alf Evers, *The Catskills: From Wilderness to Woodstock* (Garden City, N.Y.: Doubleday and Co., 1972), 698.

31. Funnell, *By the Beautiful Sea*, 4; J. Ellis Voss, "Summer Resort: An Ecological Analysis of a Satellite Community" (Ph.D. diss., University of Pennsylvania, 1941), 39, 49; Cleveland Amory, *The Last Resorts* (New York: Harper and Row, 1952).

32. Barrett, *Good Old Summer Days*, 166; Buckingham, *America*, 2:430–31; Samuel DeVeaux, *The Traveller's Own Book to Saratoga Springs, Niagara Falls, and Canada* (Buffalo, N.Y.: Faxon and Read, 1843), 88; Waller, *Saratoga*, 78–79; Snow and Wright, "Coney Island," 964. See also Funnell, *By the Beautiful Sea*, 78, 94–95; Voss, "Summer Resort," 46–49, 136.

33. Ann Vincent Fabian, *Card Shops, Dream Books, and Bucket Shops: Gambling in Nineteenth Century America* (Ithaca, N.Y.: Cornell University Press, 1990), 42–43.

34. Even New York's well-known reformer and staunch champion of Victorian morality, Anthony Comstock, placed gambling rather low on his list of offensive vices, especially given the schizophrenic stance of state laws that permitted horse-race betting while opposing all other forms of gambling. On this, see Heywood Broun and Margaret Leech, *Anthony Comstock: Roundsman of the Lord* (New York: Albert and Charles Boni, 1927), 202–3; Fabian, *Card Shops, Dream Books, and Bucket Shops*, 38–39, 42–43, 46–53.

35. Funnell, *By the Beautiful Sea*, 29–31.

36. David Katzman, *Before the Ghetto: Black Detroit in the Nineteenth Century* (Urbana: University of Illinois Press, 1973), 159; Willard B. Gatewood, *Aristocrats of Color: The Black Elite, 1880–1920* (Bloomington: University of Indiana Press, 1990), 200–202.

37. Voss, "Summer Resort," 39. See, for example, *The Negro Traveler's Green Book* (New York: Victor H. Green and Co., 1961), 56–57.

38. Carroll Greene Jr., "Summertime—In the Highland Beach Tradition," *American Visions* 1 (May/June 1986): 46–50; Benjamin C. Wilson, "Idlewild: A Black Eden in Michigan," *Michigan History* 65 (1981): 33–37; Gatewood, *Aristocrats of Color*, 201–2; Adelaide M. Cromwell, "The History of Oak Bluffs as a Popular Resort for Blacks," *Dukes County Intelligencer* 26 (Aug. 1984): 3–4; Marsha Dean Phelts, *An American Beach for African-Americans* (Gainesville: University Press of Florida, 1997), esp. 1–12.

39. Wilson, "Idlewild," 33–37; Phelts, *An American Beach*, 10–11.

40. Voss, "Summer Resort," 39, 49; Cromwell, "History of Oak Bluffs," 4; Funnell, *By the Beautiful Sea*, 14, 29.

41. See the occupational distribution figures for blacks in northern cities in George Edmund Haynes, *The Negro at Work in New York City* (New York: Columbia University Press, 1912), 42; Harold X. Connolly, *A Ghetto Grows in Brooklyn* (New York: New York University Press, 1977), 12: Kenneth L. Kusmer, *A Ghetto Takes Shape: Black Cleveland, 1870–1930* (Urbana: University of Illinois Press, 1978), 10; Katzman, *Before the Ghetto*, 62; Funnell, *By the Beautiful Sea*, 14. For evidence of the attraction of resort-town jobs for blacks in the South, see David F. Colburn, *Racial Change and Community Crisis: St. Augustine, Florida, 1877–1980* (New York: Columbia University Press, 1985), 18.

42. Eighth Census of the United States, 1860 (ms.), microfilm reels 856, 857, National Archives, Washington, D.C.; Jay Coughtry, *The Notorious Triangle: Rhode Island and the African Slave Trade* (Philadelphia: Temple University Press, 1981), 5–21; Irving H. Bartlett, *From Slave to Citizen: The Story of the Negro in Rhode Island* (Providence, R.I.: Urban League of Greater Providence, 1954), 5–7, 9, 11; Lorenzo Johnston Green, *The Negro in Colonial New England* (New York: Atheneum, 1969), 87–88.

43. Calculations based on U.S. Census, 1860 (ms.).

44. Ibid.

45. Herman D. Bloch, *The Circle of Discrimination: An Economic and Social Study of the Black Man in New York* (New York: New York University Press, 1964), 19–31; Robert J. Cottrol, *The Afro-Yankees: Providence's Black Community in the Antebellum Era* (Westport, Conn.: Greenwood Press, 1982), 119.

46. Van Renssalaer, *Our Social Capital*, 342; Cornelius E. Durkee, *Reminiscences of Saratoga* (reprinted from the *Saratogian;* Saratoga Springs, N.Y., 1928), 203; Stone, *Reminiscences of Saratoga*, 337; Evelyn Barrett Britten, *Chronicles of Saratoga* (Saratoga Springs, N.Y.: Evelyn Barrett Britten, 1959), 475; "Music of Frank Johnson," 13; Stewart is cited in Stone, *Reminiscences of Saratoga*, 169.

47. Sue Eakin and Joseph Logsdon, eds., *Twelve Years a Slave: Solomon Northrup* (Baton Rouge: Louisiana State University Press, 1977), 9.

48. William W. Fox and Mae G. Banner, "Social and Economic Contexts of

Folklore Variants: The Case of Potato Chip Legends," *Western Folklore* 42 (1983): 114–26; Bradley, *Such Was Saratoga*, 122–23; Durkee, *Reminiscences of Saratoga*, 66, 250.

49. Bartlett, *From Slave to Citizen*, 52; Rosalind Wiggins, *The Past: Black Business in Rhode Island from the 1700s into the Twentieth Century* (Providence: Opportunities Industrialization Center of Rhode Island, 1983), 44–47; Charles A. Battle, "Negroes on the Island of Rhode Island" (ms.), Rhode Island Black Heritage Society, Providence, 1932, 35.

50. S. A. M. Washington, *George Thomas Downing: Sketch of His Life and Times* (Newport, R.I.: Milne Printery, 1910), 1–6, 16–17; Lawrence Grossman, "George T. Downing and Desegregation of Rhode Island Public Schools, 1855–1866," *Rhode Island History* 36:4 (1977): 99, 101; Bayles, *History of Newport County*, 594–95.

51. Calculations based on U.S. Census, 1860 (ms.).

52. Gideon Sjoberg, *The Pre-Industrial City* (Glencoe, Ill.: Free Press, 1960), 91–105; David Ward, *Cities and Immigrants: A Geography of Change in Nineteenth-Century America* (New York: Oxford University Press, 1971), 105–7; Sylvester, *History of Saratoga County*, 153.

53. Rhode Island Historical Preservation Committee, "Kay Street–Catherine Street–Old Beach Road Neighborhood," 16; Rhode Island Historical Preservation Committee, "The West Broadway Neighborhood, Newport, Rhode Island" (ms.), Rhode Island Historical Preservation Committee, Providence, 1977, 17–18, 25. See Gary B. Nash, *Forging Freedom: The Formation of Philadelphia's Black Community, 1720–1840* (Cambridge, Mass.: Harvard University Press, 1988), 167, 169, 267, on the role of black churches in black neighborhood formation.

54. U.S. Census, 1860 (ms.); Daniel M. Johnson and Rex R. Campbell, *Black Migration in America: A Social Demographic History* (Durham, N.C.: Duke University Press, 1981), 24–27, 34–35, 37–38.

55. Durkee, *Reminiscences of Saratoga*, 203; Stone, *Reminiscences of Saratoga*, 337; George Champlin Mason, *Reminiscences of Newport* (Newport, R.I.: C. E. Hammett Jr., 1884), 106–7; Van Renssalaer, *Our Social Capital*, 344.

56. Stone, *Reminiscences of Saratoga*, 219–20.

57. George M. Frederickson, *The Black Image in the White Mind: The Debate on African-American Character and Destiny, 1817–1914* (New York: Harper and Row, 1971), 97–129; Stone, *Reminiscences of Saratoga*, 219; Van Renssalaer, *Our Social Capital*, 342.

58. Leon Litwack, *North of Slavery: The Negro in the Free States, 1790–1960* (Chicago: University of Chicago Press, 1961). Melvin Leighton Heimer, *Fabulous Bawd*, 94; Stone, *Reminiscences of Saratoga*, 167; *Saratoga Whig*, 3 Aug. 1855, 3; Howard E. Brooks, "The Negro in Newport, Rhode Island: A Short History" (ms.), Rhode Island Black Heritage Society, Providence, 1946, n.p.; James J. Gordon, "Black Institution Building: A Short History of the Free African Union Society and African Benevolent Society—Newport, Rhode Island, 1780–1824" (ms.), Rhode Island Black Heritage Society, Providence, 1978, 46; Colored Union Church File, Rhode Island Black Heritage Society, Providence; Lee Bensen, *The Concept of Jacksonian Democracy* (Princeton, N.J.: Princeton University Press, 1961), 315, 318; Cottrol, *Afro-Yankees*, 68–77.

59. Anderson, *Our County and Its People,* 280; Sylvester, *History of Saratoga,* 178, 185–86; Durkee, *Reminiscences of Saratoga,* 190.

60. Battle, "Negroes on the Island of Rhode Island," 16; William H. Robinson, ed., *Proceedings of the African Union Society* (Providence: Urban League of Rhode Island, 1976), viii, 1–15; Robert L. Harris, "Early Black Benevolent Societies," *Massachusetts Review* 20 (1979): 609–14; "Report on Newport's Black Churches: 1840–1960" (ms.), Rhode Island Black Heritage Society, Providence, 1985, 6–7.

61. Bartlett, *From Slave to Citizen,* 12; Mason, *Reminiscences of Newport,* 154–56; Van Renssalaer, *Our Social Capital,* 343–44.

62. Cited in Mason, *Reminiscences of Newport,* 156.

63. Ibid., 158–59.

64. Battle, "Negroes on Rhode Island," 17.

65. Ibid.

66. Robinson, *Proceedings of the African Union Society,* 1–15; Harris, "Early Black Benevolent Societies," 609–14.

67. Robinson, *Proceedings of the African Union Society,* 153–96; "Report on Newport's Black Churches," 11–13; Harris, "Early Black Benevolent Societies," 615.

68. Brooks, "Negro in Newport," n.p.; Gordon, "Black Institution Building," 46; Colored Union Church File.

69. Colored Union Church File.

70. Brooks, "Negro in Newport," n.p.; Mt. Zion A.M.E. Church File, Rhode Island Black Heritage Society, Providence; Shiloh Baptist Church File, Rhode Island Black Heritage Society, Providence.

71. Eakin and Logsdon, *Twelve Years a Slave,* 10.

72. Battle, "Negroes on Rhode Island," n.p.; Bartlett, *From Slave to Citizen,* 52; Bradley, *Such Was Saratoga,* 131; Britten, *Chronicles of Saratoga,* 229–31, 336–37, 339–40.

73. Larry Gara, *The Liberty Line: The Legend of the Underground Railroad* (Lexington: University of Kentucky Press, 1961), 2–4; Britten, *Chronicles of Saratoga,* 229–30; Battle, "Negroes on Rhode Island," n.p.; Bartlett, *From Slave to Citizen,* 52.

74. John Hope Franklin, *A Southern Odyssey: Travelers in the Antebellum North* (Baton Rouge: Louisiana State University Press, 1976), 133–34, 143–44, 269.

75. Bartlett, *From Slave to Citizen,* 44.

76. Dudley Taylor Cornish, *The Sable Arm: Negro Troops in the Union Army, 1861–1865* (New York: W. W. Norton, 1966), 6–7, 105–6, 253–54; Sylvester, *History of Saratoga,* 222, 226, 249, 252; Joan Baldwin, "Saratoga County Blacks in the Civil War," *Grist Mill* 21:4 (1987): n.p.; Bartlett, *From Slave to Citizen,* 47–49; Bayles, *History of Newport County,* 428; Benjamin Quarles, *Black Abolitionists* (New York: Oxford University Press, 1960).

77. Washington, *George Thomas Downing,* 1–4; Grossman, "George T. Downing," 100–101.

78. Grossman, "George T. Downing," 101–4. See Cottrol, *Afro-Yankees,* 68–85, on the black-Whig coalition in Rhode Island.

79. On Downing's involvement in antebellum Rhode Island politics, see Cottrol,

Afro-Yankees, 92, 95—96, 98—99, 106. On the black-abolitionist alliance in Rhode Island, especially surrounding the Dorr Rebellion—the antebellum suffrage struggle between working-class blacks and whites—see Cottrol, *Afro-Yankees,* 63—64, 68—85, and Marvin Gettleman, *The Dorr Rebellion: A Study of American Radicalism, 1833—1849* (New York: Random House, 1973), 44—49, 53, 104, 129—30. On the civil rights component of black abolitionism, see Benjamin Quarles, *Black Abolitionists* (New York: Oxford University Press, 1969); C. Peter Ripley, Roy E. Finkebine, Michael F. Hembree, and Donald Yacovone, eds., *Witness for Freedom: African American Voices on Race, Slavery, and Emancipation* (Chapel Hill: University of North Carolina Press, 1993), 65—68. On abolitionist activity among Boston blacks specifically, see James Oliver Horton and Lois E. Horton, *Black Bostonians: Family Life and Community Struggle in the Antebellum North* (New York: Holmes and Meiers Publishers, 1979), 93—96. General overviews of abolitionism and the centrality of Boston include Martin Duberman, ed., *The Anti-Slavery Vanguard: New Essays on the Abolitionists* (Princeton, N.J.: Princeton University Press, 1965) and Aileen S. Kraditor, *Means and Ends in American Abolitionism: Garrison and His Critics on Strategy and Tactics, 1834—1850* (New York: Pantheon Books, 1969).

Chapter 2: They Removed and Occupied a House

1. The manuscript schedules of the federal census were consulted for the following years: 1870, 1880, 1900, and 1910. State census figures for New York and Rhode Island, generally gathered deciduously five years after the federal census during the period under investigation here, were targeted as substitutes for the missing 1890 federal census and for those post-1910 manuscript federal census records unavailable at the time of my census research in the early 1980s. For the 1890s, I therefore examined the 1892 New York State manuscript census schedules. The unusual timing of this particular state census is explained by the fact that an 1885 state census had not been taken because of the inability of state officials to agree on enumeration questions. A consensus was not reached until after 1890, when officials decided to proceed quickly with a census in 1892 and forego an 1895 count. No Rhode Island State census was available for the decade of the 1890s, however. New York and Rhode Island state manuscript census records were consulted for 1925 as well.

2. Daniel M. Johnson and Rex R. Campbell, *Black Migration in America: A Social Demographic History* (Durham, N.C.: Duke University Press, 1981), 57—58; Margo J. Anderson, *The American Census: A Social History* (New Haven, Conn.: Yale University Press, 1988), 68—69, 89—90.

3. Ninth Census of the United States, 1870 (ms.), microfilm reels 1088, 1089, National Archives, Washington, D.C.; Tenth Census of the United States, 1880 (ms.), microfilm reels 928, 929, National Archives, Washington, D.C.; Eighth Census of the United States, 1860 (ms.), microfilm reels 856, 857, National Archives, Washington, D.C.; Emma Waite Diary, 1870, New York State Library, Manuscripts and Special Collections, Albany, N.Y.; Melville DeLancey Landon, *Saratoga, 1901* (New York: Sheldon and Co., 1872), 37.

4. Margaret Daggs Caron, interview by author, June 1992. During this interview, Ms. Caron recalled her friendship with the mother of black 1950s rock-and-roll star Frankie Lymon, who owned a summer house in the Bryantville section of Saratoga Springs.

5. New York State Census, 1925 (ms.).

6. Hugh Francis Bradley, *Such Was Saratoga* (New York: Doubleday, Doran, and Co., 1940), 182; Grace Maguire Swanner, *Saratoga: Queen of the Spas* (Utica, N.Y.: North Century Books, 1988), 150–68.

7. George Waller, *Saratoga: Saga of an Impious Age* (Englewood Cliffs, N.J.: Prentice-Hall, 1966), 228.

8. Ibid.

9. Ibid., 132, 134, 140–41, 160, 228.

10. Ibid., 228–29.

11. Laws on horse-race betting for the period are reviewed and summed up in the 1938 report of the New York State Constitutional Convention Committee, *Problems Relating to Legislative Organization and Powers*, chap. 15, 420–31.

12. Waller, *Saratoga*, 233, 235, 268–69, 272; Richmond Barrett, *Good Old Summer Days: Newport, Narragansett Pier, Saratoga, Long Branch, Bar Harbor* (Boston: Houghton Mifflin, 1952), 203–23, 221; Bradley, *Such Was Saratoga*, 231, 256–62.

13. Heywood Broun and Margaret Leech, *Anthony Comstock: Roundsman of the Lord* (New York: Albert and Charles Boni, 1927), 206. Some historians have suggested that Canfield expected the casino's closing to result in a noticeable drop-off in the local trade—which would then force business-minded authorities to relent in their campaign against gambling—but that this strategy was undermined by the success of the track. This plan might have worked had track and casino interests been linked as they had been under John Morrissey, who owned both, and whose arrangement continued after his death until his successor, William Spencer, sold 90 percent of the track to Gottfried Waldbaum in 1890. On this, see Bradley, *Such Was Saratoga*, 226; Waller, *Saratoga*, 232.

14. Bradley, *Such Was Saratoga*, 203–5, 223; Waller, *Saratoga*, 228–29, 232, 269.

15. Waller, *Saratoga*, 282–93; Bradley, *Such Was Saratoga*, 281–301.

16. See Cleveland Amory, *The Last Resorts* (New York: Harper and Bros., 1952), 340, on black workers in one of the new resorts; see Lena Williams, "Rebuilding a Haven Called Ninevah," *New York Times*, 12 May 1994, C1, C10, on the black community of Sag Harbor, Long Island. In a piece providing job-related information for waiters, the black newspaper *Freeman*, 15 Sept. 1900, 3, reported that "Saratoga Springs, N.Y. was at one time America's greatest summer resort, but it may now be classed as a 'has been'."

17. Waller, *Saratoga*, 293–96; Hansi Durlach and Stuart M. Blumin, *The Short Season of Sharon Springs: Portrait of Another New York* (Ithaca, N.Y.: Cornell University Press, 1980), 56–57.

18. Florette Henri, *Black Migration: Movement North, 1900–1920* (Garden City, N.Y.: Anchor Press, 1975), 49–80, 132–73.

19. Amory, *Last Resorts*, 181–85, 188–89.

20. Richard O'Connor, *The Golden Summers: An Antic History of Newport* (New York: G. P. Putnam's Sons, 1974), 105; Barrett, *Good Old Summer Days*, 38–43; Ward McAllister, *Society As I Have Found It* (New York: Cassell Publishing, 1890), 355–56; Amory, *Last Resorts*, 200.

21. McAllister, a member of the Georgia branch of the Rhode Island and New England Ward clan, bought Bayside Farm, a Newport estate, in 1853. In the immediate postbellum period, McAllister joined with Caroline (Mrs. William Backhouse) Astor, wife of the grandson of New York patrician John Jacob Astor, to mediate the mounting scuffle among America's social elite—divided among "nobs"—wealthy descendants of early American aristocrats—and "swells"—industrialist nouveaux riches and their families. In 1872, at Mrs. Astor's prompting, McAllister produced a list of "patriarchs" to form a committee for the purpose of composing the guest rosters for all society functions. As the undisputed society leader, Mrs. Astor held final veto and affirmation power concerning those admitted to the privileged circle of the fashionable. On this, see O'Connor, *Golden Summers*, 37–66; May King Van Rensselaer, *Newport: Our Social Capital* (Philadelphia: J. B. Lippincott Co., 1905), 33; May King Van Rensselaer, *The Social Ladder* (New York: Henry Holt and Co., 1924), 228–30, 232–41; McAllister, *Society As I Have Found It*, 3–10, 31–74, 107–20, 123–36, 207–17, 335–45; Barrett, *Good Old Summer Days*, 15–18, 34–36; Amory, *Last Resorts*, 185–90.

22. This is fully documented in the next chapter's discussion of blacks as steamboat workers.

23. O'Connor, *Golden Summers*, 287–90; Amory, *Last Resorts*, 228; *Newport Mercury*, 22 June 1918, 1; Nancy F. Cott, *The Grounding of Modern Feminism* (New Haven, Conn.: Yale University Press, 1987), 55–56, 75, 78, 128.

24. Council of Community Services of Northeastern New York, *West Side Neighborhood Needs Assessment* (Saratoga Springs, N.Y.: Council of Community Services of Northeastern New York, 1981), 10–11.

25. Ibid, 11.

26. *Saratoga Journal*, 2 June 1883, 3; Ernest P. Jackson, interview by author, 30 June 1983; Edna Bailey Miller, interview by author, 21 June 1983.

27. Gary B. Nash, *Forging Freedom: The Formation of Philadelphia's Black Community, 1720–1840* (Cambridge, Mass.: Harvard University Press, 1988), 167–69.

28. *Saratogian*, 22 Feb. 1988, 1A.

29. Miller, interview by author, 21 June 1983.

30. See Waller, *Saratoga*, 335–36, on the exhaustion of the springs.

31. New York State Census, 1925 (ms.); tax records for the City of Saratoga Springs, New York 1925, Office of the City Historian, Saratoga Springs, N.Y. (In the city tax records for 1920 and 1925, the name of this area is "Out Brandeville."); Miller, interview by author, 21 June 1983.

32. Edna Anderson, interview by author, 16 Oct. 1987; Margaret Daggs Caron, interview by author, 16 Oct. 1987.

33. Joseph John Jackson, interview by author, 20 June 1983.

34. Rhode Island Historical Preservation Committee, "West Broadway Neighborhood, Newport, Rhode Island," 17–20, 30.

35. William Bradford, interview by Regina Anderson, 25 July 1977, Rhode Island Black Heritage Society, Providence; Leonard Panaggio, interview by author, 25 July 1983.

36. "West Broadway Neighborhood, Newport, Rhode Island," 25.

37. Richard Berry, interview questionnaire to the author, 20 Jan. 1992; Richard Berry, interview questionnaire to the author, 11 Mar. 1992; Rhode Island State Census, 1925 (ms.).

38. Panaggio, interview by author, 25 July 1983; George Turville, *Newport Down Under* (Wakefield, R.I.: HELPS Secretarial Service, 1977), 18.

39. Turville, *Newport Down Under*, 18–19. The West, Tabb, Ross, Tate, and Wigginton families were confirmed as black residents of Edgar Court in the Rhode Island Census, 1925 (ms.).

40. Turville, *Newport Down Under*, 15. The Yates, Williams, Major, and Sutler families, along with Mrs. Leadbetter and Mrs. Harris, were confirmed as black residents of De Blois Street in the Rhode Island State Census, 1925 (ms.).

41. Colored Union Church file, Rhode Island Black Heritage Society, Providence; H. N. Jeter, *Historical Sketch of the Shiloh Baptist Church at Newport, R.I., and the Pastors Who Have Served* (Newport, R.I.: B. W. Pearce–Newport Enterprise, 1891), 11; Lyle Matthews, interview by Regina Anderson, July 1977, Rhode Island Black Heritage Society, Providence. The U.S. Census, 1900 (ms.) confirms that Thomas Glover was a landlord.

42. *Saratogian*, 15 June 1888, 5; *Newport Mercury*, 22 June 1901, 1.

43. The 1925 New York State census *did* include a question on nativity, but the enumerator simply indicated *country* of birth rather than state of birth.

44. Here, the "Upper South" includes Maryland, Virginia, the District of Columbia, Delaware, West Virginia, and North Carolina. See Johnson and Campbell, *Black Migration*, 77, for discussion of regionally determined destinations of northward-bound African Americans.

45. *New York Age*, 10 May 1890, 4; Miller, interview by author, 21 June 1983; Edna Bailey Miller, interview by author, 26 June 1989. Amory, *Last Resorts*, 340, refers to "the colored servants who worked in the hotel."

46. Carole Marks, *Farewell—We're Good and Gone: The Great Black Migration* (Bloomington: Indiana University Press, 1989), 20–25.

47. Henry N. Jeter, *Twenty-five Years Experience with the Shiloh Baptist Church: Her History* (Providence, R.I.: Remington Printing Co., 1901), 89; Matthews, interview by Regina Anderson, July 1977; U.S. Census, 1900 (ms.); U.S. Census, 1910 (ms.); Lynda J. Morgan, *Emancipation in Virginia's Tobacco Belt, 1850–1870* (Athens: University of Georgia Press, 1992), 25, 208, 229, 283.

48. Peter Gottlieb, *Making Their Own Way: Southern Blacks' Migration to Pittsburgh, 1916–30* (Urbana: University of Illinois Press, 1987), 22–23, 26; Matthews, interview by

Regina Anderson, July 1977; *Providence Sunday Journal*, 20 July 1986, A13; U.S. Census, 1900 (ms.).

49. Lewis Phillips, interview by staff member of the Rhode Island Black Heritage Society, 29 Aug. 1979; U.S. Census, 1910 (ms.).

50. Amy Weston, interview by staff member of the Rhode Island Black Heritage Society, 28 Aug. 1979; Rhode Island State Census, 1925 (ms.).

51. Henri, *Black Migration*, 68; Clyde Vernon Kiser, *Sea Island to City: A Study of St. Helena Islanders in Harlem and Other Urban Centers* (New York: Columbia University Press, 1932), 94; Bradford, interview by Regina Anderson, 25 July 1977. The Orange and Alexandria Railroad, which cut a 75-mile, southwest-to-northeast path through the middle of the northern piedmont region in which Culpeper was located, had Alexandria, just across the Potomac River from the nation's capital, as its northern terminus. From there, it was easy to transfer to any of the steamboat lines to the North. On this, see Morgan, *Emancipation in Virginia's Tobacco Belt*, 5.

52. Department of the Interior, Census Office, *Statistics of the Population of the United States at the Tenth Census* (Washington, D.C.: Government Printing Office, 1883), 378. Johnson and Campbell, *Black Migration*, 59, 63–69.

53. Johnson and Campbell, *Black Migration*, 68.

54. These figures are based on a random sample (N=130 for each year) of the black populations of Newport and Saratoga Springs as recorded in the manuscript federal census for the years 1870, 1880, 1900, and 1910. In addition, a similar sample was used in the case of the state census manuscripts for Saratoga Springs for the years 1892 and 1925.

55. Many of those recorded in the census as both black and Portuguese may not have been of European birth but Cape Verdeans or enumerators simply naming the mother country as the place of birth. On Cape Verdean migration to the United States, see Antonio Carreira, *The People of the Cape Verde Islands: Exploitation and Emigration* (London: C. Hurst and Co., 1982), 4–24, 42–55; Raymond A. Almeida, *Cape Verdeans in America* (Boston: American Committee for Cape Verde, 1978), 48–51; Rhett Jones, "The Beginning of the Road: Patterns of Black Migration into Rhode Island" (ms.), Rhode Island Black Heritage Society, Providence, 1983, 2; Raymond A. Almeida and Patricia Nyhan, *Cape Verde and Its People: A Short History* (Boston: American Committee for Cape Verde, 1976), 20–21; Ministry of Economic Development, *Cape Verde Islands* (Paris: Editions Delroisse, n.d.), xxii; Marilyn Halter, *Between Race and Ethnicity: Cape Verdean American Immigrants, 1860–1965* (Urbana: University of Illinois Press, 1993), 3–17, 163–77.

56. Herbert Gutman, *The Black Family in Slavery and Freedom, 1750–1925* (New York: Vintage Books, 1976), 443–44, 448, 451–52, 454–56, 511, 515; Elizabeth H. Pleck, "The Two-Parent Household: Black Family Structure in Late Nineteenth Century Boston," *Journal of Social History* 6 (Fall 1972): 21; Paul J. Lammermaier, "The Urban Black Family of the Nineteenth Century: A Study of Black Family Structure in the Ohio Valley, 1850–1880," *Journal of Marriage and the Family* 35 (Aug. 1973): 451; Frank F. Furstenberg Jr., Theodore Hershberg, and John Modell, "The Origins of the

Female-Headed Black Family: The Impact of the Urban Experience," *Journal of Interdisciplinary History* 7 (Autumn 1975): 215; Darrel E. Bigham, "The Black Family in Evansville and Vandenburgh County, Indiana, in 1880," *Indiana Magazine of History* 75 (June 1979): 136; Darrel E. Bigham, "The Black Family in Evansville and Vandenburgh County, Indiana: A 1900 Postscript," *Indiana Magazine of History* 78 (June 1982): 162.

57. U.S. Census, 1880 (ms.); New York State Census, 1925 (ms.); Rhode Island State Census, 1925 (ms.).

58. John Modell and Tamara K. Hareven, "Malleable Household: An Examination of Boarding and Lodging in American Families," in Michael Gordon, ed., *The American Family in Social-Historical Perspective* (New York: St. Martin's Press, 1978), 56; Gottlieb, *Making Their Own Way*, 72; U.S. Census, 1880 (ms.); U.S. Census, 1900 (ms.).

59. U.S. Census, 1880 (ms.).

60. E. Jackson, interview by author, 30 June 1983; U.S. Census, 1900 (ms.).

61. U.S. Census, 1880 (ms.).

62. Emma Waite Diary, 9, 13, 14, 15, 16 May 1870.

63. *Saratogian*, 14 Aug. 1888, 5.

64. David Katzman, *Seven Days A Week: Women and Domestic Service in Industrializing America* (New York: Oxford University Press, 1978), 95–222.

65. Modell and Hareven, "Malleable Household," 63.

66. Phillips, interview by staff member of Rhode Island Black Heritage Society, 29 Aug. 1979.

Chapter 3: Common Labors

1. U.S. Senate Documents, vol. 66, *Reports of the Immigration Commission: Immigration in Cities* (Washington, D.C.: Government Printing Office, 1911), 1:130, 132.

2. Joseph John Jackson, interview by author, 20 June 1983; Edna Bailey Miller, interview by author, 21 June 1983; Joseph Smith, *Reminiscences of Saratoga or Twelve Seasons at the "States"* (New York: Knickerbocker Press, 1897), 105; Ernest P. Jackson, interview by author, 30 June 1983.

3. Lyle Matthews, interview by Rowena Stewart, [1977?], Rhode Island Black Heritage Society, Providence.

4. Roger Williams McAdam, *The Old Fall River Line* (New York: Stephen Daye Press, 1955), 86; *Fall River Line Journal*, Jan. 1921, 7; Edwin L. Dunbaugh, *The Era of the Joy Line: A Sage of Steamboating on Long Island Sound* (New York: Greenwood Press, 1982), 15–27, 292–310.

5. Roger Williams McAdam, *Priscilla of Fall River* (New York: Stephen Daye Press, 1956), 34.

6. Erick Taylor, interview by Rowena Stewart, 13 July 1977, Rhode Island Black Heritage Society, Providence.

7. Richard Berry, written response to the author's questionnaire, 20 Jan. 1992; Edwin L. Dunbaugh, interview by author, 19 Oct. 1991.

8. Dunbaugh, interview by author, 19 Oct. 1991.

9. Ibid. For a full description of a steward's responsibilities at this time, see John Tellman, *The Practical Hotel Steward* (Chicago: Hotel Monthly, 1900) and John Tellman, *The Practical Hotel Steward*, 4th ed. (Chicago: Hotel Monthly, 1913).

10. Ninth Census of the United States, 1870 (ms.), microfilm reels 1088, 1089, 1472, National Archives, Washington, D.C.; Tenth Census of the United States, 1880 (ms.), microfilm reels 928, 929, 1210, National Archives, Washington, D.C.; Twelfth Census of the United States, 1900 (ms.), microfilm reels 1159, 1505, National Archives, Washington, D.C.; Thirteenth Census of the United States, 1910 (ms.), microfilm reels 1076, 1077, 1437, National Archives, Washington, D.C.; New York State Census, 1925 (ms.); Harvey W. Reid Sr., interview by author, 28 June 1989.

11. Emma Waite Diary, 1870, New York State Library, Manuscripts and Special Collections, Albany, N.Y.; *Saratogian*, 1 Sept. 1874, 2; ibid., 7 July 1904, 5; U.S. Census, 1910 (ms.); *Saratoga Springs Directory, 1895* (Saratoga Springs, N.Y.: Saratogian Co., 1895), 98; *Saratoga Springs Directory, 1905* (Saratoga Springs, N.Y.: Saratogian Co., 1905), 67; *Saratoga Springs Directory, 1915* (Saratoga Springs, N.Y.: Saratogian Co., 1915), 72; U.S. Census, 1880 (ms.); Dunbaugh, interview by author, 19 Oct. 1991. During a slightly earlier period, an 1868 visitor to Newport noted a "sleek mulatto stewardess" who, on receiving women boarding the steamship, "with the pomposity of her dusky lineage, ministers to their various wants" (see "An American Watering Place and Its Frequenters," *London Society* 14 [Sept. 1868], 207).

12. U.S. Census, 1870 (ms.); U.S. Census, 1880 (ms.); U.S. Census, 1900 (ms.); U.S. Census, 1910 (ms.); New York State Census, 1892 (ms.); New York State Census, 1925 (ms.); Rhode Island State Census, 1925 (ms.).

13. Melville DeLancey Landon, *Saratoga, 1901* (New York: Heldon and Co., 1872), 9, 12, 13; D. Evans Saunders, "When Negro Jockeys Ruled the Sport of Kings," *Negro Digest* 10:8 (June 1961), 42–45; Richmond Barrett, *Good Old Summer Days: Newport, Narragansett Pier, Saratoga, Long Branch, Bar Harbor* (Boston, Houghton Mifflin, 1952), 152; Jesse Lynch Williams, "Saratoga and Its People," *Outing* 41 (Dec. 1920), 269, 275; *Saratogian*, 2 June 1888, 3; Edna Bailey Miller, interview by author, June 1992; Miller, interview by author, 21 June 1983.

14. U.S. Census, 1870 (ms.); U.S. Census, 1880 (ms.); U.S. Census, 1900 (ms.); New York State Census, 1925 (ms.); *Saratoga Journal*, 3 Aug. 1882, 7; *Saratogian*, 30 July 1920, 1.

15. H. A. Stewart, "We Get Ours in August," *World Outlook* 6 (Jan. 1920): 12; George Waller, *Saratoga: Saga of an Impious Age* (Englewood Cliffs, N.J.: Prentice-Hall, 1966), 275; *Eye on Saratoga*, Feb. 1988, 17; Harvey W. Reid Sr., interview by author, 28 June 1989.

16. E. Jackson, interview by author, 30 June 1983. See Robert S. Wickham, *A Saratoga Boyhood* (Syracuse, N.Y.: Orange Publishing Co., 1948), 18, for a description of the morning newsboy hustle.

17. Edward Pilkington, interview by author, 25 June 1983.

18. U.S. Census, 1910 (ms.); New York State Census, 1925 (ms.); E. Jackson, interview by author, 30 June 1983; Pilkington, interview by author, 25 June 1983.

19. *This Week in Saratoga Life* 2:2 (12 Aug.–19 Aug. 1938): 22; *Directory of Saratoga Springs, 1925* (Saratoga Springs, N.Y.: Saratogian Co., 1925), 46; Paulette Thomas, "Congress Street: It Was Up All Night Long," *Saratogian*, 24 Feb. 1985, sec. A, 1–4; *Inter-state Tattler*, 10 Aug. 1924, 13; ibid., 12 Aug. 1927, 14; ibid., 19 Aug. 1927, 14; *Eye on Saratoga*, Feb. 1988, 17; Anna Massey, interview by author, 23 June 1983; Pilkington, interview by author, 25 June 1983; *Providence Sunday Journal*, 20 July 1986, A-13; Henry N. Jeter, *Twenty-five Years Experience with the Shiloh Baptist Church and Her History* (Providence, R.I.: Remington Printing Co., 1901), 86–87; U.S. Census, 1900 (ms.).

20. William H. Robinson, "Blacks in Nineteenth Century Rhode Island: An Overview" (ms.), Rhode Island Black Heritage Society, Providence, n.d., 134; U.S. Census, 1900 (ms.); U.S. Census, 1910 (ms.); New York State Census, 1925 (ms.); Harvey Fred Reid, interview by author, 27 June 1989; Harvey W. Reid Sr., interview by author, 28 June 1989; *Inter-state Tattler*, 12 Aug. 1927, 14.

21. Harvey Fred Reid, interview by author, 27 June 1989; Harvey W. Reid Sr., interview by author, 28 June 1989. Miller, interview by author, 21 June 1983; Miller, interview by author, 26 June 1989.

22. Jacqueline Jones, *Labor of Love, Labor of Sorrow: Black Women, Work, and the Family from Slavery to the Present* (New York: Basic Books, 1985), 77–78, 90, 111, 128, 184; Elizabeth H. Pleck, "A Mother's Wages: Income Earning among Married Italian and Black Women, 1896–1911," in Michael Gordon, ed., *The American Family in Social-Historical Perspective* (New York: St. Martin's Press, 1978), 495; E. Jackson, interview by author, 30 June 1983.

23. Miller, interview by author, 21 June 1983.

24. Harvey W. Reid Sr., interview by author, 28 June 1989.

25. New York State Census, 1925 (ms.); *Directory of Saratoga Springs, 1925*, 46–47.

26. U.S. Census, 1870 (ms.); George Baker Anderson, *Our County and Its People: A Description and Biographical Record of Saratoga County, New York* (Boston: Boston History Co., 1899), 519–20; New York vol. 560, 348, R. G. Dun & Co. Collection, Baker Library, Harvard University Graduate School of Business Administration, Cambridge, M.A.; *Boyd's Saratoga Springs Directory, 1874–75* (Albany, N.Y.: Andrew Boyd, 1874), 115, 147; *Saratoga Springs Directory, 1875–76* (Saratoga Springs, N.Y.: J. H. Lant, 1875), 117; *Boyd's Saratoga Springs Directory, 1876–77* (Albany, N.Y.: Andrew Boyd, 1876), 149; *Boyd's Saratoga Springs Directory, 1880–81* (Saratoga Springs, N.Y.: Fred Boyd, 1880), 129; *Saratoga Daily Journal*, 29 June 1983, 3.

27. *Kirwin and Williams' Saratoga Springs Directory, 1884–85* (Saratoga Springs, N.Y.: Kirwin and Williams, 1884), 203.

28. *Kirwin and Williams' Saratoga Springs Directory, 1886–87* (Saratoga Springs, N.Y.: Kirwin and Williams, 1886), 203.

29. *Saratoga Weekly Journal*, 22 June 1882, 6.

30. New York State Census, 1925 (ms.); Pilkington, interview by author, 25 June 1983.

31. U.S. Census, 1880 (ms.); U.S. Census, 1900 (ms.); *The Mercantile Agency Reference*

Book, vol. 187 (New York: R. G. Dun & Co., 1919), n.p.; Matthews, interview by Regina Anderson, July 1977; Jeter, *Twenty-five Years Experience*, 89.

32. U.S. Census, 1880 (ms.); U.S. Census, 1900 (ms.); U.S. Census, 1910 (ms.); George Turville, *Newport Down Under* (Wakefield, R.I.: HELPS Secretarial Office, 1977), 6; State of Rhode Island and Providence Plantations, *Second Annual Report of the Factory Inspectors: Inspection of Factories, Mercantile Establishments, and Workshops* (Providence, R.I.: E. L. Freeman and Son, State Printers, 1896), 21; State of Rhode Island and Providence Plantations, *Twelfth Annual Report of the Factory Inspectors: Inspection of Factories, Mercantile Establishments, and Workshops* (Providence, R.I.: E. L. Freeman and Son, State Printers, 1906), 29; State of Rhode Island and Providence Plantations, *Seventeenth Annual Report of the Factory Inspectors: Inspection of Factories, Mercantile Establishments, and Workshops* (Providence, R.I.: E. L. Freeman and Son, State Printers, 1911), 40; State of Rhode Island and Providence Plantations, *Twenty-Second Annual Report of the Factory Inspectors: Inspection of Factories, Mercantile Establishments, and Workshops* (Providence, R.I.: E. L. Freeman and Son, State Printers, 1916), 36; Jeter, *Twenty-five Years Experience*, 84–87; *The Mercantile Agency Reference Book*, vol. 83 (New York: R. G. Dun & Co., 1889), n.p.; *The Mercantile Agency Reference Book*, vol. 88 (New York: R. G. Dun & Co., 1890), n.p.; *The Mercantile Agency Reference Book*, vol. 91 (New York: R. G. Dun & Co., 1891), n.p.; *The Mercantile Agency Reference Book*, vol. 95 (New York: R. G. Dun & Co., 1892), n.p.; *The Mercantile Agency Reference Book*, vol. 181 (New York: R. G. Dun & Co., 1913), n.p.; *Mercantile Agency Reference Book*, vol. 187, n.p.

33. J. Ellis Voss, "Summer Resort: An Ecological Analysis of a Satellite Community" (Ph.D. diss., University of Pennsylvania, 1941), 77, 108–30.

34. U.S. Census, 1880 (ms.); U.S. Census, 1900 (ms.); U.S. Census, 1910 (ms.).

35. Richard O'Connor, *The Golden Summers: An Antic History of Newport* (New York: G. P. Putnam's Sons, 1974), 152–53; William S. Swift, *The Negro in the Offshore Maritime Industry* (Philadelphia: Industrial Research Unit, Wharton School, University of Pennsylvania, 1974), 58–59, 74–75; Walter L. Beasley, "U.S. Naval Training School of Newport," *Scientific American* 92 (18 Feb.1905): 144, 146; U.S. Census, 1880 (ms.); U.S. Census, 1900 (ms.); U.S. Census, 1910 (ms.); Rhode Island State Census, 1925 (ms.). While the 1925 Rhode Island State Census did not generally record occupations, it did specify assignments in the case of naval personnel.

36. U.S. Census, 1880 (ms.); U.S. Census, 1900 (ms.); U.S. Census, 1910 (ms.); Rhode Island State Census, 1925 (ms.); Matthews, interview by Regina Anderson, July 1977.

37. U.S. Census, 1900 (ms.); U.S. Census, 1910 (ms.).

38. U.S. Census, 1900 (ms.); Van Horne Family File, Rhode Island Black Heritage Society, Providence; U.S. Census, 1910 (ms.); Rice Family File, Rhode Island Black Heritage Society, Providence; Black Policeman File, Rhode Island Black Heritage Society, Providence.

39. W. Jeffrey Bolster, " 'To Feel Like a Man': Black Seamen in the Northern States, 1800–1860," *Journal of American History* 76 (Mar. 1990): 1192–99; Martha S.

Putney, "Black Merchant Seamen of Newport, 1803–1865: A Case Study in Foreign Commerce," *Journal of Negro History* 57:2 (1972): 165–68; Lorenzo J. Greene and Carter G. Woodson, *The Negro Wage-Earner* (1930; rpt., New York: AMS Press, 1970), 113; U.S. Census, 1900 (ms.); U.S. Census, 1910 (ms.). For a discussion of the precarious states of black sailors even during the antebellum peak of their involvement in maritime work, see W. Jeffrey Bolster, *Black Jacks: African-American Seamen in the Age of Sail* (Cambridge, Mass.: Harvard University Press, 1997), 158–89.

40. Berry, written response to the author, 20 Jan. 1992; Dunbaugh, interview by author, 19 Oct. 1991; U.S. Census, 1900 (ms.); U.S. Census, 1910 (ms.).

41. The details concerning black churches and their ministers are discussed more fully and documented in the next chapter.

42. Van Horne Family File, Rhode Island Black Heritage Society, Providence; Anna Amelia Smith, *Reminiscences of Colored People of Princeton, N.J.* (Philadelphia: P. V. Baugh, 1913), 8; Jeter, *Twenty-five Years Experience*, 15–16, 48–49; Jeter Family File, Rhode Island Black Heritage Society, Providence.

43. U.S. Census, 1870 (ms.); U.S. Census, 1880 (ms.); New York State Census, 1892 (ms.); U.S. Census, 1900 (ms.); U.S. Census, 1910 (ms.); New York State Census, 1925 (ms.); Miller, interview by author, 21 June 1983.

44. U.S. Census, 1880 (ms.); U.S. Census, 1900 (ms.); U.S. Census, 1910 (ms.); Rhode Island State Census, 1925 (ms.); Marcus F. Wheatland File, Rhode Island Black Heritage Society, Providence; Alan E. Oestreich, "Centennial History of African-Americans in Radiology," *American Journal of Roentgenology* 166:1 (Jan. 1996): 255.

45. Calculations based on U.S. Census, 1870 (ms.); U.S. Census, 1880 (ms.); U.S. Census, 1900 (ms.); U.S. Census, 1910 (ms.); New York State Census, 1925 (ms.); Rhode Island State Census, 1925 (ms.); Stephan Thernstrom, *Poverty and Progress: Social Mobility in a Nineteenth-Century City* (New York: Atheneum, 1977), 84–90.

46. Leslie Woodcock Tentler, *Wage-Earning Women: Industrial Work and Family Life in the United States, 1900–1930* (New York: Oxford University Press, 1979), 59, 139, 142–45; Jones, *Labor of Love, Labor of Sorrow*, 162–64; U.S. Census, 1910 (ms.).

47. William Hamilton Harris, *The Harder We Run: Black Workers since the Civil War* (New York: Oxford University Press, 1982), 24; Jones, *Labor of Love, Labor of Sorrow*, 162; Alice Kessler-Harris, *Out to Work: A History of Wage-Earning Women in the United States* (New York: Oxford University Press, 1982), 123; U.S. Census, 1880 (ms.); U.S. Census, 1910 (ms.). Both Jones and Kessler-Harris discuss this relationship between work opportunities for men, household poverty, and labor-force participation rates for black wives. Also see U.S. Senate Documents, vol. 66, *Reports of the Immigration Commission* (1911), 139.

48. Cleveland Moffett, "Luxurious Newport," *Cosmopolitan* 43 (Aug. 1907): 349–58; Barrett, *Good Old Summer Days*, 32, 115; O'Connor, *Golden Summers*, 255; David Katzman, *Seven Days a Week: Women and Domestic Service in Industrializing America* (New York: Oxford University Press, 1978), 225; Faye E. Dudden, *Serving Women: Household*

Service in Nineteenth-Century America (Middletown, Conn.: Wesleyan University Press, 1983), 108–14; Daniel E. Sutherland, *Americans and Their Servants: Domestic Service in the United States from 1800 to 1920* (Baton Rouge: Louisiana State University Press, 1981), 13–14, 48–49; Greene and Woodson, *Negro Wage-Earner*, 91–92; Matthews, interview by Rowena Stewart, [1977?].

49. Douglas Henry Daniels, *Pioneer Urbanites: A Social and Cultural History of Black San Francisco* (Philadelphia: Temple University Press, 1980), 35–40; Greene and Woodson, *Negro Wage-Earner*, 94–95; Emma Waite Diary, 2, 3 June 1870; S. R. Stoddard, *Lake George (Illustrated) and Lake Champlain: A Book of Today* (Glens Falls, N.Y.: S. R. Stoddard, 1892), 22A. Despite its title, Stoddard's Lake George area guidebook contained information on Saratoga Springs as well.

50. Landon, *Saratoga, 1901*, 9, 12, 13; D. Evans Saunders, "When Negro Jockeys Ruled the Sport of Kings," *Negro Digest* 10:8 (June 1961): 42–45; Barrett, *Good Old Summer Days*, 152; Williams, "Saratoga and Its People," *Outing* 41 (Dec. 1902): 269, 275; *Saratogian*, 2 June 1888, 3.

51. Swift, *Negro in the Offshore Maritime Industry*, 58–59, 74–75; Beasley, "U.S. Naval Training School," 144, 146; U.S. Census, 1880 (ms.); U.S. Census, 1900 (ms.); U.S. Census, 1910 (ms.); Rhode Island State Census, 1925 (ms.). While the 1925 Rhode Island State Census did not generally record occupations, it did specify assignments in the case of naval personnel.

52. Bolster, "To Feel Like a Man," 1192–99; Putney, "Black Merchant Seamen of Newport," 165–68; Greene and Woodson, *Negro Wage-Earner*, 113; U.S. Census, 1900 (ms.); U.S. Census, 1910 (ms.).

53. U.S. Census, 1870 (ms.); U.S. Census, 1880 (ms.); New York State Census, 1892 (ms.); U.S. Census, 1900 (ms.); U.S. Census, 1910 (ms.); Greene and Woodson, *Negro Wage-Earner*, 98–99, 244–45; New York State Census, 1925 (ms.).

54. Robinson, "Blacks in Nineteenth Century Rhode Island," 149; Dorothy C. Salem, ed., *African-American Women: A Biographical Dictionary* (New York: Garland Publishing, 1993), 569; Pilkington, interview by author, 25 June 1983.

55. Stuart Blumin, *The Emergence of the Middle Class: Social Experience in the American City, 1760–1900* (Cambridge: Cambridge University Press, 1989), 258–75; U.S. Census, 1870 (ms.); U.S. Census, 1880 (ms.); New York State Census, 1892 (ms.); U.S. Census, 1900 (ms.); U.S. Census, 1910 (ms.); New York State Census, 1925 (ms.); Mahlon Van Horne, "The Negro in Rhode Island: His Past, Present, and Future" (ms.), Van Horne Family File, Rhode Island Black Heritage Society, Providence, [1880?].

56. Abram L. Harris, *The Negro as Capitalist: A Study of Banking and Business among American Negroes* (New York: Negro Universities Press, 1936), 55, 168–69; Ivan Light, *Ethnic Enterprise in America: Business and Welfare among Chinese, Japanese, and Blacks* (Berkeley: University of California Press, 1972), 19–23, 36–61, 107–69; Charles A. Battle, "Negroes on the Island of Rhode Island" (ms.), Rhode Island Black Heritage Society, Providence, 1932, 35.

57. Rhode Island vol. 1, 62; Rhode Island vol. 3, 123, 230; New York vol. 560, 316, 348; New York vol. 561, 144, 403, all in R. G. Dun & Co. Collection, Baker Library, Harvard University Graduate School of Business Administration, Cambridge, Mass.

58. Pilkington, interview by author, 25 June 1983.

59. Jones, *Labor of Love, Labor of Sorrow*, 164. It should be noted, however, that during the late nineteenth and the early twentieth centuries, black men began to outnumber black women in domestic service occupations in the North; and, in the country as a whole, black men began entering domestic and personal service work at higher rates than did black women between 1890 and 1900 as the former faced restrictive competition in other more remunerative work in their efforts to hold chief breadwinner status within their families. On this, see Greene and Woodson, *Negro Wage-Earner*, 75–76, 78.

60. Donna L. Van Raaphorst, *Union Maids Not Wanted: Organizing Domestic Workers, 1870–1940* (New York: Praeger, 1988), 102.

61. Matthews, interview by Rowena Stewart, [1977?].

62. Hugh Francis Bradley, *Such Was Saratoga* (New York: Doubleday, Doran, and Co., 1940), 310; Stewart, "We Get Ours in August," 13; Waller, *Saratoga*, 362; Robert Sims, interview by author, 9 June 1983; Massey, interview by author, 23 June 1983; E. Jackson, interview by author, 30 June 1983.

63. Miller, interview by author, 21 June 1983; Pilkington, interview by author, 25 June 1983.

64. Mora E. Hammonds, "Newport Blacks in Business" (ms.), Rhode Island Black Heritage Society, Providence, 1982.

65. *Saratogian*, 7 July 1879, 2; E. Jackson, interview by author, 30 June 1983; U.S. Census, 1910 (ms.).

66. Emma Waite Diary, 5 Oct. 1870; J. Jackson, interview by author, 20 June 1983; Smith, *Reminiscences of Saratoga*, 8; Landon, *Saratoga, 1901*, 35.

67. William H. Grimshaw, *Official History of Freemasonry among the Colored People in North America* (1903; rpt., New York: Negro Universities Press, 1969), 241; Richard M. Bayles, *History of Newport County, Rhode Island* (New York: L. E. Preston and Co., 1888), 554; *The Newport Directory, 1885* (Newport, R.I.: Sampson, Murdock, and Co., 1885), 319; *The Newport Directory, 1890* (Newport, R.I.: Sampson, Murdock, and Co., 1890), 288–89, 297; *Newport Directory, 1895* (Newport, R.I.: Sampson, Murdock, and Co., 1895), 322–23.

68. *Newport Directory, 1900* (Newport, R.I.: Sampson, Murdock, and Co., 1900), 343–44, 350; *The Newport Directory, 1905* (Newport, R.I.: Sampson, Murdock, and Co., 1905), 26–29, 33; *The Newport Directory, 1910* (Newport, R.I.: Sampson, Murdock, and Co., 1910), 42–44, 48; *The Newport Directory, 1920* (Newport, R.I.: Sampson, Murdock, and Co., 1920), 115, 117–20; *The Newport Directory, 1925* (Boston: Sampson and Murdock Co., 1925), 36–38; *The Newport Directory, 1930* (Boston: Sampson and Murdock Co., 1930), 42–44.

69. Harris, *Negro as Capitalist*, 21, 47–48; Rhode Island Loan and Investment

Company File, Rhode Island Black Heritage Society, Providence; Matthews, interview by Regina Anderson, July 1977; U.S. Census, 1910 (ms.).

70. U.S. Census, 1900 (ms.); U.S. Census, 1910 (ms.); Matthews, interview by Regina Anderson, July 1977.

71. *Saratoga Springs Directory, 1874–1875*, 153–154; *Boyd's Saratoga Springs Directory, 1880–81*, 216; *Saratoga Springs Directory, 1885–1886* (Saratoga Springs, N.Y.: Henry Huling, 1885), 29; *Kirwin and Williams' Saratoga Springs Directory, 1890* (Saratoga Springs, N.Y.: Kirwin and Williams, 1890), 20–21; *Greater Saratoga Directory, 1895–1896* (Saratoga Springs, N.Y.: Mingay and Regan, 1895), 1:18; *Saratoga Springs Directory, 1895*, 19–20; *Saratoga Springs Directory, 1900* (Saratoga Springs, N.Y.: Saratogian Co., 1900), 22–24; *Saratoga Springs Directory, 1905*, 13; *Saratoga Springs Directory, 1910* (Saratoga Springs, N.Y.: Saratogian Co., 1910), 14–15; *Saratoga Springs Directory, 1915*, 15–16; *Saratoga Springs Directory, 1920* (Saratoga Springs, N.Y.: Saratogian Co., 1920), 19–20; *Saratoga Springs Directory, 1925*, 16–17; *Saratoga Springs Directory, 1930* (Saratoga Springs, N.Y.: Saratogian Co., 1930), 16–17.

72. Harris, *Negro as Capitalist*, 49–53; *Providence Advance*, 28 Aug. 1908, 1.

73. *Saratoga Journal*, 27 July 1882, 7.

74. Clifford L. Miller, "A Negro Student's Summer Vacation," *Independent* 56 (16 June 1904): 1364–65.

75. Miller, interview by author, 21 June 1983; Pilkington, interview by author, 25 June 1983. It is difficult to know what proportion of hotel waiters were college students. A check of the average age of waiters in Saratoga Springs in 1870, 1900, and 1925 yielded the figures twenty-seven, thirty-one, and forty-eight, respectively—figures far too high for a college-age population. Perhaps because they were a distinguished and unusual group among the blacks, the summer waiters who *were* college students stood out in the memories of longtime village residents more than the "ordinary" hotel worker did. It is also possible that these students, as nonresidents of Saratoga Springs, were omitted from the census while in fact constituting a large portion of hotel staffs.

76. Dudden, *Serving Women*, 19–20, 80. U.S. Census, 1900 (ms.); Greene and Woodson, *Negro Wage-Earner*, 80; U.S. Census, 1910 (ms.).

77. Greene and Woodson, *Negro Wage-Earner*, 79–80; Miller, interview by author, 21 June 1983.

78. William Henry Rogers, letter to Dolly Smith, Dolly Smith Papers, Historical Society of Saratoga Springs, Saratoga Springs, N.Y.

79. *Saratogian*, 22 May 1873, 3; Sims, interview by author, 9 June 1983.

80. Miller, "Negro Student's Summer Vacation," 1364.

81. *Inter-state Tattler*, 10 Aug. 1924, 13; Maccannon, *Commanders of the Dining Room: Biographic Sketches and Portraits of Successful Head Waiters* (New York: Gwendolyn Publishing Co., 1904), 65, 81, 83, 163, 169.

82. Stoddard, *Lake George (Illustrated) and Lake Champlain*, 22A; Maccannon, *Commanders of the Dining Room*, 13–19. (This organization's name was changed in 1903 to

Head, Second, and Side Waiters' National Benefit Association after it decided to incorporate side waiters as well.) Burton J. Bledsoe, *The Culture of Professionalism: The Middle Class and the Development of Higher Education in America* (New York: W. W. Norton, 1978), 86–120, 156–57.

83. U.S. Census, 1870 (ms.); U.S. Census, 1880 (ms.); U.S. Census, 1910 (ms.); Landon, *Saratoga, 1901*, 35–37; Maccannon, *Commanders of the Dining Room*, 66–67, 82–83, 162–64, 168–70; McAdam, *Old Fall River Line*, 86; *New York Globe*, 16 June 1883, 3; *(Harrisburg, Pa.) State Journal*, 12 July 1884, 4; *New York Age*, 3 May 1890, 3; ibid., 10 May 1890, 4; ibid., 5 July 1890, 1; *Saratoga Sentinel*, 6 June 1872, 3; *Saratogian*, 1 June 1876, 3; ibid., 25 June 1891, 5.

84. *Newport Directory, 1925* (Boston: Sampson and Murdock Co., 1925), 25; U.S. Census, 1880 (ms.); U.S. Census, 1900 (ms.); U.S. Census, 1910 (ms.); Rhode Island State Census, 1925 (ms.).

85. Turville, *Newport Down Under*, 14.

86. U.S. Census, 1870 (ms.); U.S. Census, 1880 (ms.); New York State Census, 1892 (ms.); U.S. Census, 1900 (ms.); U.S. Census, 1910 (ms.); Greene and Woodson, *Negro Wage-Earner*, 98–99, 244–45; New York State Census, 1925 (ms.).

87. Van Raaphorst, *Union Maids Not Wanted*, 55–94, 100–102, 126–27, 186–219.

88. Van Horne File, Rhode Island Black Heritage Society, Providence.

89. Stephanie J. Shaw, *What a Woman Ought to Be and to Do: Black Professional Women Workers during the Jim Crow Era* (Chicago: University of Chicago Press, 1996), 135–54.

90. Landon, *Saratoga, 1901*, 37; Jeter, *Twenty-five Years Experience*, 84–85.

91. Pilkington, interview by author, 25 June 1983.

92. Ibid.

93. *Saratogian*, 5 July 1908, 2; ibid., 24 July 1918, 2; ibid., 25 Aug. 1908, 2.

94. Smith, *Reminiscences of Saratoga*, 1–2, 4–7.

95. Ibid., 105–6.

96. Katzman, *Seven Days a Week*, 269–79; Maccannon, *Commanders of the Dining Room*, 17.

97. Sutherland, *Americans and Their Servants*, 14–15, 26–34.

98. The historical and sociological literature on the meaning of class within the African-American community is vast. David M. Katzman's *Before the Ghetto: Black Detroit in the Nineteenth Century* (Urbana: University of Illinois Press, 1973), esp. 104–74, 213–16, provides an excellent case study of the historical protocols determining class and caste in the black community. A more recent historical monograph, Stephanie J. Shaw's *What a Woman Ought to Be and to Do: Black Professional Women Workers during the Jim Crow Era*, 135–54, charts the strategies adopted by African-American female professionals in an attempt to resolve the discrepancy between their high-class standing within the black community and their low status in the larger society. The seminal sociological work on class dynamics in African America, E. Franklin Frazier's *Black Bourgeoisie* (New York: Free Press, 1957), by adopting the white bourgeoisie as a standard, is extremely critical of the conventions and self-assessments of the black middle-class world during the segregationist era of American race rela-

tions. This study of Newport and Saratoga Springs, in stark contrast, attempts to explicate the logic and consciousness of black elites within and toward their racialized community.

99. Maccannon, *Commanders of the Dining Room*, 10.

100. Cited in Thomas, "Congress Street," 1A, 4A.

101. Landon, *Saratoga, 1901*, 35, 37; *Saratogian*, 27 Aug. 1888, 3.

102. Cited in McAdam, *Old Fall River Line*, 86.

103. Roger Williams McAdam, *Priscilla of Fall River* (New York: Stephen Daye Press, 1956), 35–36, 95; *Newport Mercury*, 23 July 1892, 1.

104. For a pertinent discussion of leadership culture among late nineteenth-century white professionals, see Bledsoe, *Culture of Professionalism*, 123.

Chapter 4: Common Hopes and Loves

1. George M. Fredrickson, *The Black Image in the White Mind: The Debate on Afro-American Character and Destiny, 1817–1914* (New York: Harper and Row, 1971), 283–319.

2. *Saratogian*, 9 July 1890, 3; ibid., 2 July 1883, 3; ibid., 5 June 1876, 3.

3. Ibid., 22 June 1928, 4; ibid., 23 June 1928, 4; ibid., 27 July 1928, 4.

4. Ibid., 8 May 1924, 2.

5. *Saratoga Daily Journal*, 2 July 1885, 3.

6. *Seventh Annual Report of the Commissioners of the State Reservation at Saratoga Springs, 1916* (Albany: J. B. Lyon Co., 1916), 23.

7. Edward Pilkington, interview by author, 25 June 1983; Melville DeLancey Landon, *Saratoga, 1901* (New York: Heldon and Co., 1872), 4; *Saratogian*, 4 Aug. 1874, 3.

8. May King Van Renssalaer, *Newport: Our Social Capital* (Philadelphia: J. B. Lippincott Co., 1950), 342–43.

9. Lyle Matthews, interview by Regina Anderson, July 1977.

10. Joseph Hergesheimer, "Marble Lily," *Saturday Evening Post* 203 (15 Nov. 1930): 42.

11. W. C. Brownell, "Newport," *Scribner's Magazine* 16 (Aug. 1894): 135, 143.

12. Gouverneur Morris, "Newport the Maligned," *Everybody's* 19 (Sept. 1908): 312.

13. *Newport Mercury*, 21 July 1888, 1; Matthews, interview by Regina Anderson, July 1977; *Newport Journal*, 4 July 1913, 3; ibid., 11 July 1913, 8; Irving H. Bartlett, *From Slave to Citizen: The Story of the Negro in Rhode Island* (Providence, R.I.: Urban League of Greater Providence, 1954), 64–65.

14. Earl Lewis, *In Their Own Interests: Race, Class, and Power in Twentieth-Century Norfolk, Virginia* (Berkeley: University of California Press, 1991), 90–92.

15. George Anderson, *Our County and Its People: A Descriptive and Biographical Record of Saratoga County, New York* (Boston: Boston History Co., 1899), 280; Evelyn Barrett Britten, *Chronicles of Saratoga* (Saratoga Springs, N.Y.: Evelyn Barrett Britten, 1959), 547; Henry H. Jeter, *Historical Sketch of the Shiloh Baptist Church at Newport, R.I., and the Pastors Who Have Served* (Newport, R.I.: R. W. Pearce-Newport Enterprise, 1891), 21, 24; Henry H. Jeter, *Twenty-five Years Experience with the Shiloh Baptist Church and Her History* (Providence, R.I.: Remington Printing Co., 1901), 15; Colored Union Church File;

Mt. Zion African Methodist Episcopal (A.M.E.) Church File; "Report on Black Churches" (ms.), Rhode Island Black Heritage Society, Providence, n.d., 8–20. On the separate foundings of the A.M.E. and A.M.E. Zion churches, see C. Eric Lincoln and Lawrence H. Mamiya, *The Black Church in the African-American Experience* (Durham, N.C.: Duke University Press, 1990), 50–60.

16. *Saratogian*, 28 June 1872, 3; ibid., 16 June 1904, 5; ibid., 2 July 1906, 3; ibid., 27 July 1910, 5; ibid., 17 June 1914, 5; ibid., 6 Aug. 1918, 5; ibid., 16 Aug. 1924, 5; *Newport Mercury*, 1 July 1876, 2; ibid., 19 June 1880, 2; ibid., 2 Aug. 1924, 1; ibid., 4 July 1930, 1. At patch parties, participants sewed patches on a pair of large overalls that had been hung from some height.

17. Lincoln and Mamiya, *Black Church*, 11, 15.

18. Ibid., 6, 15; *Newport Mercury*, 11 Aug. 1888, 1; *Saratogian*, 17 June 1908, 5; ibid., 27 Aug. 1906, 5; ibid., 30 Aug. 1902, 3; ibid., 14 Aug. 1920, 5.

19. *Newport Mercury*, 11 Aug. 1888, 1; *Saratogian*, 31 Aug. 1916, 5. On the general concern among blacks with deportment and etiquette (although mainly focused on black elites), see "The Genteel Performance" (chap. 7), Willard B. Gatewood, *Aristocrats of Color: The Black Elite, 1880–1920* (Bloomington: Indiana University Press, 1990).

20. Lincoln and Mamiya, *Black Church*, 26–28; Jeter, *Twenty-five Years Experience*, 42–48; Lincoln and Mamiya, *Black Church*, 42.

21. Britten, *Chronicles of Saratoga*, 551; *Saratoga Daily Journal*, 21 July 1883, 3; ibid., 28 July 1883, 3; ibid., 4 Aug. 1883, 3; *Saratogian*, 13 Aug. 1902, 5; ibid., 2 July 1904, 5; ibid., 18 Aug. 1904, 5; ibid., 6 June 1908, 5; Hattie Heath, "The History of Mt. Olivet Baptist Church," Mt. Olivet Baptist Church Records, Saratoga Springs, N.Y., n.d., n.p.; Certificate of Incorporation for Mt. Olivet Baptist Church, 17 Dec. 1910, Deed Records, Saratoga County Clerk's Office, Ballston Spa, N.Y.; U.S. Census, 1900 (ms.); U.S. Census, 1910 (ms.). On the concentration of black Baptists in the South and for numbers of black Baptists, see Lincoln and Mamiya, *Black Church*, 23, 31.

22. William A. Muraskin, *Middle-Class Blacks in a White Society: Prince Hall Freemasonry in America* (Berkeley: University of California Press, 1975), 75–85, 161, 123–35; Mary Ann Clawson, *Constituting Brotherhood: Class, Gender, and Fraternalism* (Princeton, N.J.: Princeton University Press, 1989).

23. Muraskin, *Middle-Class Blacks*, 161–62; Betty M. Kuyk, "The African Derivation of Black Fraternal Orders in the United States," *Comparative Studies in Society and History* 25 (Oct. 1983): 591. Clawson, in *Constituting Brotherhood*, 249–59, finds that white fraternities also had a classless character.

24. Myra B. Young Armstead, "The History of Blacks in Resort Towns: Newport, Rhode Island, and Saratoga Springs, New York, 1870–1930" (Ph.D. diss., University of Chicago, 1987), 204–6.

25. Clawson, *Constituting Brotherhood*, 178–210.

26. Muraskin, *Middle-Class Blacks*, 108–122; Lincoln and Mamiya, *Black Church*, 165.

27. Pilkington, interview by author, 25 June 1983; Ernest P. Jackson, interview by author, 30 June 1983; Edna Bailey Miller, interview by author, 26 June 1989; New York State Census, 1925 (ms.).

28. Pilkington, interview by author, 25 June 1983; Miller, interview by author, 26 June 1989; U.S. Census, 1910 (ms.); New York State Census, 1925 (ms.); Gatewood, *Aristocrats of Color*, 272–99.

29. Leslie H. Fishel Jr., "The Negro in Northern Politics, 1870–1900," *Mississippi Valley Historical Review* 42 (Dec. 1955): 467; *Saratogian*, 28 Apr. 1870, 1.

30. *Saratogian*, 11 Apr. 1871, 3.

31. Fishel, "Negro in Northern Politics," 470–72.

32. George M. Mayer, *The Republican Party, 1854–1966* (New York: Oxford University Press, 1967), 179–83; *Saratogian*, 13 July 1872, 2; ibid., 3 Aug. 1872, 2; ibid., 5 Aug. 1872, 2.

33. Van Horne File, Rhode Island Black Heritage Society, Providence; Downing File, Rhode Island Black Heritage Society, Providence; Fishel, "Negro in Northern Politics," 472–78; S. A. M. Washington, *George Thomas Downing: Sketch of His Life and Times* (Newport, R.I.: Milne Printery, 1910), 4, 11–17.

34. For an overview of the shifting nature of black political leadership at the turn of the century, see August Meier, *Negro Thought in America, 1880–1915: Racial Ideologies in the Age of Booker T. Washington* (Ann Arbor: University of Michigan Press, 1963), 85–118, 130, 172, or John Hope Franklin and Alfred A. Moss Jr., *From Slavery to Freedom: A History of Negro Americans*, 6th ed. (New York: Alfred A. Knopf, 1988), 235–38, 244–51. On Washington specifically, see Louis R. Harlan, *Booker T. Washington: The Wizard of Tuskegee, 1901–1915* (New York: Oxford University Press, 1983).

35. *Saratogian*, 14 Aug. 1905, 1, 3; Harlan, *Booker T. Washington*, 128–29, 385.

36. *Saratogian*, 9 June 1906, 1.

37. Ibid., 14 Aug. 1905, 1, 3; Harlan, *Booker T. Washington*, 128–29, 385; *Saratogian*, 9 June 1906, 1; George Waller, *Saratoga: Saga of an Impious Age* (Englewood Cliffs, N.J.: Prentice-Hall, 1966), 335, 352–53; Grace Maguire Swanner, *Saratoga, Queen of Spas: A History of the Saratoga Spa and the Mineral Springs of the Saratoga and Ballston Areas* (Utica, N.Y.: North Country Books, 1988), 198, 206; *Saratoga Springs Directory, 1911* (Saratoga Springs, N.Y.: Saratogian, 1911), 217; *Saratoga Springs Directory, 1912* (Saratoga Springs, N.Y.: Saratogian, 1912), 210; *Saratoga Springs Directory, 1913* (Saratoga Springs, N.Y.: Saratogian, 1913), 207; *Saratoga Springs Directory, 1917* (Saratoga Springs, N.Y.: Saratogian, 1917), 191; *Saratoga Springs Directory, 1921* (Saratoga Springs, N.Y.: Saratogian, 1921), 209; *Saratoga Springs Directory, 1930* (Saratoga Springs, N.Y.: Saratogian, 1930), 221; Louise Ware, *George Foster Peabody: Banker, Philanthropist, Publicist* (Athens: University of Georgia Press, 1951), 116–17, 145–47.

38. *Saratogian*, 13 July 1920, 5; ibid., 16 July 1920, 5; ibid., 20 July 1920, 3; ibid., 26 Aug. 1926, 2; ibid., 19 July 1930, 5.

39. Anderson, *Our County and Its People*, 280; Britten, *Chronicles of Saratoga*, 547; "Biographical Materials, Caroline Phelps Stokes," "Biographical Material on Olivia E. P. Stokes (1847–1927)," "Correspondence Re: Miscellaneous Philanthropic Activities, 1898–1928," box 162, folders 1 and 2, Phelps-Stokes Fund Records, Manuscripts, Archives, and Rare Books Division, Schomburg Center for Research in Black Culture, New York Public Library, Astor, Lenox, and Tilden Foundations. While

the Schomburg's Phelps-Stokes papers do not expressly reveal the donor to the Saratoga Springs church, they do demonstrate similar charitable acts by family members to churches, missionary work, and black efforts.

40. *Newport Mercury*, 1 July 1896, 1; Paula Giddings, *When and Where I Enter: The Impact of Black Women on Race and Sex in America* (New York: Bantam Books, 1985), 95–131; Sheila Rothman, *Woman's Proper Place: A History of Changing Ideals and Practices, 1870 to the Present* (New York: Basic Books, 1978), 13–132. See Evelyn Brooks Higginbotham, *Righteous Discontent: The Women's Movement in the Black Baptist Church, 1880–1920* (Cambridge, Mass.: Harvard University Press, 1993), 60–62, 188, 194–96, for a discussion of similar self-help leanings among contemporary black Baptist women.

41. Marcus F. Wheatland, "Getting Along under Difficulties," *Colored American Magazine*, 14:4 (Apr. 1908): 191–92, 194; Harlan, *Booker T. Washington*, 41; Alan E. Oestreich, M.D., "A Medical History: Marcus Fitzherbert Wheatland," Department of Radiology, Children's Hospital Medical Center, Cincinnati, Ohio, 1995, 1–3.

42. Jeter, *Twenty-five Years Experience*, 15–16, 48–49; Jeter File, Rhode Island Black Heritage Society, Providence; *Newport Mercury*, 8 July 1916, 1.

43. Gatewood, *Aristocrats of Color*, 304–5; Van Horne File, Rhode Island Black Heritage Society, Providence; *Providence Advance*, 26 Jan. 1912, 5; Bartlett, *From Slave to Citizen*, 64.

44. *Providence Advance*, 2 June 1911, 1.

45. Wheatland File, Rhode Island Black Heritage Society, Providence; *Thirty-third Annual Report of the Charity Organization Society of Newport, R.I., 1911*, 22; *Thirty-sixth Annual Report of the Charity Organization Society of Newport, R.I., 1915*, 22; *Fortieth Annual Report of the Charity Organization Society of Newport, R.I., 1918*, 24; *City Documents of the City of Newport, R.I., for the Year 1910* (Newport, R.I.: Mercury Publishing Co., 1911), 19, 67; Oestreich, "Medical History," 8; Alan E. Oestrich, "Centennial History of African-Americans in Radiology," *American Journal of Roentgenology* 166:1 (Jan. 1996): 255.

46. Charles Flint Kellogg, *NAACP: A History of the National Association for the Advancement of Colored People* (Baltimore: Johns Hopkins University Press, 1967), 1:91; Clifford Miller, letter to NAACP Headquarters, 29 Oct. 1913, and Marcus Wheatland, letter to W. E. B. Du Bois, 7 Jan. 1914, NAACP Branch Files—Newport, R.I., group 1, box G-195, Library of Congress, Washington, D.C.; Matthews, interview by Regina Anderson, July 1977; N. A. Marriott, letter to R. Shillard, 14 Nov. 1919, R. Shillard, letter to N. A. Marriott, 17 Nov. 1919, and Charles A. Battle, letter to M. Johnson, 8 Dec. 1919, NAACP Branch Files—Newport, R.I., group 1, box G-195, Library of Congress, Washington, D.C.; Charter Application, NAACP Branch Files—Newport, R.I., Library of Congress, Washington, D.C.

47. *Newport Mercury*, 11 Aug. 1920, 1; *Newport Daily News*, 9 Aug. 1920, 1; Cromwell West, letter to Walter White, 2 July 1923, Joseph G. LeCount, letter to Walter White, 16 July 1923, and Cromwell West, letter to NAACP Secretary, 26 Nov. 1923, NAACP Branch Files—Newport, R.I., Library of Congress, Washington, D.C.

48. Charter Application, NAACP Branch Files—Saratoga Springs, N.Y., group 1, box G-136, Library of Congress, Washington, D.C.; *Saratogian*, 1 Aug. 1922, 5; New York State Census, 1925 (ms.).

49. *Triangle* 1 (Mar. 1920): 1, 24, Rhode Island Black Heritage Society, Providence; "Dedication Services of Community Baptist Church—April 16, 1983," Community Baptist Church File, Rhode Island Black Heritage Society, Providence; *Triangle* 1 (Mar. 1920): 3, 5, 7—8, 10—13, 15, 17, 19, 20.

50. Cromwell West, letter to NAACP Secretary, 26 Nov. 1923, NAACP Branch Files—Newport, R.I., group 1, box G-195, Library of Congress, Washington, D.C.; *Newport Mercury*, 31 Aug. 1928, 2; August Meier and Elliott Rudwick, *Black History and the Historical Profession, 1915–1980* (Urbana: University of Illinois Press, 1986), 8—10, 49—50. On the erection of the monument in 1976, see Rowena Stewart, *A Heritage Discovered: Blacks in Rhode Island* (Providence: Rhode Island Black Heritage Society, n.d.), 12.

51. Miller, interview by author, 21 June 1983. Miller did not recall the exact year in which this incident occurred, but since her father was pastor of Dyer-Phelps A.M.E. Church from 1924 to 1928, it is safe to assume that it occurred during his tenure.

52. Lyle Matthews, interview by Rowena Stewart, [1977?]; *Providence Advance*, 12 Aug. 1908, 1; Harvey F. Reid, interview by author, 27 June 1989. On black Republicanism, see Nancy Weiss, *Farewell to the Party of Lincoln: Black Politics in the Age of FDR* (Princeton, N.J.: Princeton University Press, 1983).

53. *Providence Advance*, 12 Aug. 1908, 1.

54. Kathryn Grover, *Making a Way Somehow: African-American Life in a Northern Community, 1790–1965* (Syracuse, N.Y.: Syracuse University Press, 1994), 238—49.

55. *Saratogian*, 25 June 1929, 2; ibid., 26 Sept. 1929, 1.

56. David L. Lewis, *When Harlem Was in Vogue* (New York: Oxford University Press, 1981), 162—97; Gilbert Osofsky, *Harlem: The Making of a Ghetto* (New York: Harper and Row, 1971), 179—80, 184—87; Lewis Erenberg, *Steppin' Out: New York Nightlife and the Transformation of American Culture, 1890–1930* (Chicago: University of Chicago Press, 1984), 255—59; Robert Sims, interview by author, 9 June 1983; Paulette Thomas, "Congress Street: It Was Up All Night Long," *Saratogian*, 24 Feb. 1985, sec. A, 1, 4; E. Jackson, interview by author, 30 June 1983.

57. Thomas, "Congress Street," *Saratogian*, 24 Feb. 1985, sec. A, 1, 4.

58. E. Jackson, interview by author, 30 June 1983.

59. Pilkington, interview by author, 25 June 1983; E. Jackson, interview by author, 30 June 1983.

60. E. Jackson, interview by author, 30 June 1983.

61. *Inter-state Tattler*, 10 Aug. 1924, 1, 10.

62. Lewis, *When Harlem Was in Vogue*, 59—60, 126, 217; Osofsky, *Harlem*, 161—68.

63. Miller, interview by author, 21 June 1983; Miller, interview by author, 26 June 1989; Miller, interview by author, June 1992; *Saratogian*, 24 July 1926, 2; ibid., 7 Aug. 1926, 3; ibid., 9 July 1930, 5.

64. *Saratogian*, 15 Aug. 1908, 5; ibid., 28 Aug. 1920, 5; ibid., 26 Aug. 1922, 5; ibid., 16 Aug. 1924, 5; ibid., 23 Aug. 1924, 2; ibid., 14 Aug. 1926, 5; ibid., 21 Aug. 1926; ibid., 23 Aug. 1930, 3.

65. Ibid., 25 Aug. 1874, 2; *Saratoga Daily Journal*, 15 Aug. 1883, 3; *Saratogian*, 1 Aug. 1883, 3; ibid., 10 Aug. 1888, 5; ibid., 17 Aug. 1888, 5; *The Saratogian Almanac for 1897* (n.p.: n.d.).

66. Oestereich, "Medical History," 10.

67. For examples of summer social activity in Newport, see the *New York Freeman*, 6 Sept. 1884; Pilkington, interview by author, 25 June 1983.

68. *Saratogian*, 13 July 1872, 2; U.S. Census, 1870 (ms.); U.S. Census, 1880 (ms.).

69. Marcus Wheatland to May Childs Nerny, 22 Mar. 1915, NAACP Branch Files—Newport, R.I., group I, box G-195, Library of Congress, Washington, D.C.

70. *Newport Mercury*, 11 Aug. 1920, 1; *Newport Daily News*, 9 Aug. 1920, 1.

71. NAACP Chief Accountant, letter to Saratoga branch, 23 Sept. 1926, and H. J. McKinney, letter to R. W. Bagnall, 12 Aug. 1930, NAACP Branch Files—Saratoga Springs, N.Y., group I, box G-136, Library of Congress, Washington, D.C.

72. Z. Marshall Cochrane, letter to NAACP headquarters, 18 Oct. 1926, ibid.

Conclusion

1. Sue Eakin and Joseph Logsdon, eds., *Twelve Years a Slave: Solomon Northup* (Baton Rouge: Louisiana State University Press, 1977), 4–10.

2. Ibid., 10–11.

INDEX

MYRA B. YOUNG ARMSTEAD, an associate professor of history at Bard College in Annandale-on-Hudson, N.Y., teaches American history, American studies, and multiethnic studies. Her academic research interests are in nineteenth-century U.S. social history and African-American history, and she regularly engages in public historical work for local, state, and national museums, historical societies, and funding agencies.